CULTURES OF UNEMPLOYMENT

POLITICAL CULTURES
Aaron Wildavsky, Series Editor

Political cultures broadly describe people who share values, beliefs, and preferences legitimating different ways of life. This series will be distinguished by its openness to a variety of approaches to the study of political cultures; any defensible comparison, definition, and research method will be considered. The goal of this series is to advance the study of political and social life.

A single set of common concerns will be addressed by all authors in the series: what values are shared, what sorts of social relations are preferred, what kinds of beliefs are involved, and what the political implications of these values, beliefs, and relations are. Beyond that, the focal points of the studies are open and may compare cultures within a country or among different countries, including or excluding the United States.

BOOKS IN THE SERIES

*Cultures of Unemployment: A Comparative Look
at Long-Term Unemployment and Urban Poverty*
Godfried Engbersen, Kees Schuyt, Jaap Timmer, and Frans Van Waarden

Culture and Currency: Cultural Bias in Monetary Theory and Policy
John W. Houghton

A Genealogy of Political Culture
Michael E. Brint

Cultural Theory
Michael Thompson, Richard Ellis, and Aaron Wildavsky

District Leaders: A Political Ethnography
Rachel Sady

*The American Mosaic: The Impact of Space, Time, and Culture on
American Politics*
Daniel J. Elazar

CULTURES OF UNEMPLOYMENT

A Comparative Look
at Long-Term Unemployment
and Urban Poverty

Godfried Engbersen
Kees Schuyt
Jaap Timmer
Frans Van Waarden

with a Foreword
by William Julius Wilson

Westview Press
BOULDER, SAN FRANCISCO, & OXFORD

Political Cultures

Copyright © 1993 by Westview Press, Inc.

Published in 1993 in the United States of America by Westview Press Inc., 5500 Central Avenue, Boulder, Colorado 80301-2877, and in the United Kingdom by Westview Press, 36 Lonsdale Road, Summertown, Oxford OX2 7EW

Library of Congress Cataloging-in-Publication Data
Cultures of unemployment: a comparative look at long-term
    unemployment and urban poverty / Godfried Engbersen . . . [et al.].
        p. cm. — (Political Cultures)
    Includes bibliographical references and index.
    ISBN 0-8133-8603-9
    1. Unemployment—Cross-cultural studies. 2. Poverty—Cross-
cultural studies. I. Engbersen, Godfried. 1958– . II. Series.
HD5708.C85 1993
331.13—dc20   93-3010
                                                                                CIP

Printed and bound in the United States of America

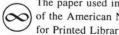

The paper used in this publication meets the requirements of the American National Standard for Permanence of Paper for Printed Library Materials Z39.48-1984.

10   9   8   7   6   5   4   3   2   1

Contents

**PART THREE
ANALYSIS AND COMPARISONS**

Tables and Figures

Tables

Figures

Foreword

Metropolitan areas in the United States feature a much greater decentralization of business and selective suburbanization than those in Europe. In the past several decades, America's central cities have experienced a significant outmigration of more affluent families to the suburbs and, at the same time, a sharp increase in the number and proportion of lower income families. American metropolises have also suffered the growth of highly concentrated poverty areas or ghettos populated by millions of disadvantaged minorities.

Europe has also experienced the process of selective suburbanization, but unlike America, the city centers remain very desirable places to reside because of much better and more accessible public transportation and effective urban renewal programs. Moreover, cheap public transportation makes suburbanized employment sites accessible. Moreover, good public education in the city centers still is much more available to the poor and disadvantaged in Europe than it is in the United States.

Nonetheless, although they have not yet reached the degree of poverty concentration along ethnic and racial lines that is typical of metropolises in the United States, cities in Europe are developing pockets of poverty that are beginning to resemble American inner cities. For example, in Rotterdam in the Netherlands, although inner-city neighborhoods are more mixed in terms of ethnicity and social class due to extensive urban renewal, there are a number of interconnected streets or block clusters where a substantial number of residents are unemployed and on public assistance. These blocks resemble many ghetto streets on the South Side of Chicago or in Harlem in New York. Also, in metropolitan Paris one will find a number of Algerian and African neighborhoods that are beginning to take on the characteristics of American inner-city neighborhoods.

In order to understand these developments it is important to recognize that countries in western Europe acquired a significant number of immigrants in the second half of the twentieth century. Since the late 1960s, western European economies have received workers from Turkey, the Maghreb countries of northwest Africa, northern Africa, the Middle East, and former British, Dutch, and

French territories. These immigrant flows have widened the cultural background differences between the immigrants and the indigenous populations.

More important, however, the economic and industrial restructuring of Europe, including the decline of traditional manufacturing areas, has decreased the need for unskilled immigrant labor. Thousands of the immigrants who had been recruited during periods of national labor shortages have been laid off by businesses. A substantial number of the new jobs in the next several decades will require levels of training and education that are beyond the reach of most immigrant minorities. Being the last hired and the first fired, immigrant minorities became unemployed at record levels during the late 1970s through the 1980s.

The creation of the Single European Market will very likely exacerbate, not alleviate, joblessness. Although the Single Market is expected to increase substantially economic growth and employment opportunities overall, the European Commission has warned that, initially at least, its creation could result in significant economic and social dislocations for some segments of the population—particularly the disadvantaged.

The recent economic and social changes of urban Europe have already created situations ripe for the demagogic mobilization of racism and anti-immigrant feelings. As economic conditions have worsened, many in the majority white population view the growth of minorities and immigrants as part of the problem. Stagnant economies and slack labor markets in Europe have placed strains on the welfare state at the very time when the immigrant population has become more dependent on public assistance for survival.

When the European economies featured tight labor markets and economic growth, the welfare state was easily financed, and welfare services, with strong popular support, were either maintained or increased. However, cries to cut back on welfare programs accompanied economic stagnation and were influenced by the growing costs of social service programs and entitlements during periods of high unemployment and limited public revenues.

In various parts of Europe ethnic and racial antagonisms have been heightened. In Germany many centers for African and Asian asylum seekers have been looted recently. Algerians and black Africans were attacked in several French cities and, to the dismay of French progressives, Le Pen's anti-immigrant National Front movement has experienced surprising electoral successes. Rioting occurred in several black neighborhoods in Britain. African immigrants have been attacked in a number of Italian cities, and tensions have surfaced in several Dutch cities between Christians and Muslims and racial minorities and whites. Unfortunately, in view of the growing economic and social dislocations in Europe, expressions of overt racism both spontaneous and organized will likely increase if the economic and social problems I have thus far described are not addressed. In many respects, the Europe that we know today may not resemble the Europe we will see at the turn of the century.

As Western Europe enters a period of economic uncertainty and experiences growing problems of poverty, poverty concentration, and joblessness among the disadvantaged, individuals concerned about preserving social citizenship rights should pay close attention to what has happened in urban America. I say this because there is growing convergence between Western Europe and the United States not only in the growth of impoverished populations, but also in the way the general public has responded to the increasing visibility and deteriorating economic and social situation of minority and immigrant populations.

For all of these reasons, *Cultures of Unemployment: A Comparative Look at Long-Term Unemployment and Urban Poverty* is an important and timely book. Godfried Engbersen, Kees Schuyt, Jaap Timmer, and Frans van Waarden brilliantly position the problems of increasing joblessness and poverty in the Netherlands within the international and American debates on urban poverty and welfare state regimes.

Indeed, *Cultures of Unemployment* is the most significant study to date on the new poverty in Europe and its consequences for the future. Basing their analysis on an "in-depth study of the daily life of unemployed in three Dutch neighborhoods with a high unemployment rate," the authors effectively relate the problems of economic restructuring in the Netherlands with the emergence of long-term unemployment and the development of cultures of unemployment. Moreover, the authors persuasively demonstrate that the combination of weak labor force attachment and social isolation may exist in certain urban environments without the same level of concentrated poverty inherent in American ghettos.

Engbersen and his colleagues provide evidence that the long-term jobless in the inner cities in the Netherlands have experienced sharply decreasing contact with conventional groups and institutions in the larger society despite levels of class and ethnic segregation far below those of the American inner cities. This development has prompted the authors to discuss the formation of an underclass in the Netherlands in precisely the theoretical terms that I have used to explain the crystallization of ghetto poverty in the United States.

In so doing they provide rich and detailed information that allows systematic cross-cultural comparisons of the formation of underclass populations in a major European country and the United States for the first time. What is even more important is that they present a framework for understanding cultures of unemployment that will be useful to American poverty analysts, especially those of us who recognize the importance of linking attitudes and other cultural traits with structural realities in the economy and the job market.

William Julius Wilson
University of Chicago

PART ONE

INTRODUCTION

CHAPTER 1

Cultures of the
Welfare State

In the 1980s, both the United States and the Netherlands were confronted with problems that had sizeable consequences for welfare states and the quality of life of vulnerable people. The people most affected were the unemployed, single-parent families, the disabled and other groups who depended on state benefits. Three developments should be cited in this connection.

First, national economies were confronted with a process of economic restructuring. The reduced role of manufacturing, the growing significance of the service industry and the internationalization of capital transfers and control over them were among the repercussions. Deindustrialization had shattering effects for whole regions and cities, particularly inner cities, which were unable to compensate for the loss of jobs in manufacturing, in particular jobs for unskilled workers (see also Bluestone and Harrison 1982, Kloosterman and Elfring 1991). At the same time, economic restructuring caused growing labor insecurity in the welfare states of Western Europe, including the Netherlands, and in the United States. This labor insecurity manifested mainly itself in high rates of long-term unemployment, particularly in the Netherlands, and in the growth of part-time, temporary and flexible work. For today's new generation of workers, the labor market no longer guarantees a secure labor career. The segmentation of the labor market has led to insecurity in other aspects of life as well. The return of poverty to such countries as Great Britain, France, Germany and the Netherlands in the 1980s was evident all over. An obvious difference however between the situation in the Netherlands and in the United States is that the majority of the Dutch poor do not work, whereas a substantial percentage of the American poor do have jobs, albeit insecure, part-time and low-paid jobs (Ellwood 1988, Jencks 1992).

Second, austerities affected national social policies in the 1980s, which will go down in history as the era of "the crisis of the welfare state." In many countries, the level of various welfare arrangements deteriorated. The United States and Great Britain are the clearest examples (Katz 1989, Dahrendorf 1988), but in the Netherlands budget cuts also affected housing, health care and public assistance, to which we further refer as "welfare." The welfare state crisis not only was expressed in retrenchment policy, but was even more obvious in the changing views on social policy in general. There was a revival of mistrust in the makability of society and growing concern about the perverse effects of social policies (see Murray 1984 and Mead 1986). A debate on the perverse repercussions of the social security system took place in the United States, and the unintended effects of the system were widely discussed in the Netherlands (Schuyt 1991, Engbersen and Van der Veen 1992). In progressive circles, it was often said that the social system was outdated, and was too focused on income replacement and not enough on reintegration into the labor market ("active or activating labor market policy").

Third, in the past few decades Europe was confronted with a growing influx of migrants. Large numbers of workers migrated with their families from the Mediterranean area to the Western welfare states. These migration flows altered the very countenance of the large cities and metropolises. Multi-cultural urban centers emerged in relatively homogeneous countries. In addition, there are now more than one million refugees in the European Community. As a result, the countries of Western Europe made their admission policies much stricter, although they were often unable to reduce the influx. In some countries, (for example in southern Italy) there has been large-scale illegal immigration. In addition, the integration of officially recognized refugees and immigrants who arrived decades ago and are already "settled" has created a wide range of problems. Many of them are now either unemployed or unable to work due to disabilities, and their children also have difficulties finding a place in the labor market. For a complex of reasons, there are now "poor immigrant" neighborhoods in the large cities where many residents are out of work. Because of the large-scale immigration, poverty has more and more become "colored." In the Netherlands, relatively few people are of non-Dutch descent, 5 percent of the population (compared to a black population of 12 percent and a Spanish-speaking population of 7 percent in the United States). But 42 percent of the immigrants in the Netherlands live in the four largest Dutch cities (WRR 1989).

The developments described here—economic restructuring, budget cuts on welfare arrangements, and the influx of migrants—have given rise to debates on new poverty, on the development of a "split level society," and on the emergence of an "underclass" and ghettoes in Europe. Recurrent concepts in these debates have been "marginalization," "social isolation," "social exclusion" and "welfare dependence." In the United States, comparable debates have addressed welfare dependence, poverty, ghettoization and the underclass, and precisely the same causes have been frequently referred to: economic transformations and social policies that are inadequate to deal with them. In addition to migration into the United States, internal migration flows have also come to play a significant role, particularly the outmigration of stable employed Afro-American families to the suburbs, leaving the most vulnerable groups behind in extreme poverty areas (see Wilson 1987).

Despite the similarities, there are obvious differences in emphasis. In Western Europe, the topic of new poverty related to long-term unemployment occupies a central position in the debate, whereas in the United States attention is mainly focused on the urban underclass and the problems of the ghetto.[1] There is, for example, the far greater visibility of urban poverty in the United States and the marked segregation of black Americans. In some European countries, there is a high level of long-term unemployment. Despite these differences, some basic research questions are more or less the same:

• Does an "underclass" emerge and what is the social composition of this underclass (see Wilson 1987 and Dahrendorf 1988)? What are the main social, economic and cultural determinants of underclass formation?
• What are the perverse effects of the social security system? Does welfare generate permanent state dependence? Are the long-term unemployed "calculating" citizens who misuse the welfare system (see Murray 1984 and Jordan et al. 1992)?
• Do the poor or the unemployed share the same values and aspirations of the wider society, or do they develop a "culture of poverty" or a "culture of unemployment" that perpetuates their marginal position (see Lewis 1968 and Gans 1991)?

These questions led to poverty debates in the 1960s and at the end of the 1980s and the beginning of the 1990s. Large numbers of studies were published that give totally different answers to these basic questions.

In this book we give some *Dutch* answers to the questions concerning the emergence of an underclass, the perverse effects of social policy and the culture and rationality of unemployment. Therefore, we make use of the cultural theory framework, developed by Mary Douglas (1978) and Michael Thompson, Richard Ellis, and Aaron Wildavsky (1990). In Chapter 10 we apply this theoretical framework to the American poverty debates and make some comparisons with regard to the cultural heterogeneity of urban poverty and unemployment.

This book is based on an in-dept study of the daily lives of unemployed individuals in three Dutch neighborhoods with high unemployment rates. In the following chapters, we describe the problem of mass long-term unemployment in the Netherlands in the 1980s and report on the coping strategies of 271 long-term unemployed in terms of work, time, money and rights and obligations. In this first chapter we portray the main dimensions of the Dutch welfare system and sketch its dynamic development. It is difficult to understand the meaning of problems of unemployment without any insight into the main characteristics of the Dutch welfare state regime. Such an analysis will show that the Dutch case has its unique dimensions but also has a resemblance with other European welfare states. Thus, the results of this unemployment study are relevant for other European countries. Here, Douglas' cultural theory is used on the level of social systems to analyze and comprehend the macro developments that have taken place within the Dutch welfare state.

In the final chapters we apply cultural theory to the level of unemployed individuals and demonstrate that they do have a certain amount of choice in how they cope with long-term unemployment. The choices they have are in part a function of two dominant cultural tendencies in the Dutch welfare state, an active individualistic one and a passive deterministic one. The macrocultural possibilities are reflected on the micro level. This analysis has enabled us to distinguish various cultures of unemployment in the wider social context of one welfare state regime. People are not simply victims of their circumstances, even if they are "hit" by long-term unemployment. In much the same vein, societies are not predestined to follow one and only one route in their development, even if they are "hit" by a lengthy recession. Welfare states are not all identical, nor do they differ in all of their characteristics. Welfare states might be described as combinations of various developmental options.

THE DUTCH WELFARE STATE IN COMPARATIVE PERSPECTIVE

Location Matters

The Netherlands is located at the crossroads of Western Europe, at the heart of the two axes of Stein Rokkan's geo-political map of Europe (Rokkan 1981): right on the city belt, which stretched since the late Middle Ages from the North Sea and the Baltic over the Alps to the Mediterranean; just distant enough from Rome to be at the boundary between protestant Northern Europe and Roman Catholic Southern Europe; and at the borderline between the Germanic and Roman cultures as well as a third, influenced by both, the Anglo-Saxon. In short, it is a comparatively small country, squeezed between the three great European nations, Britain, France, and Germany, and not too far removed from the Scandinavian world.

The country has always had good connections and communications with these surrounding nations, owing to an interrelation of geographic, economic, political, demographic, and cultural factors. Transport was facilitated by the location on the North Sea and the rivers Rhine and Meuse. Economically, trade relations have been of major importance in this seafaring state of merchant cities. Exports, whether of domestic products or of products bought elsewhere, have always been a lion's share of the national economy and currently account for over 50 percent of GNP. Political relations were established and maintained through: the economic importance of the Dutch Republic in the seventeenth and eighteenth centuries; a reputation as a tolerant haven for economic and intellectual refugees from elsewhere in Europe; and a foreign policy dictated by the desire for peace in Europe, conducive to trade, rather than by Realpolitik and empire building. The Dutch foreign policy was more recently apparent in the initiating and stimulating role the country played in the formation of supranational organizations such as the European Community (EC) and the Benelux, an intensive cooperation between the three neighboring countries Belgium, the Netherlands and Luxembourg.

Demographically, both job opportunities and comparatively high incomes on the merchant fleets and in trade and industry, as well as religious tolerance, attracted over the ages many enterprising or persecuted people (Jews, Huguenots, even the Pilgrim Fathers for a while) from the European hinterland to this country on the borders of the North Sea (see also Lucassen 1984), enriching the population. Hence many Dutchmen have German, French, or British sounding names. Finally, cultural factors conducive to communications with the surrounding countries were among others the spread of foreign language skills, and the relative tolerance and freedom, which led to an infusion of the economic and intellectual talents of refugees and made the Netherlands a major printing press for Europe. Unlike the Swiss Republic, of similar political origin, which has traditionally closed itself off (except in secret financial relations), the Dutch Republic and Kingdom have been open to the outside world.

The country once was a leader in the political and economic modernization process in Europe. Capitalism was practically invented by the Dutch, and in the sixteenth century the country was a major trade industrial center in Europe. The thousands of windmills in the Zaan region northwest of Amsterdam, grinding oilseeds for paints and sawing Scandinavian wood for housing and shipbuilding, were the giant machines of the proto-industry. The urbanization process set in early, due to the early disappearance of feudalism and the importance of trade. The rule of law, division of political power, federalism, and republicanism all were introduced early by the Dutch. The polity of the Dutch Republic was a model for the American constitution. Later, however, the country lagged in modernization. Perhaps because of its early start, it was overtaken by the surrounding countries. There is something in the theories of "braking leads" (Romein 1971).

In the eighteenth century the economy declined (De Vries 1968) and with it the economic and political power of the country. Frustrations with the cumbersome, corrupt and indecisive polity of the Republic mounted and led eventually to the dissolution of the republican polity and a shortlived backslide into near absolutist monarchy—which, however, brought political centralization. This centralization, as well as functional differentiation in the polity, both main elements of political modernization (see Huntington 1968), were late in coming, as was full suffrage. Furthermore, the country industrialized late. Recent studies may have found more economic activity in the first half of the nineteenth century than conventional wisdom recognized (Griffiths 1980, Van Zanden 1989); nevertheless, the introduction of mass production must be dated after 1865, and the real take-off of industrialization took place only in the interbellum period. Until the Second World War the Dutch economy was still based mainly on trade and on supplying the surrounding industrialized nations with agricultural products. Hence, the social problems accompanying industrialization arrived late, as did other related phenomena such as trade unions.

These three factors—geographic location, good connections, and late modernization—were conducive to foreign influences on many political, economic and cultural institutions of the Dutch. The language has borrowed and absorbed words from German, French and English. The legal system owes much to Napoleonic codification, as does the organization of the public administration. Early industrialization was borrowed from the British—complete with machines, skilled workers and training for sons of industrialists—as were the accompanying social phenomena. Originally, the Dutch used the English word "strikes" instead of the Dutch *stakingen*, as if to indicate that labor unrest was of foreign import. The emergent union movement was heavily influenced by the writings of the Webbs, and the main employers' association made a five-volume study of employers' associations in the four neighboring countries France, Britain, Germany and Belgium (an early industrializer) to learn from foreign experience.

The Dutch have often combined foreign influences, sometimes to their advantage and sometimes not. Academia has not been free from foreign influences either. Galtung (1981) has argued that Dutch intellectuals and academics are alone in being under the influence of three different intellectual styles—the Teutonic, Gallic and Saxon.

What might hold for intellectual styles certainly holds for the institutions of the Dutch welfare state, the topic of this book. It too has been under the influence of various foreign examples and has combined elements of them. One could say that the Dutch system contains elements from all three "worlds of welfare capitalism" that Esping-Andersen (1990) distinguished: the liberal, the conservative-corporatist, and the social-democratic model.

Foreign Models: Bismarck and Beveridge

Esping-Andersen's typology is related to, but does not coincide with, earlier typologies, such as that of the market, state, or church/associational model or the distinction between means- and needs-tested welfare, state compulsory social insurance for workers, and flat-rate state benefits for all citizens (Alber 1982a). These types differ in the following characteristics: principles of allocation and legitimation, institutions safeguarded, coverage of the population, universalism or particularism, criteria of eligibility, generosity and maximum duration of benefits, principle of calculation of benefits and funding-base, abuse regulations, strictness of control and punishment, presence of waiting periods, redistributive character, and state involvement in funding and implementation.

Table 1.1 gives an overview of the characteristics of the four main types of social security: welfare, voluntary insurance, compulsory insurance, and state pension. The liberal welfare state type uses the first two types: means-tested welfare supplemented by state subsidized (usually through tax exemption) voluntary social insurance. The conservative-corporatist type relies predominantly on

TABLE 1.1 Characteristics of Different Welfare State Systems

Variable	Liberal Welfare State		Conservative-Corporatist	Social-Democratic
Type of social security	means- and needs tested social assistance	state-subsidized voluntary insurance	state compulsory social insurance (workmen's compensation)	flat-rate state pension (people's insurance)
Name associated symbolically			Bismarck	Beveridge
Institution protected or central in allocation	the market	the market	family, church, private associations	government agencies
Coverage population, hence size welfare clientele	small	small	medium large	large
Criterium for eligibility: Welfare for	the poor	the affluent middle-class	employees	all citizens which satisfy objective criteria (age etc.)
Universalistic/particularistic (targeted)	universalistic	particularistic	particularistic	universalistic
Generosity:				
• Level of benefits	low	variable	high	low
• Max. duration of benefits	indefinite	variable	limited	indefinite
• Principle of calculation of benefits	flat rate, based on needs and individual means	contributions paid	former wages	flat-rate, based only on general needs
• Principle of funding	taxes	premiums paid	premiums paid	taxes
• Waiting periods	no	variable	usually	usually
• Strictness of control	high	low	low	low
• Redistributive character	vertically from rich to poor	horizontally among contributors	horizontally, within categories of contributors	horizontally and vertically
• Stigmatization	yes	no	no	no
State involvement in:				
• regulation	high	low	medium	high
• funding	high	low	low	high
• implementation	high	none	none	high
Predominant in:	USA, Australia, Canada	USA, Australia, Canada	Germany, France, Italy, Austria, the Netherlands	Sweden, Norway, Denmark, United Kingdom

Source: Alber 1982 and Esping-Andersen 1990.

state compulsory insurance for workers; and the social-democratic type combines a basic flat-rate state pension with supplementary compulsory social insurance, differentiated for various income categories.

The *liberal type* of welfare state makes the market central and is hence the least generous. Social problems should be solved primarily through the market, and only when market failure is unavoidable the state could intervene, then in such a way and to such an extent as to interfere least with the market. One problem the market can not always solve is poverty; hence, welfare by the state to the poor is a major component of this type. Benefits, however, should be as low as possible and duration as short as possible, and criteria for eligibility should be strict, as should be control and sanctioning. In this way, economic costs could be kept to a minimum and financial incentives to look for work on the labor market would not be mitigated. Benefits are in two respects means-tested. First, the only criterium for eligibility is need, or absence of any other resources for survival. It is typically meant only for the poor. Hence in principle benefits are equal—one could speak of an "equality of poverty"—and independent of, for example, former wages; that is, of former work performance or economic contributions to society. However, account is taken of any property recipients may have; in this second sense, too, it is means-tested. Property has to be sold, before benefits can be collected, or benefitlevels are lower and meant only to be supplementary. Also, welfare may vary with specific needs, such as the size of the family. In order to minimize the chance of abuse, welfare is sometimes given *in natura* or distributed in such a way that the money can be used only for specific forms of consumption, such as the American food stamps.

Usually the system is funded out of general tax income of the state. In that sense it is vertically redistributive, from the rich to the poor. Given the limited scope of the system, however, the redistributive character is also limited (see also Esping-Andersen 1990). Any additional insurance against the risks of capitalism—sickness, disability, unemployment, aging—for the better-off in society should be dealt with through the market: by private insurance companies, according to commercial criteria. The state could at most sponsor such private commercial arrangements, through tax privileges, for example. Given the voluntary nature and the unequal distribution of all risks except aging, this scheme also tends to be limited in coverage. This model of the welfare state is found mostly in countries with a strong Anglo-Saxon tradition of liberalism and individualism, but without the strong socialist labor movement of Britain itself; that is, in the immigrant countries USA, Canada and Australia.

The *conservative-corporatist type* has less of an obsession with the market. However, the institutions it wants to protect are the intermediary organizations between the individual and the state: the family, the church, and private associations. Thus the principle of subsidiarity is of central importance in this model: only where organizations of civil society "fail" can the state legitimately intervene, and then in such a way and to such an extent as to interfere least with these intermediary institutions. Similarly, the retainment of status and class differentials is important in this model. Thus rights are attached to class and status: for every social group there should be different forms of protection against the risks of capitalism. Preferably these protections should be given by the family, the church, and private associations. However, in order to solve free rider problems, the state could intervene. Thus the typical social security model in this type is that of social insurance by private associations or the church, backed by the state, which decrees compulsory participation. The name of the German chancellor Bismarck has become associated with this system of state compulsory social insurance. The criterium for eligibility is premiums paid, usually out of wage earnings. The level of benefits is related to the amount of premiums paid or formerly earned wages—which also maintain's status differentials. The duration of benefits is related to the period over which premiums have been paid or a person has worked. Thus the system is tied to work situation; it is not a general social right.

In order not to disturb the social stratification, there are programs for each category—for blue-collar workers, white-collar workers, and civil servants—each with its own set of rights and duties. In order to preserve the sanctity of the family, non-working wives are excluded from social insurance; benefits should be high enough to support a single-income family; and special social services, such as child allowances for family fathers, are provided to sustain and advance motherhood. Day-care centers are undesired and scarce. Overall this welfare state system tends to be more generous and costly than the liberal model. There is some redistribution of income, but it is usually restricted to within social strata. This type of welfare state is found in countries in which the Roman Catholic church is influential in politics and/or in countries with traditionally powerful organizations of civil society, for example, Germany, Italy and Austria.

The *social-democratic type* does not protect the market or intermediary institutions such as the family, the church, or private associations. Instead it aims to protect the individual by granting all citizens similar social rights. Thus every individual has a right to a benefit in case of sickness, unemployment or old age, and in principle all benefits are equal in level. There is no relation to length and level of premiums paid or time worked. Eligibility is solely dependent on objective criteria: age, being out of work, degree of sickness and disability. Hence these universal social security systems have been called people's insurances *(Volksversicherungen* in German) or state pensions. The state does not wait for the family or the church to provide protection. Instead, the costs of familyhood are socialized. Income transfers are given directly to children, and childcare is publicly funded. The system does not know any breadwinner principle. Individual benefits may be lower than in the corporatist type, but benefits per member of the household may be higher. In general, benefits are high and the system is the most generous around. Unlike the liberal system, there is equality not of minimal needs but of high standards of living. Usually this system funded out of general tax income but sometimes also out of contributions of workers and employers. Whether the system is vertically redistributive depends on the progression of taxes or premiums. Usually the state itself is directly responsible for distribution.

Major supporters of this system have been the social-democrats, and the British labor politician Beveridge has become the symbol for it. It is, however, found mostly in the Scandinavian countries, countries which lack a historically strong stratified society (rural countries with independent farmers), a Roman Catholic church, and a belief in self-made individualism typical of immigrant countries, but which have a traditionally strong labor movement. Lately, these Scandinavian countries have modified their systems somewhat to adapt to the emergence of the new middle classes and to preserve their legitimacy. Thus a luxurious second tier has been added to the system, a universal income-differentiated insurance scheme on top of the flat-rate egalitarian one. Given the high costs of the system, it must have an active labor force participation policy. The concomitant of the individualization of generous benefits is that every individual, including women, has in principle the obligation to seek work. In order to help them, the state engages in an active labor market policy. "Perhaps the most salient characteristic of the social-democratic regime is its fusion of welfare and work. It is at once genuinely committed to a full-employment guarantee, and entirely dependent on its attainment. On the one side, the right to work has equal status to the right of income protection. On the other side, the enormous costs of maintaining a solidaristic, universalistic, and decommodifying welfare system means that it must minimize social problems and maximize revenue income. This is obviously best done with most people working, and the fewest possible living off of social transfers" (Esping-Andersen 1990:28).

The Compromise-Character of the Dutch Welfare State

Typically for the Netherlands, its welfare system incorporates elements of all three models. At the crossroads of Europe, and late in modernization and industrialization, the country borrowed freely from different foreign examples. Bismarck's introduction of compulsory insurance for workers in Germany against sickness (1883), accidents (1884), invalidity and aging (1889) stimulated the social and parliamentary discussion in the Netherlands around the turn of the century, inspired the enactment of the first compulsory accident insurance in 1901, and provided the model for various additional accident and disability plans (the original one covered only 22 percent of the working population, Alber 1982) as well as the first sickness act of 1930 and some old-age pension plans enacted before the Second World War.

Although the social-democratic model of flat-rate state pensions did play a role in the prewar political discussions on social insurance, it was not realized until the first comprehensive old-age and widow plans of 1957 and 1959. These were significantly influenced by the British Beveridge plan. The plans were originally prepared during the war by a committee chaired by Van Rhijn and appointed by the government in exile in London, one of the first to include social-democrats. This physical closeness has probably enhanced the influence of Beveridge on the Dutch *volksverzekeringen*.

The influence of the liberal model was probably more of a historical-domestic nature. The Dutch Republic from before 1795 was one of the first liberal-plural-istic nations, in which liberal merchant interests dominated politics (see also Van Waarden 1992). Since then the liberal model has been an influence, albeit a minority one, in Dutch politics. It has influenced the older Dutch poor laws and still finds its expression in the National Assistance Act of 1965, the ABW, further referred to as "welfare," which replaced the older poor laws, as well as in the partly voluntary health insurance system.

The different models did not influence the Dutch welfare state edifice only through foreign examples; all three ideologies were present in the country itself, each in a minority position, partly due to the location of the country. The dividing line between northern protestant regions and southern Roman Catholic ones goes straight through the country, along the Rhine. Furthermore, the early urbanization in the city belt produced an age-old and well-established commercial elite har-boring liberal sentiments. The later industrialization laid the foundations for a socialist movement, which, however, was limited in its expansion by the com-peting Christian trade union organizations, which in turn owed their continued existence to the fact that they also were part of emancipation movements of social minorities. These enduring social cleavages lie at the base of the well-known Dutch "pillarization." They have found expression in political parties as well as in interest groups: religious and social-democratic trade unions, Christian and liberal business associations and farmers' organizations. Thus the various ideol-ogies were present in different political arenas: parliament, the coalition-cabinets, and the many corporatist organizations surrounding the state.

As Lijphart (1975) has argued, the fact that the various pillars were all in a minority position necessitated concertation and pacification between the groups, exemplified in the coalition-cabinets that have governed the country since the late nineteenth century. This was enhanced by an old tradition, going back to the days of the Dutch Republic, of pluralist concertation, tolerance of minorities, consensualism and compromise, and was related to the pluralistic structure of the merchant elites, as Daalder has argued (1966 and 1981). Thus the Dutch wel-fare state is a typical product of consociational concertation and compromise. All the different ideological and social groups, liberals, social-democrats, Calvinists, and Roman Catholics had to realize something of their ideology and interests in the policy output. The influence of the religious groups with their principles of subsidiarity (Roman Catholics) and "sovereignty in own circle" (Calvinists) was probably greatest, as they occupied the political center, at one time forming an alliance with the liberals, at another time with the social-democrats.

The compromise character is, first, apparent both in content and form. Com-pulsory workmen's insurance has been the guiding principle in the various accident insurance plans (1901, 1919, 1922); the invalidity insurance (1919); the postwar general disability plan, WAO, that replaced all these and extended coverage to all wage earners; the first sickness insurance (1930); and the postwar unemployment provisions (WW, WWV, RWW). The social-democratic ideal of universal state pensions has been realized in the general old age and widow insurance providing a basic flat-rate benefit, enough to survive on in relative comfort, and in the children's allowance plans. It also has guided a plan for exceptional health costs, such as stays in nursing homes (the AWBZ). The liberal model of welfare found expression in the National Assistance Act (ABW) of 1965, which replaced the poor law of 1854 and 1912 and which transformed welfare from a favor to a right and made it a complete state, rather than a mixed state-church responsibility. The liberal idea of subvention of voluntary insurance found expression in the 1917 and 1938 Acts on support of unemployment insurance funds of trade unions. Furthermore, liberalism is still present in the health insurance system, which is still partly private (for people above a certain income), as well as in supplementary old age pensions. As a result of its specific history, the Dutch system of social security has become highly differentiated, befitting the corporatist idea of social differentiation and maintenance of status differences. Altogether there are now 39 different insurance plans (Ministry of Social Affairs and Employment 1981). However, the largest part of them cover only small and specialized categories such as the mentally disabled or war victims.

Second, the compromise-character of the system has affected the level of benefits. The social-democrats wanted direct support and protection of workers. The confessional pillars demanded child allowances, orphan protection, and the breadwinner principle: a family father should receive a benefit high enough to feed a family. Furthermore, the various pillars were kept together internally through paternalism and clientelism. These structural principles were carried over the general state, and that too has influenced the benefit level. The Roman Catholic, Protestant, and social-democratic pillars were founded on an implicit contractual relation akin to feudalism and ideally exemplifying political contract theory. The leaders of the pillars acquired the uncritical and loyal adherence of their followers in implicit exchange for the protection of these followers, for the caring of their spiritual as well as material interests within the nation as a whole. Carried over the state, this implied that state legitimacy required state care for its citizens. This philosophy, together with the competition between the various pillars, has successively increased the levels of benefits to such an extent that they are now among the most generous in the western world. Most workers' insurance plans now provide benefits of 70 percent of formerly earned wages, compared to 40-65 percent in most other democratic-capitalist nations (until 1987 it was 80 percent in the Netherlands). Furthermore, there is a minimum benefit level, related to the statutory minimum wage. The flat-rate benefits under the General Old Age Pensions Act and the General Disability Benefits Act AAW are also at the net-minimum wage level. All of these benefits are corrected annually for inflation and also for the increase in general prosperity. They are attached to the wage levels in a number of important industry-wide collective agreements.

Third, the compromise-character has produced a complex system of implementation agencies. The flat-rate people's insurance plans, following liberal and social-democratic preferences, are implemented by government agencies, the industrial insurance boards. Welfare is provided by municipal welfare agencies. And, in accordance with confessional corporatist preferences, the workers' insurance plans are implemented by semi-state agencies governed by representatives of trade unions and employers' associations. Corporatism is furthermore of major importance in the implementation of social policy, such as social work, health, public housing, and education. Voluntary agencies implement "the primary service delivery system, based on the principle of subsidiarity, with government almost exclusively as financier, having only a residual role in service delivery. Governmental subsidies for administration and social insurance payments provide at least 90 percent of the income of voluntary agencies" (Kramer 1985:135). This is quite unlike the systems in Britain and the U.S., countries where in general the principle of voluntariness is praised, but where in social service delivery voluntary agencies merely "supplement a dominant, governmental system that uses a variety of service providers" (Kramer 1985:135).[2]

Fourth, the compromise-mixture of public and private responsibilities is also apparent from the way the system is being financed. On the surface, this seems to be rather corporatist. The state funded in 1974 only 9.5 percent of the expenses out of taxes, the lowest percentage among 13 EC/EFTA countries (Alber 1982). (The second lowest was France with 10 percent, the highest Denmark with 88 percent). In the Netherlands, as of 1987, the insured workers themselves paid most of the premiums, for some programs the employers pay the premiums and for some other regulations the premiums are shared. However, because of the comprehensive character of most plans, as well as the income-dependent premiums, the latter do not differ very much from progressively graded taxes. The more so as the state, and not the private interest associations, determine the amount of most premiums to be paid. Symbolic in this respect is the fact that the state tax offices collect the premiums that workers pay for the flat-rate people's insurances.

Fifth, the Dutch system is generous not only in the level of benefits, but also in its conditions for eligibility, and this might also be a consequence of its compromise-character. Take, for example, the disability plans WAO (for employees) and AAW (self-employed and handicapped). These have been the fastest growing plans in terms of volume. Whereas in 1970 there were 295,000 recipients, by 1990 the number had risen to 862,000. But this growth has stopped now. In percentage terms, the number of disabled persons increased between 1970 and 1990 from 6 percent to 12 percent of the insured population. This increase cannot be caused by a decreasing health of the population. One reason is likely to be that the WAO has been an attractive alternative for lay offs during the economic restructuring in 1970s and the early 1980s. Another is the lenient criteria for eligibility. In the Netherlands a person has to be only 15 to 25 percent disabled in order to be admitted to the plan, but in Germany 50 percent is required and in Belgium 67 percent.

Another example of lenient admission criteria is provided by the unemployment insurance. The Dutch cherish the importance of the voluntary character of labor. Hence there is only limited pressure on unemployed individuals to look for work, to accept any work they can get, or to follow vocational training courses. Forms of "workfare," although seriously debated at the moment, are probably not acceptable within Dutch culture. Hence, while officially being obliged to apply for work, someone can remain eligible for unemployment benefit or (later) welfare, even without actively looking for work. In line with this conception, the Dutch system has no active labor market policy to integrate or reintegrate individuals into the labor market (Therborn 1986). The Dutch regime compensates the loss or non-existence of a job, but is not able to conduct an effective labor market strategy. Many "able-bodied" people are permanently dependent on the Dutch welfare state. The result is a high long-term unemployment rate in comparison with other OECD countries, as well as a low level of labor force participation. An active labor market policy is a major difference between the Dutch and the Swedish welfare systems. Both are well developed and costly. However, Swedish labor force participation is much higher than the Dutch, and unemployment much is lower. The Swedish costs mainly reflect the individualization of benefits; the Dutch high costs reflect a high volume of benefit receivers.

Like the criteria for eligibility, neither the rules against nor the sanctions on abuse are very strict. Detected fraud is punished at most with one—or two—month withholding of benefits. Even where there are rules, they are rarely observed or applied. The implementation agencies are not very active in investigating and prosecuting abuse (Engbersen 1990, Van der Veen 1990). Dutch street-level bureaucrats have a comparatively large discretionary authority. They "do not go by the books" as their American counterparts do. They have a relative freedom to differentially apply general rules to individual cases, to give exemptions, or even to give preferential treatment.[3] Hence their policy style is more like that of British than of American civil servants, as described by Vogel (1986) in his comparison of U.S. and British environmental policies: informal, flexible, cooperative, consensual rather than adversarial, relying more on persuasion than on coercion, and willing to take account of specific circumstances of individual clients.

The discretionary power of civil servants may produce arbitrary implementation and enhance feelings of injustice and dependence among welfare clients. However, it also implies advantages for the clientele: the possibilities of manipulation and favorable treatment are greater. Fraud is furthermore facilitated by the differentiation and the complexities of the system. As a consequence, the more "calculating" and "enterprising" clients of the system, who know their way through the labyrinth of facilities and rules better and are less inhibited about getting the maximum benefit out of the system, will succeed better in profiting from it than the less "enterprising." Socialist and universalistic in conception and legal form, the Dutch system turns out to be more liberal and particularistic in its actual workings and factual distribution (see also Schuyt, Groenendijk and Sloot 1976). In this sense, too, it is a combination of social-democracy and liberalism.

The compromise-character of the Dutch welfare state between the liberal, corporatist, and social-democratic regime models is reflected in the medium scores of the Netherlands in Esping-Andersen's rank-ordering of countries by conservative-corporatist and by liberal regime attributes (1990).

First, the system is, as argued, the product of foreign influences, which became so great because of the location and late modernization of the country. Second, the content and form of the Dutch welfare state were influenced by specific longtime characteristics of Dutch society and polity, some of which date back to the time of the Dutch Republic; for example: pluralism among segments of the merchant oligarchies and later between societal pillars, consociationalism and consensualism, a central political position of confessional groups, absence of a red-green alliance as in Scandinavia, late mass participation in politics, and subsidiarity and corporatism. Third, although the Dutch welfare state was late in coming, the country had a long-time tradition of collective care for the poor. At the end of the Dutch golden age of capitalism, around 1800, one-quarter of the population of Holland was on welfare. This tradition has survived till this day.

Compromise, Pork-Barrel, and Expansion of the System

The compromise-character has enhanced the complexity, generosity, and costs of the Dutch welfare system. The competition between the pillar-elites drove up the level of benefits and eased the criteria for eligibility. Policy formation was a case of Dutch pork-barrel politics, of distributive politics in terms of Lowi's well-known typology (1972). In the U.S., pork-barrel was the result of territorial decentralization and absence of integrative mechanisms such as party discipline. The Dutch version was the result of vertical segmentation or pillarization. In the consociational tradition, for every minority group there had to be something in the barrel.

Furthermore, the Dutch system was also the result of functional decentralization: policy formulation and implementation by corporatist bodies, controlled by the church and other interest organizations, but externalization of the costs to the collective whole, the state (see also Wassenberg 1982). All kind of pillar-linked organizations claimed their right of existence and independence, while the state was generally supposed to bear the costs. The subsidiarity principle of the dominant confessional groupings translated into the slogan "Boss in own house, and the house on costs of the state," which also refers to the heavy subsidizing of privately owned houses through tax deduction (Van Doorn 1978:29). Since the famous consociational pacification of 1917, every local pillar-group had a constitutional right to its own schools, hospitals, domestic stationary health care, public housing associations, social work agencies, etc. This produced of course duplication and inefficiencies—the more so as competition and social comparisons between the pillars increased the level of social services—but these costs were to be born by the state. The same was the case with the system of social security. The cooperation of trade unions and employers at the sectoral level also externalized costs to the collectivity. An example is the growth of the disability plan. Trade unions and employers agreed to place many workers, laid off by industrial restructuring and disappearance of declining industries, in the more generous disability plans instead of in the less costly but less client-friendly unemployment insurance plans. Until 1987 unemployment paid 80 percent of workers' former salary for two years, but disability plans could pay the same amount until their sixty-fifth birthday. (After the revision of the social security system in 1987, unemployment benefits paid 70 percent of workers' last earned salary for five months to five years depending on their seniority.) This policy was at least partly responsible for the rapid expansion of the disability plan.

The corporatist institutional separation of costs and benefits, of collection and distribution of money, facilitates spending, it has been argued. "An explanation for this striking difference [high growth in the Netherlands and low in Switzerland, countries with similar political histories] appears to lie in the forms of funding and control of services in both countries. Financing and control at local and associative levels appears to result in a much slower and better balanced expansion than in the case of control by organizations which do not raise their own funding. This may be especially true when they are in competition with each other and use the institutions for clientelistic purposes" (Flora 1986:xix). The leniency in implementation of the Dutch system could reflect such clientelistic intentions.

Finally, the structural differentiation and categorization of the system, in corporatist tradition, will have increased the role differentiation in society and thus the opportunities for mutual comparisons of rights and benefits between groups. This will have contributed to a revolution of rising expectations and continuing political pressure for more and better social provisions, or at least pressure against curtailing the autonomous growth of the system due to increased use (Schuyt 1978).

From Laggard to Leader

Thus compromise-character of the Dutch welfare state is responsible for its enormous size. However, this size is only of recent date. The Dutch welfare state was, like other dimensions of modernization, also late in coming. It was for many years behind in "regulation (labor legislation), supplementation (social security systems), and replacement (social services) of markets by state bureaucracies" (Flora and Alber 1982:40). In 1900 it was the only country among 12 European countries with no social security provision whatsoever. Zero percent of the population was covered, while in Germany already 40 percent was entitled to some form of social security (Alber 1982). But here the opposite took place as in general modernization: from laggard the Netherlands leaped to become leader (Cox 1992 and Wilensky 1975). "In no other West European country has the welfare state expanded to such an extent after World War II" (Flora 1986:xix). The first social security law (on disability) passed parliament in 1901, but coverage was no more than symbolic until 1917. In 1958 the Netherlands overtook with one set of measures all others except Britain, Sweden and Norway in the extent of principled coverage of the population (Flora and Alber 1982).

The greatest expansion took place in the period between 1958 and 1967—the "golden age of the welfare state" (Flora 1986:xii)—when major new laws on state pensions, unemployment insurance, sickness and disability plans, and welfare were introduced. In 1977 it was second only to Norway in extent of coverage. After the system of provisions and regulations was constructed in such a comprehensive way, it grew in financial size especially after the 1970s, when more and more people had to fall back on the various provisions. In terms of public expenditure, an often used but criticized indicator for welfare state development, the Dutch were by 1975 the leading welfare state, with over 54 percent of GNP spent on government consumption and social security (see Table 1.2). The latter accounted for 26 percent of GNP, again the highest percentage among all OECD countries. By 1980 these figures had risen to 60.6 and 28 percent (Cameron 1985).[4] Table 1.2 shows that this growth has taken place after 1950. In this year the Netherlands still occupied an average position in terms of public expenditure. Sweden, Germany, Britain, France, Italy, and even the U.S. spent more. However, in the period 1950-1975 the Netherlands had the highest annual growth rate, both of public expenditure and social transfer expenditures.

TABLE 1.2 Public Expenditures and Social Transfer Expenditures as Percentage of GNP (1950 and 1975) (rank-ordered by public expenditures 1975)

	Public Expenditures as percentage of GNP			Social Transfer Expenditures as percentage of GNP		
Country	1950	1975	Average Annual Change	1950	1975	Average Annual Change
Netherlands	27.0	54.3	+1.04	6.6	26.1	+0.74
Sweden	37.5	51.0	+0.82	6.3	16.6	+0.39
Denmark	19.4	47.5	+1.03	5.8	15.0	+0.31
Norway	25.5	46.5	+0.91	4.9	16.0	+0.38
United Kingdom	30.4	46.1	+0.53	5.7	11.1	+0.24
Germany	30.8	45.6	+0.45	12.2	16.7	+0.10
Belgium	26.3	44.9	+0.81	9.6	18.9	+0.38
Italy	27.8	43.1	+0.67	9.3	19.6	+0.47
France	28.4	42.4	+0.38	11.3	20.0	+0.29
Canada	26.8	41.2	+0.55	5.8	10.4	+0.22
Austria	25.0	40.3	+0.49	7.8	13.9	+0.21
Finland	26.9	37.2	+0.55	5.8	8.8	+0.17
United States	27.4	36.2	+0.37	3.3	11.5	+0.39
Switzerland	20.8	27.4	+0.66	5.9	10.2	+0.33

Source: Kohl 1982:310, 317.

The expansion in the 1970s and 1980s was due to an enormous rise in number of people acquiring a right to a benefit in one of the various plans. Table 1.3 describes this trend in detail.

- The WW is the Unemployment Insurance Act (1952) which supplies 70 percent (80 percent before 1987) of the last-earned wage for a period of several months up to several years, depending on the work career of the beneficiary.
- The RWW (State Group Regulations for Unemployed Persons, in the sequence of the study referred to as "welfare") is part of the National Assistance Act (ABW). It provides an income for those who are no longer entitled to any other unemployment benefit. This so called "social minimum" is derived from the legal minimum wage and amounts up to 70 percent for singles, 90 percent for single parents and 100 percent for couples.
- The WWV (Unemployment Benefit Act) was abolished in 1987. Until then, unemployed who's WW benefit was exhausted were entitled to a 70 percent WWV benefit for a maximum period of two years.
- The IOAW (Act on Income for Older and Partly Disabled Workers, 1987) provides a supplementary income for unemployed workers aged 50 and more.
- The ZW (Sickness Benefits Act, 1930) provides for a 70 percent sickness and maternity benefit for a maximum period of twelve months.
- The WAO (Disability Insurance Act, 1967) covers 70 percent of the last wage, if necessary until the age of 65. One can also be diagnosed as partly disabled and provided with a certain percentage of the full benefit.
- The AAW (General Disability Benefits Act, 1976) provides an (partly) income on the level of the legal minimum wage for self-employed and people handicapped and therefor unable to work since their youth.
- The AOW (General Old Age Pensions Act, 1957, 1947 provisional) provides every citizen of the Netherlands 65 years of age and older with an income more or less along the same system as the RWW and the ABW.
- The AWW (General Widows and Orphans Act, 1959) provides children who have lost both parents with an income and adults who have lost their partner with a minimum income for the time they have to maintain dependent children.

TABLE 1.3 Number of Benefit Receivers of the Most Important Insurance Plans (in thousands)

Plan	1960	1965	1970	1975	1980	1985	1990
WW (unemployment insurance)		21	31	73	65	76	205
WWV/RWW/IOAW (welfare related)		6	21	109	168	570	370
total unemployment benefits	22	27	52	182	233	646	575
ZW (sickness)	93	122	205	245	269	225	292
WAO/AAW (disability)	161	221	295	406	696	772	862
AOW/AWW (state pensions)	927	1,063	1,213	1,361	1,504	2,025	2,043
ABW (welfare)	–	209	292	376	280	217	215
Total	1,203	1,642	2,057	2,570	2,982	3,885	3,987

Source: CBS 1990.

TABLE 1.4 Benefit-Receivers as Percentage of Total Population by Age-Category in the Netherlands (1988)

Age Category	Percentage Benefit Receivers
00-14	0.0
15-19	2.5
20-24	13.3
25-29	14.2
30-34	13.8
35-39	14.0
40-44	14.9
45-49	20.2
50-54	27.3
55-59	36.4
60-64	58.9
65+	100.0

Source: WRR 1990:109.

* The ABW (National Assistance Act, 1965, in the sequence of the study also referred to as "welfare") replaces the 1912 Poor Law. It supplies the income of people who receive less than the social minimum and provides income when there is not any. See further RWW.

A somewhat more accurate indication of growth is the "benefit-volume," or the full benefit years paid. In 1960 the benefit-volume was 1.2 million on a labor-volume of 4.2 million, or 29 percent. By 1990 these figures had increased to 4.0 million benefit-volume versus 6.9 million labor-volume (58 percent). Recalculated in full-time equivalents, for every four full-time working people there are now three full-time benefit-receivers (WRR 1990). A major share of the latter are those who receive state pension. However, if one disregards these, there is still a benefit-volume of 1.9 million, or 28 percent of the labor-volume: for every three workers one benefit-receiver. Most of these are older people, but quite a substantial amount of younger ones also live on a benefit, as Table 1.4 shows.

The concomitant of the benefit-volume is a low labor force participation rate. Table 1.5 shows that among OECD countries only Belgium has a lower labor force participation rate than the Netherlands. The same holds true for Ireland and the three Mediterranean EC countries—Italy, Greece and Spain. In the other highly developed welfare states, Sweden and the UK, a much larger percentage of the population is economically active.

The labor force participation in the Netherlands remained more or less constant between 1960 and 1988, around 60 percent. However, the aggregate figure hides important differences between men and women. (Table III in Appendix I shows the development of female participation over time for several countries.) Traditionally, the Netherlands has a low participation rate for women. In 1960 only 26 percent had a job outside the home. By comparison, the average for Scandinavia was 50 percent in the same year, and the average for Western Europe (Germany, France, Austria, Belgium, Luxembourg, Switzerland) was 47 percent (WRR 1990). The Dutch figure rose from 26 to 44 percent between 1960 and 1988.

TABLE 1.5 Net Labor Force Participation (percentages of real persons and full-time equivalents, 1987)

	Men + Women		Men		Women	
	Persons	FTE	Persons	FTE	Persons	FTE
Netherlands	58	47	73	65	42	26
United States	71	–	80	–	62	–
Sweden	80	–	82	–	78	–
Belgium	56	53	69	70	44	36
France	59	53	70	68	48	38
United Kingdom	68	56	77	74	58	37
West Germany	63	60	77	78	50	41
EC average	59	53	73	72	45	35

Source: OECD 1990 and WRR 1990.

The increase in the participation rate of women was completely offset, however, by a similar decrease in the rate for men. In 1960 men's participation was very high, 96 percent, or 5.5 percent above the OECD-average. In traditional Dutch society the man was the breadwinner and the wife stayed at home. (In 1937 the Roman Catholic party tried in vain to push a law through parliament which forbade married women to work. Until the 1960s it was common practice for employers to fire women as soon as they got married.) The welfare state programs brought the male participation rate drastically down: from 97 percent to 74 percent in 1988. From being above OECD average the Netherlands fell to 4.5 percent below average, one of the lowest positions.

FIGURE 1.1 Unemployment Trends from 1960 to 1992 (in percentages of the total work force of the Netherlands, the EC, the OECD and the United States)

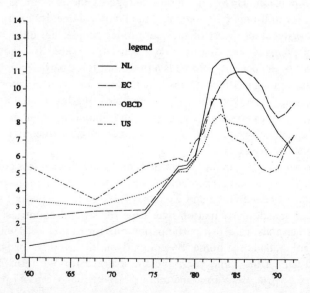

Source of data: OECD 1991 and 1992.

TABLE 1.6 Long-Term Unemployment in a Number of OECD Countries (12 months and longer, 1980-1990, percentage of total unemployment)

	1980	*1984*	*1985*	*1986*	*1987*	*1988*	*1989*
Netherlands	35.9	54.5	58.7	59.5	53.2	51.7	49.9
Belgium	61.5	68.4	69.2	70.3	74.5	–	76.3
France	32.6	42.3	46.8	47.8	45.5	44.8	43.9
Japan	16.4	15.1	13.1	17.2	20.2	20.2	18.7
United Kingdom	29.5	48.1	48.1	45.0	45.2	–	40.8
United States	4.2	12.3	9.5	8.7	8.1	7.4	5.7
West Germany	28.7	45.1	47.9	48.9	48.1	–	49.0
Sweden	5.5	12.4	11.4	8.1	8.2	8.2	6.5

Source: SCP 1990 and OECD 1991.

TABLE 1.7 Unemployment Among Immigrants (in percentages)

	Men	*Women*	*Total*
Indigenous Dutch	12	16	13
Surinamese	27	25	27
Antilleans	21	27	23
Turks	40	58	44
Moroccans	41	49	42
Italian, Greek, Portuguese and Spanish	18	21	18
Other non-EC Subjects (incl. refugees)	35	38	36

Source: WRR 1989.

Part of the inactive population is made up of unemployed. Figure 1.1 shows the unemployment trends as percentages of the working populations in the period from 1960 to 1992 compared with the figures for the European Community, the OECD and the United States.[5] In the Netherlands, there was a sharp rise after 1980, and the figures did not start to fall again until 1984. However, there are some European countries with higher unemployment rates, e.g. Belgium (7.9 percent), France (9.0 percent) and Spain (15.9 percent in 1990, OECD 1990). Various additional facts should be mentioned. In various European countries the unemployment rates for women are much higher than for men, in the Netherlands and Belgium even half as high. Throughout the EC, as well as in Sweden, the United States and Japan youth unemployment (under 25) is often one and a half times as high as for people over that age (SCP 1990).

Figure 1.1 suggests that the Dutch labor market has continued to do very well, while in other western economies unemployment has already started to rise again. This trend, however, does not reveal the fast-growing number of disabled workers in the Netherlands. At least an estimated one-third to one-half of these workers are thought to have been placed in the generous disability insurance plan in order to be prevented from falling victim to unemployment.

Unlike in the United States, the continuous high unemployment rate in the Netherlands and the very low turnover within the unemployed has been responsible for a rapid rise in the number of registered long-term unemployed people. The Netherlands compares unfavorably in this respect, as Table 1.6 shows. In the

1980s, the number of persons unemployed for more than two years rose from 10 percent in 1982 to 36 percent in 1987 and stayed at a high level after that.[6]

Increasingly, long-term unemployment is becoming concentrated among members of ethnic minorities. Table 1.7 provides an impression of registered unemployment among certain immigrant groups. The rate of unemployment varies considerably among immigrant groups, being much higher among Turks, Moroccans and citizens from non-EC countries than it is among Surinamese and Antilleans —although unemployment among the latter two groups is still much higher than among indigenous Dutch persons.

Economic and Social Consequences of a Highly Developed Welfare State

The welfare state has to be paid for, of course. A major consequence of the generous Dutch welfare system is high labor costs.

Table 1.8 shows that the difference between labor costs and net wages is in comparative terms very high in the Netherlands: employers have to pay more while workers get less.[7] Dutch workers take home on average no more than 51 percent of the money the employer spends on them. In no other EC country is this percentage so low. Gross wages in the Netherlands are among the highest in the OECD world. If one recalculates labor costs per full labor-year, only three OECD countries have higher wage costs per worker; the USA, Norway and Canada (WRR 1990). Net wages, however, are among the lowest in Europe. Of all EC countries, only Danish workers take home less.

High labor costs to a certain level do pose problems for a country's competitive position on the world market. So it may be amazing that an economy that is so dependent on exports as the Dutch (more than 50 percent of GNP is sold abroad) can afford to have such high labor costs. However, the welfare state is not only a curse to Dutch capitalists, but also a blessing. It is largely responsible for the very high degree of labor productivity.

TABLE 1.8 Net Wages as Percentage of Total Wage Sum per Labor-Year (1984)

Country	Wage Sum in ECU	Net Wages in ECU	Net Wages as Pct of Wage Sum
Netherlands	1891	968	51.2
Luxembourg	1574	1217	77.3
United Kingdom	1417	954	67.3
Italy	1545	986	63.8
Ireland	1423	899	63.2
France	1734	1096	63.2
Belgium	1719	1009	58.7
West-Germany	2008	1141	56.8
Denmark	1732	882	50.9

Net wages = wages minus employers' contributions to social security, employee contributions, and direct taxes; plus children's allowances, study and housing subsidies, and a few other benefits for a single-income family with two children.

Source: WRR 1990:123.

The Netherlands is one of the richest countries in the world. It occupies the sixth place in the rank-order of EC countries by "GNP per head of the population" (1987 data). However, it has the highest GNP per labor-year (WRR 1990): 118 percent of EC-average, above all other EC countries (e.g., Germany and Denmark 99 percent of EC-average, Britain 104 percent; only France comes close to the Netherlands with 116.) Even Sweden and Japan have a lower GNP per labor-year (WRR 1990). Only the U.S. is higher on the scale. This figure indicates a high labor-productivity rate in the Netherlands. The welfare state is responsible in two ways. First, all less-productive workers have been shut out off the production process by means of the unemployment and disability regulations. Second, the high labor costs motivate if not force employers to look for ways to increase labor productivity, invest in the latest technology, restructure and streamline production organization, etc.—with success, as the high labor productivity indicates. Competition is often hailed by economists as necessary for keeping business on its toes and economically efficient. However, costly welfare state programs seem to provide a similar pressure to an economy exposed to international competition.

The welfare state does not only provide economic efficiency, it also produces equity. The income transfers have made income equality in the Netherlands the highest among 10 OECD countries on which Stephens (1979) could find data.[8] In addition, the incidence of poverty in the Netherlands was one of the lowest among EC countries (see Table 1.9).

Nevertheless, in spite of the Dutch comprehensive social security system, poverty still exists. In the 1980s the number of households who had to make do with the social minimum income mushroomed from 300,000 in 1980 to between 800,000 and 900,000 in 1989, which is 13-15 percent of the total number of households (SCP 1990).

TABLE 1.9 Poverty Rates of Individuals and Households (in percentages)

	Eurostat 1985[a]		O'Higgins 1985[b]	
	Individuals	Households	Individuals	Households
Netherlands	9.6	6.9	5.3	7.4
Belgium	7.1	6.3	7.2	6.3
Denmark	7.9	8.0	14.7	14.7
Germany	10.5	10.3	8.5	7.4
United Kingdom	14.6	14.1	11.7	11.7
France	19.1	18.0	17.5	14.5
Ireland	18.4	18.5	17.5	14.5
Spain	20.9	20.3	20.0	20.0
Greece	21.5	20.5	24.0	24.0
Portugal	32.4	31.4	28.0	28.0
EC Average	14.7	14.0	13.9	12.1

[a] Eurostat 1990. The poverty line has been defined as 50 percent of the average equivalent household expenditure of single adults. Equivalence scale: first adult 1.00, second adult 0.7, child 0.5 (<14 years old).

[b] O'Higgins and Jenkins 1990. The poverty line has been defined as 50 percent of the average equivalent household income. Equivalence scale: 1.00 - 0.7 - 0.5.

Source: Deleeck and Van den Bosch 1992:112.

This rise had to do with the growing numbers of long-term unemployed and with the growing numbers of old age pensioners and the fact that there were more and more single mothers on social security. The permanent dependence on social security of large numbers of people; the absence of an active labor market policy; budget cuts pertaining to such state facilities as public health care, rent subsidies and legal aid; and the loss of purchasing power have once again made poverty an issue.

In the period after 1985, various studies were published that made mention of new poverty in the Netherlands.[9] The new poverty in the Netherlands can be generally described as the structural exclusion of citizens from social participation accompanied by permanent dependence on the state. The effects of these two interrelated processes are evident in the seven features of new poverty: little money (only one minimum benefit per household), social isolation, lack of benefit from some public facilities (especially education), permanent dependence on government agencies, feelings of relative deprivation, concentration in the old inner cities, and emergence of a culture of welfare dependence (see Engbersen and Van der Veen 1987). An examination of the features show that, although multiple deprivation is definitely involved, the emphasis has clearly shifted from the material dimensions to the social ones. A crucial feature of the new poverty is permanent dependence on the care of the state. This feature is a reflection of the profit-and-loss account of the welfare state. In one column is the automatic right to benefits, and in the other is the reduction of independence due to permanent intervention in the lives of individuals who receive benefits.

Welfare benefits produce more than socially beneficial consequences. A large percentage of the population may have been "decommodified," to use Esping-Andersen's terms: they no longer have to sell their labor power on the market in order to survive. However, the dependence on capitalist entrepreneurs and labor markets has been replaced by a dependence on state bureaucracies and private welfare agencies. Furthermore, the generous benefits seems to hinder re-entry into the labor market. It is often economically more rational to remain a benefit-receiver than to accept a job that pays about the same or even less, for example part-time and flexible jobs. The more so, as the Netherlands does not (yet) have an active labor participation policy as Sweden does (although it is presently being debated; see WRR 1990).

TABLE 1.10 Development of Unemployment by Duration-category, 1984-1990 (in thousands)

Category	1984	1990	mutation in %
less than 1 year	387	311	− 20
1-2 years	185	106	− 43
2-3 years	121	60	− 50
3-4 years	73	38	− 48
more than 4 years	56	115	+ 105
Total	822	630	− 23

Source: WRR 1990:163.

Unemployed individuals are in practice hardly forced to accept any kind of work, to do public works, or to follow vocational training courses. The relatively generous benefits and lenient conditions could partly explain why long-term unemployment is becoming a larger share of total Dutch unemployment, as Table 1.10 shows.

Another social disadvantage could be that many "decommodified" people feel left out of the economy and left out of society. Society is in danger of being split in half: a productive side and an unproductive side. Labor force participation can be considered as a form of social participation that contributes integration into society (Jahoda 1982). In the Netherlands, many people are excluded from labor force participation. The social and psychological repercussions and the financial problems long-term unemployment entails (especially among those who receive only a minimum income) have put some categories of people in a situation of social isolation (see also Oude Engberink 1984 and 1987).

CHANGES OVER TIME

The various international comparative studies have to restrict themselves to comparing different systems at one or two points in time. Hence they tend to produce relatively static analyses and to underemphasize changes that may take place within individual systems over time. Domestic authors, often absorbed by short-term changes in their "direct environment," tend to overemphasize the importance of differences over time in their own countries and take less notice of the enduring and specific properties of one system in comparison with others. The latter might be more visible to a foreign observer, whose lack of detailed knowledge about one specific foreign system in combination with knowledge on other systems might facilitate the identification of important peculiarities of this foreign system.

Nevertheless, changes over time do take place and may transform one type of welfare state gradually into another type. For such a dynamic analysis, the Netherlands is an interesting case. It has not always been the mixture of systems it is today. At different times in history, each of the three models identified in the literature has been dominant. The present combination of elements of three different types has been the product of such a sequence of phases, in which proponents of different models dominated in politics and in which their position was fortified by specific economic and societal developments. In the successive phases, new elements were superimposed over older ones, without obliterating the latter. Elements of older types have survived later changes.

One could divide the history of the Dutch welfare state into six periods of about 20 years each (apart from the first one, which is longer), as is done in Table 1.11. In the early phases, the main policy problem was, as in most countries, the alleviation of the risks accompanying capitalist development: sickness, disability, unemployment, old age, and social inequality.

TABLE 1.11 Periods of the Dutch Welfare State

Economic Conditions	Political Conditions/ Events	Socio-Structural, Cultural Conditions	The Dutch Welfare State		
			Programs, content	Organization	Relations with clientele
PERIOD 1: 1848-1903 • since 1870: beginning of industrialization • since 1880: emergence of first trade unions, Protestant, Roman Catholic, socialist	• 1848: reduction power of king; intro. ministerial responsibility to parliament • liberal cabinets • heyday of liberal night-watch state • gradual extension suffrage	• Protestant elite society • beginning emancipation of Roman Catholics (formerly secondary) citizens and lower-middle-class Calvinist • beginning pillarization	• 1854: Poor Act • self-help unemployment/sickness fund of unions • 1874: first social legislation (protection of child labor)	• Poor Act implemented by churches etc. • voluntary associations • local police, later state factory inspectorate	• social assistance a charity, sometimes church attendance required • rights dependent on membership and payment into fund
PERIOD 2: 1901-1919 • economic growth • creation of modern peak associations of trade unions and employers' associations • 1919: very tight labor market	• 1903: Christian parties first time in cabinet • dominance Christian parties in politics • 1917: full suffrage • 1917: consociational pacification between pillars: state payment of private education, welfare, etc. • 1919: revolutionary threat	• strengthening of socio-cultural pillarization	• 1901: first social security act (accident insur.) • 1913: failed sickness insurance, conflict over org. of implementation • 1917: state subsidy for unempl. funds of unions • 1917-1919: major new social legislation	• compulsory insurance but freedom of organization: implem. by private assoc. or state Councils of Labor • voluntary associations	• insurance organizations competing for employers as customers • workers for insurance dependent on preferences employers • provision of subsidized unempl. insurance by unions raises union density ratios considerably
PERIOD 3: 1920-1939 economic crisis 1921, 1929+	• Christain-democratic dominance in government • heyday of corporatism and consensualism • 1938 amendment to the con-	• heyday pillarization	• 1930: finally introduction Sickness Benefits Act • 1931-1936: far-reaching regulation of the economy, e.g. generally	• again compulsory insurance but choice of organizations • state with assistance associations	• stigmatization of unemployed benefit receivers of private interest

	Economic conditions	Politics	Society/culture	Legislation	Implementation	Effects
PERIOD 4: 1940–1959:	• postwar reconstruction • high economic growth • high productivity, low wages • low unemployment	stitution, allowing delegation of state powers to private associations • Social Democrats in all coalition cabinets • corporatist concertation between peak trade unions and empl. assoc. • consensualism still strong	• still traditional society (pillars, family, authorities, etc.)	binding declaration of cartels and collective wage agreements • attempts at economic planning; Keynesian econ. policy • 1957: Gen. Old Age Pensions Act • 1959: Gen. Widow + Orphan Act • 1952: Unempl. Insurance Act	• state planning bureau impl. by government agencies • compulsory unempl. ins., no more freedom of organization but control by social partners	• welfare state provisions for the first time presented and experienced as a right instead of a favor
PERIOD 5: 1960–1976:	• still high economic growth but beginning of industrial restructuring in sunset industries • significant wage increases, capital investm. replacing labor • fast rising standard of living • shortage of labor supply, import of foreign workers	• alternating Christian-liberal and Christian-soc. democr. coalitions • breakdown of macro-corporatist concertation, social contracts • polarization, conflictualism replacing consensualism temporarily • new social movements in politics	• breakdown of pillarization • crisis of authority ('68) • family less important • new assertiveness of particularistic inter. groups	• 1963: Gen. Fam. Allow Act • 1965: Nat. Assistance Act • 1967: Disability Ins. Act • 1966: Health Ins. Act • 1968: Except. Med. Expenses Act • beginning expansion use of welfare state	• Nat. Ass. Act implemented by municipal agencies • Disab. Ins. still controlled by social partners • Med. Exp. by private Sickness Funds, but regulated by state	• revolution of rising expectations
PERIOD 6: 1976–1992:	• econ. stagnation till 1986 • continued industrial restruction • increasing public budget deficits • mass unemployment • rising costs of social security	• mostly liberal-Christian-democratic coalitions • world-wide liberal backlash also in the Netherlands • retreat in econ. intervention • renewed consensualism	• individualization of life-styles	• 1976: last major new provision: Gen. Disability Benefits Act • expanded use and demand for programs • attempts at austerity and redirection of programs	• professionalization and bureaucratization of implementation agencies • attempts to reduce influence of corporatist organizations	• dependence large numbers of recipients on bureaucratic state and corporatist agencies • also new assertiveness of welfare clientele • continued rising expect.

These social problems have been countered successively in different ways. In the first phase, from 1848 until 1903, liberals dominated in politics. Hence their welfare models, assistance for the poor and voluntary insurance, characterized the system. Between 1903 and 1940 the Roman Catholic and protestant parties were in the center of political power, sometimes alone, sometimes in co-alition with liberals. In this period the Bismarck model of compulsory workmen's insurance found a good reception in Dutch politics. However, it was overlaid with specific Social Christian elements: subsidiarity and freedom of organization. Liberal elements survived in state subsidization for voluntary unemployment in-surance by trade unions (introduced in 1917).

Between 1940 (in the government in exile in Britain) and 1959, the Social Democrats formed various coalition governments with the Christian Democrats. It was in this period that the foreign model of Beveridge, flat-rate state pension, was introduced in the Netherlands. However, again, elements of the older models persisted and were introduced in new legislation: liberal elements in the National Assistance Act of 1965 and the Health Insurance Act of 1966; Christian-corporatist elements in the Unemployment Insurance Act of 1952 and the Disability Insurance Act of 1967. During the second till fourth periods, pillarization characterized society and politics and influenced the outcome of welfare-state politics. Coexistence of social and religious minorities led to corporatist, consociational, and consensual policy styles and policy networks, which in turn worked together to produce a comprehensive system of programs, covering every conceivable category of disadvantage.

Notwithstanding the consensual tradition, the development of the Dutch welfare state was phenomenal, so much that it belied concepts of incremental policy change. According to Cox, it was a clear case of policies changing in a non-incremental fashion (Cox 1992). He cites the sizable extension in coverage of the system from 1957 to 1959. Other periods in which the system expanded drastically were in 1917 and in 1965-1968.

While the first two phases were phases of construction of the welfare state, the last ones were (also) phases of stabilization and reorientation. They were first of all characterized by increasing use of the system, created during the earlier phases. Several interrelated developments were responsible for this: economic restructuring and disappearance of sunset industries, technological modernization and replacement of labor by capital, stagnating economic growth, rising and per-sistent unemployment, decline of pillarization, crisis of traditional authority, breakdown of existing institutions between state and individual such as the family and pillarized interest associations, individualization of social relations and life-styles, increasing particularism in interest intermediation, failure of macro-corporatist cooperation and rising expectations directed at the state.

Second, the welfare state was less and less able to satisfy the demands put to it, precisely because it was called upon so much. Thus policy problems changed. The old problems, such as social inequality, disability and old-age, were taken care of. The new problems became persistent long-term unemployment, economic slow-down, rising costs of the welfare state system, bureaucratization of welfare state agencies, and dependence of large parts of the population on these agencies. This led in the last phase to a reorientation, which coincided with and was influenced again by foreign examples: the world-wide liberal backlash, manifesting itself in attempts at deregulation, privatization, and so on, and in general in a retreat of the state. The existing consociational and corporatist institutions and political culture in the Netherlands, however, proved to be rather persistent and retarded and minimized the domestic effect of this universal trend. The Dutch welfare state may have become somewhat tougher and more liberal in comparison with former times; in comparison with "real" liberal welfare states, such as the U.S. or Australia, the Netherlands still cannot be called liberal.

CULTURES OF THE WELFARE STATE

The changes during the last phases of the Dutch welfare state could be interpreted with reference to Douglas' group/grid model. The significance of the work of Douglas lies in her effort to demonstrate how changes in forms of social organization lead to changes in the way individuals think and act.[10] She adhered to the classical sociological maxim that the way individuals think and behave (and justify their thoughts and behavior) is influenced by and simultaneously influences the social environment they are part of. In her comparative classification model, two dimensions were distinguished: group and grid. The *group dimension* pertains to the extent a person's life is affected by the fact that he or she is a member of a group. This dimension can vary from weak to strong. In a strong group, there is more of a focus on the difference between "us" and "them," between the insiders and the outsiders. The borderline between the two is sharply marked. Group members are supposed to associate mainly with each other and strict social control is exerted to prevent them from doing otherwise. Being a member of a strong group implies loss of personal autonomy. In weak groups, the borders between "us" and "them" are much more diffuse and vague. Social dividing lines are less clear. Instead, there are altering coalitions; whether or not one is a member of a particular group depends on the particular situation. Weak groups have no clear group identity and individuals exert little social control over each other.

The *grid dimension* pertains to the extent a person's life is affected by regulations. Like the group dimension, the grid dimension is a continuum from weak to strong. A strong grid entails a refined system of roles with the appropriate status differences. Since a system of classifications regulates and curtails social intercourse of all kinds, individual freedom of action is limited. The Indian caste system is a good example of a rather extreme form of this. The Dutch pillarization system is another example.

FIGURE 1.2 Mary Douglas' Group/Grid Model

+	Atomized Subordination B	Hierarchy C
Grid	Individualism	Factionalism
−	A	D

| | − | Group | + |

Source: Douglas 1982:4.

Social scaling systems of this kind determine how people interact or fail to interact with each other. In a social environment with a strong grid, individuals are expected to behave according to their social classification. A weak grid does not have set classifications of this kind. Rights and obligations, roles and status have to be constantly negotiated.

Douglas summarized the distinction between group and grid as follows: "Group means the outside boundary that people have erected between themselves and the outside world. Grid means all the other social distinctions and delegations that they use to limit how people behave to one another" (Douglas 1982:138). In a recent application of the group/grid model Douglas formulated the distinction between group and grid in this way (see Figure 1.2): "*Grid*, a vertical dimension indicating degrees of autonomy; complete at zero where structure is minimal, and restricted at the top by structures imposed by various forms of organization. *Group*, a horizontal dimension, indicating degrees of incorporation, minimal at zero, complete at the far right" (Douglas 1992:106). The group dimension pertains to the face-to-face contact people have with one another and is evident in the social coercion people exert on each other in direct confrontations. The grid dimension is more complicated. The rules and regulations that influence people's behavior can come from outside the person's own social environment. In a modern society, rules and regulations often come from distant, anonymous official institutions.

The two dimensions can be combined in the following ways: A weak group, weak grid; B, weak group, strong grid; C, strong group, strong grid; and D, strong group, weak grid. These combinations are ideal types in a two-by-two table. The group and grid dimensions can be used to classify the social environment people live in. Each specific social environment has its own cultural bias or cosmology (see Figure 1.2).[11] Square A corresponds with a pragmatic bias. The weak group boundaries and grid allow for individualist behavior styles. In matters of ethics, an opportunistic attitude prevails.

Square B forms an environment where people are subject to binding prescriptions but are excluded from group membership. This combination makes for an atomized social context. Individuals are confined within a highly developed body of rules and are by definition excluded from the dominant institutions. They are not part of any collective frameworks and do not have any group identity. They accept the social order as something beyond their control. Square B is therefore characterized by a fatalistic bias.

Square C is the site with clear group boundaries and a highly developed internal social stratification. Differences and conflicts can be dealt with easily in an atmosphere of this kind. There is a system of distributive justice that legitimizes the hierarchical order. In this environment a hierarchical or ritualist bias dominates, in which the proper application of rules and strict adherence to them are of central importance.

Square D has a dichotomous bias with a strong us/them perspective (factionalism). The freedom of the individual is subordinate to the interest of the group. Individual social life is synonymous with public life. Because of this public aspect and social control, privacy is virtually non-existent. Since there are so few alternatives open to individuals here, the strong social control can result in tension and hostility. Conflicts are solved by scapegoating and ostracism.

In terms of the group/grid model, the Dutch welfare state has developed from a hierarchic and authoritarian social environment with strong group boundaries, fixed roles and internal differentiations (pillarization) into a system with strong role differentiation and vague boundaries between groups. This has been partly the result of the "juridization" of the social programs, which has produced a great variety of categories of people who receive certain benefits or have certain rights.

Two developments have come to characterize post-war society. First, it has developed from a hierarchic social environment to a more individualized environment as a result of the de-pillarization and democratization processes (from C to A). The number of behavioral prescriptions has been reduced and the number of options increased. Someone who is born into a Roman Catholic home in 1990 is no longer expected to play football at a Roman Catholic club or obliged to join a Roman Catholic labor union and marry someone who is Roman Catholic. He or she no longer has to listen to the Roman Catholic radio station and refrain from ever tuning to the socialist television program.

Second, there has been a shift from a hierarchical social environment where people know their place to a fragmented social environment where isolated individuals are expected to behave in accordance with guidelines set down by professionals and bureaucrats (from C to B). This development resulted from a combination of diminishing interpersonal social ties and the explosive growth of rules that regulate conduct. This process has particularly affected people who are permanently dependent on the state or dependent on it for lengthy periods of time. They become isolated and fall under the influence sphere of bureaucratic agencies that regulate many things they do. It should be noted, however, that rules and regulations do not only impose restrictions on individuals. They can also promote individuals' autonomy and freedom, formally by granting rights to categories of people who did not have them, and informally by enabling people with bureaucratic skills to benefit from bending the rules in their own interest. In other words, an increase in rule-density does not imply a strong grid for everyone. This is why a cultural trend has also been observed from B to A (see Figure 1.2).

The two dominant developments have affected the way people think and live. The hierarchical, law-abiding cosmology characteristic of the pillarization period has been replaced by two other cosmologies, a more pragmatic and individualized one and a more passive and fatalistic one. In addition, remnants of the law-abiding cosmology are still in evidence, especially among the older generation. The welfare state thus offers people a variety of adaptation possibilities. They can be active and go their own way, actively utilizing the possibilities the regime has presented them with. Or they can adopt a more passive attitude, obey the instructions of officials, and stick to the precepts of care arrangements. The *extent* to which various cultures come into being and the *frequency* with which this takes place are empirical questions.

THE RELEVANCE OF THE DUTCH CASE

The Dutch welfare state is worthy of study in comparative work, as several authors already have remarked.[12] First, in quantitative terms it is the most highly developed welfare state around. Second, what makes the "Dutch case" especially interesting are some of its structural characteristics. The Dutch welfare state is a product of different foreign influences, intermediated and mixed through the Dutch political institutions, consociationalism, corporatism, and consensualism, and given specific Dutch touches in the process. It combines elements of the liberal, conservative-corporatist and social-democratic welfare states. The structural characteristics thus acquired have produced a rather comprehensive but complicated, generous and lenient system of regulations and implementation organizations. And it is these characteristics that are largely responsible for the enormous size the welfare state programs have acquired. Furthermore, the Dutch welfare state could be interesting theoretically because it undermines some popularly held beliefs and accepted theories; for example that the welfare state is the product of social-democratic political domination (Cox 1992).

Third, given the size of the welfare state, its consequences—in terms of low labor force participation, high costs, economic efficiency, equity, and dependence on government agencies—are also extreme. Therefore the Dutch system could be a good case for studying welfare state-related problems, which also occur in less-developed welfare states.

Nevertheless, in the English-speaking world little is known about the Dutch welfare state, certainly much less than about another well-developed and small welfare state, Sweden. For foreign scholars, the language could provide difficulties of access. Comparative work on the welfare state has been done in Germany, Britain and the USA but not in the Netherlands—with the exception of De Swaan (1988). This study is an attempt to break out of the self-chosen isolation of Dutch social science. We want to present one aspect of the Dutch welfare state to a foreign audience: some of the social consequences.

Given the large numbers of economically inactive people, questions of major social importance are how they live and how they experience their existence. Do they feel stigmatized, ashamed, useless, or do they experience decommodification as a liberation? How do they spend their time? How do they manage with the little money they have? Do they still want to work, and do they look for work? How do they experience their dependence on welfare agencies? Money, time, work, and dependence—these are the themes of this investigation. We selected only a subcategory for study, the long-term unemployed. They have an official relation to the labor market, in the sense that in order to be eligible for a welfare benefit they still have the duty to look for work. However, given the time they are already out of the labor process—if they have ever worked—it will be difficult for them to get a job again. Factually, then, their condition is similar to other permanent clients of the welfare state such as the aged and disabled; little money, plenty of time, dependence on the state. Their situation is even more problematic because they are under pressure to look for work, even if such a search is hopeless, and could be subject to stigmatization. Thus this group is an extreme case of dependence on welfare state agencies. We have tried to find out how they live and feel. Do they form one homogeneous group, or does the category long-term unemployed hide a plurality of subgroups?

THE PLAN OF THE BOOK

In the first two chapters, we clarify the aims of this book. After the positioning of the Dutch welfare state, we pay attention to mass unemployment in the Netherlands and outline the design of our study in Chapter 2.

Chapters 3 through 7 constitute the core of the book. They are mainly of a descriptive nature. Each chapter opens with references to some important American studies. Chapter 3 deals with the trends in the labor market and with the impact of losing a job. Chapter 4 focuses on the first problem of the long-term unemployed: shortage of money. It describes the financial repercussions of the loss of work and reports on the various methods used by the unemployed to try and make ends meet. Chapter 5 is focused on the surplus of time and describes how the long-term unemployed spend and perceive time. The subject of Chapter 6 is how they deal with the lack of work and with finding a job. It contains an extensive account of the behavior, experiences and attitudes of the long-term unemployed on the labor market. Chapter 7 reviews the relationships of unemployed people with government agencies, particularly the welfare department. These relationships are discussed within the theme of this chapter: new forms of social dependence and independence.

The last three chapters constitute the theoretical and comparative part of this book. In Chapter 8, we present the sociological typology of the long-term unemployed produced by our research. Certain types of unemployed individuals fit well into certain cultural settings, which perpetuate the adherence to specific behavior patterns. The "cultures of long-term unemployment" described here contrast with many current depictions, often based solely on statistical variables such as age or level of education. However, they clearly show similarities with typologies and analyses in the American ethnographic literature, which becomes clear in Chapter 10. But first, the Dutch long-term unemployed are portrayed in their capacity as rational problem solvers. Chapter 9 illustrates that for a better understanding of the cost-benefit analyses made by unemployed, attention should be focused not only on the economic costs and benefits but on the social ones as well. In Chapter 10, we turn back to the initial questions of this study. We put the findings of the study into a comparative perspective by reviewing some American ethnographic studies. We demonstrate the relevance of cultural theory for the poverty debates on the culture of poverty, the underclass, and the unintended consequences of social policy.

NOTES

1. See for the United States: Ken Auletta, *The Underclass*, New York: Random House, 1982; William Julius Wilson, *The Truly Disadvantaged: The Inner City, The Underclass, and Public Policy*, Chicago: The University of Chicago Press 1987; Christopher Jencks and Paul E. Peterson (eds.), *The Urban Underclass*, Washington, D.C.: The Brookings Institute, 1991; Lawrence Mead, *The New Politics of Poverty: The Nonworking Poor in America*, New York: Basic Books 1992.

See for Europe: Ralf Dahrendorf, *The Modern Social Conflict: An Essay on the Politics of Liberty*, London: Weidenfeld and Nicolson, 1988; David Fryer and Philip Ullah (eds.), *Unemployed People, Social and Psychological Perspectives*, Milton Keynes Philadelphia: Open University Press, 1987; R. Teekens and B. van Praag (eds.), *Analysing Poverty in the European Community*, Luxembourg: Eurostat News Special Edition 1990; Herman Deleeck and Karel van den Bosch, Poverty and Adequacy of Social Security in Europe: a Comparative Analysis, in: *Journal of European Social Policy*, 1992, Vol. 2, no. 2:107-120.

2. The question who was to implement social security plans has for a long time been a major point of political conflict, and it has retarded social security legislation considerably. The introduction of sickness insurance was for example retarded from 1913—when a first draft was introduced in parliament—to 1930 when the Netherlands, as one of the last countries finally introduced sickness insurance. This long-time principle conflict over state or corporatist implementation hence partly explains the late development of the Dutch welfare system.

3. There are, however, important differences between the various agencies which implement and administer the various social security schemes. The case workers of the Municipal Welfare Departments have a certain amount of discretionary power, but the officials of the industrial insurance boards have very little discretionary power. The professionals (among others medical doctors) who work at the agency which advises the industrial insurance boards in implementing the disability acts have a high amount of discretion (see Romke J. van der Veen, *De sociale grenzen van beleid: Een onderzoek naar de uitvoering en effecten van het stelsel van sociale zekerheid*, Leiden/Antwerpen: Stenfert Kroese BV, 1990.

4. The sharp increase in expenditure on social security in the 1970s was followed by stabilization after 1983. In 1989 the proportion of net national income spent on social security was 2 percent less than in 1980. The amount of expenditure is determined both by the number of claimants and changes in the average amount of benefit. This was substantially lowered in 1987 (revision of the social security system), when the level of benefits under the Disability Insurance Act (WAO), the Unemploy-

ment Insurance Act (WW) and the Sickness Benefits Act (ZW) were reduced from 80 percent to 70 percent of the last earned wage (SCP 1990) and the state contributions to the insurances were stopped.

5. For the 1992 figure we have taken the unemployment rate for May 1992, OECD, *Employment Outlook 1992*, Paris: OECD, 1992. The first part of the figure is only four-yearly, starting from 1978, it is based on yearly unemployment rates. The fieldwork of our study was carried out in 1987.

6. In Chapter 3 more information is presented about the Dutch labor market. In Appendix I, we present some more detailed comparative information about unemployment and the labor market.

7. ECU, European Currency Unit, is the still theoretical monetary unit of the European Community. One ECU is worth 1.2 U.S. dollar. The exchange rate of the dollar to the guilder is 1.8.

8. These countries include the Netherlands, Luxembourg, Great Britain, Italy, Ireland, France, Belgium, West-Germany and Denmark.

9. See Gerard Oude Engberink, *Minima zonder marge*, Rotterdam: GSD, 1984; Gerard Oude Engberink, *Minima zonder marge: de balans 3 jaar later*, Rotterdam: GSD, 1987; Godfried Engbersen and Romke van der Veen, *Moderne armoede: overleven op het sociaal minimum*, Leiden/Antwerpen: Stenfert Kroese BV, 1987; Henk Jan Dirven and Jos Berghman, *Poverty, Insecurity of Subsistence and Relative Deprivation in the Netherlands*, Report 1991: Tilburg: Department of Social Security Studies, 1991; Ruud Muffels, Jos Berghman and Henk-Jan Dirven, A Multi-Method Approach to Monitor the Evolution of Poverty, in: *Journal of European Social Policy*, 1992, Vol.2, nr.3: 193-213.

10. See for the dynamic use of the group/grid model Douglas' analysis of Max Weber's 'The Rise of the Protestant Ethic and the Spirit of Capitalism', in: Mary Douglas and Baron Isherwood, *The World of Goods*, New York: Basic Books, 1979; and Aaron Wildavsky, *The Nursing Father: Moses as a Political Leader*, Alabama, University of Alabama Press, 1984.

11. In the foreword to *Essays in the Sociology of Perception*, Douglas defined the term "cosmology" as follows: 'The ultimate justifying ideas to be invoked as if part of the natural order and yet which, since we distinguish four kinds of cosmology, are evidently not at all natural but strictly a product of social interaction' Mary Douglas (ed.), *Essays in Sociology of Perception*, London/Boston: Routledge & Kegan Paul/Russell Sage Foundation, 1982, 5.

12. Robert H. Cox, 'Can Welfare States Grow in Leaps and Bounds? Non-Incremental Policymaking in the Netherlands', in *Governance. An International Journal of Policy and Administration*, Vol. 5, No. 1, January, pp. 68-87; Peter Flora, 'Introduction', in Peter Flora (ed.) *Growth to Limits: The Western European Welfare States Since World War II*, Berlin: De Gruyter, 1986; Walter Korpi, *The Working Class and Welfare Capitalism*, London: Routledge and Kegan Paul, 1980; John D. Stephens, *The Transition from Capitalism to Socialism*, London: Macmillan: 1979.

CHAPTER 2

The Central Issues
of the Study

As the Dutch post-war welfare state took shape in the 1950s and 1960s, three things were taken for granted. First, there were going to be jobs for everyone. Due to temporary friction in the labor market or perhaps seasonal fluctuations, at most a few people would be out of work for short periods of time. Second, the social security system was to be linked to employment. Premiums were based on the wage-sum and benefits-rights were related to length of former employment. Third, wages and benefits were almost automatically equated with family income, that is, the income a working man needed to support his wife and children. Nowadays, these three premises are no longer taken for granted. Changes in the employment system and other developments in society have made them obsolete.

THREE WELFARE STATE PREMISES

Long-Term Unemployment

Since 1970, the discrepancy between supply and demand on the labor market has grown. Unemployment stayed relatively low until the mid-1970s. From 1960 to 1980, the loss of industrial jobs was compensated for by the growth of employment in the public sector, but since 1980 this has no longer been the case. After an initial growth of the public sector from 12 percent of the total work force in 1970 to 15 percent in 1980, this growth nearly ceased because of government cutbacks. As the number of jobs decreased, every year approximately 50,000 teenagers left secondary school and looked for jobs. This annual increase is expected to continue until 1995. Finally, many of the country's two million unemployed housewives would like a job if they could find one (WRR 1987 and 1990). Although unemployment has decreased since 1984, the figure is still high (see Table I in Appendix I). In sum, given the recovery of the labor market and the socio-cultural and demographic developments, full employment will not be restored in the near future. In other words, for some time to come, labor supply will continue to be overabundant.

The combined effects of the restructuring of the economy and the compromise character of the Dutch welfare system are most evident in the long-term unemployment in the Netherlands. The number of long-term unemployed has risen sharply in the past ten years. In 1980, over 40 percent of recipients of State Group Regulations for Unemployed Persons (welfare for unemployed people) received benefits for over a year; eight years later the figure has risen to almost 70 percent. In 1988 one in five recipients claimed benefits for over five years (SCP 1990). The latter category includes the hard core of the long-term unemployed.

Living on Welfare or Unemployment Benefits

The second assumption as the welfare state took shape has also become problematic. The social security system had been linked mainly to the jobs people had. The implication is that as fewer people work and more people need benefits, the pressure on the system increases. In two ways, the unemployed suffer the repercussions of this link between work and welfare. First, the economic costs of welfare benefits are often claimed to be an obstacle to economic recovery. According to this view, the extensive social security system has made labor so expensive, thus leading to a replacement of people by machines. Second, a relation is assumed to exist between the level of benefits and the potential willingness to look for work. The unemployed are suspected to be not really willing to work when benefits are "so high." And the larger and longer unemployment is, the more pressure there will be to keep benefits down.

Furthermore, the rules of the social security system are so strict that if a person engages in any kind of activity or does any kind of paid work on the side, he gets penalized; it affects his income position and the way he is allowed to spend his time. This could discourage unemployed individuals from taking any such initiative, thus perpetuating their long-term unemployment. No one knows just exactly how the unemployed, particularly the long-term unemployed, spend their time. Do they sit back and wait, or do they make good use of their "free" time and take all kinds of initiatives?

The link between work and social security, between income earned and the benefits received, entail extra problems for the long-term unemployed. The reality of the 1950s, when workers would only be dependent on unemployment benefits only for short periods of time, have been superseded by a situation of long-term dependence on government agencies.

Individualization

The level of benefits people receive and their subsequent standard of living are now also subject to pressure from society itself. In the 1950s, benefits were assumed to represent a family income. (This was not the case in countries like Great Britain or West Germany, where percentages of working women were higher and where unemployment benefits were lower.) However, in recent years the family as a social unit has decreased in importance. Divorce is more frequent than in the 1950s, and more people stay single. In the Netherlands, the category of single households has increased in proportion to the total population—from 3 percent in 1960 to 11 percent in 1985—and its importance will continue to grow in the future. By the middle of the next century one quarter of the population will be living alone, and half of all households will consist of one person only, some demographers predict (Van Imhoff 1991).

Partially influenced by the social security system, a socio-cultural individualization process has taken place. More people have left home at an increasingly younger age and have continued life singly than two or three decades before. Since the National Assistance Act fixed the benefit for a single person at 70 percent of the family allowance, it became more advantageous for welfare receivers not to share one income and not to live together, at least officially. Thus the social security system has come to implicitly encourage the disintegration of social relations and has made fraud tempting. These phenomena have been referred to as "the moral hazards of the welfare state." People who are dependent for the longest periods are most prone to these hazards. Emerging patterns of dependence on benefits combined with emerging patterns of socio-cultural or purely administrative individualization can become an important factor in the perpetuation of unemployment, regardless of whether or not this is consciously desired. What is more, their social environment can directly influence the financial position of unemployed people. The process of individualization and the growing ambiguity of formal and informal social relations have combined to make it difficult to gain realistic insight into the income position of people who live on welfare.

The Demise of the Premises

Thus there is less and less reason to take the three premises of the welfare state for granted. Even if rapid economic recovery were to place, full employment is not apt to return soon. The link between welfare and the number of jobs, and between the "do not work on the side" rule and eligibility for a benefit, will become more and more of a problem. The socio-cultural trend will make it increasingly difficult for authorities to know just exactly who is and who is not eligible for just exactly how much of a benefit. It is against this background that the problem of large-scale and long-term unemployment should be examined. This study, therefore, is an effort to address the consequences of long-term unemployment. The study does not deal with the economic causes of long-term unemployment. It primarily focuses on the consequences of long-term unemployment and on how such individuals perceive and experience their situation. These consequences were studied in connection with the possibilities for the individuals' return to the official labor market and in relation to the social context they were part of. By way of a detailed sociological description of the individual and collective processes accompanying long-term unemployment, we have tried to provide new insights into a social phenomenon that is still largely unfathomed.

LOOKING BACK ON MARIENTHAL

There was a significant time gap as far as research into unemployment is concerned. Important studies were conducted in the 1930s, when the Depression turned unemployment into a major problem. Marie Lazarsfeld-Jahoda and Hans Zeisel wrote *Die Arbeitslosen von Marienthal* (1933) about mass unemployment in a small Austrian factory town, a study that has since become a classic. Bakke wrote his monumental work, *The Unemployed Man* (1933), about the adjustment problems of unemployed men and their families in a small American town. References are still made to this literature. In the 1940s and 1950s, there was little interest in unemployment, as World War Two and the post-war period gave rise to quite different problems and fields of interest. Social science literature barely mentioned of unemployment. It was not until the 1970s that articles on the topic once again began to appear. In the 1980s an increasing amount of attention was focused on unemployment and numerous publications appeared on what had emerged as a serious problem.[1]

In 1982, Marie Jahoda picked up where she had left off and drew a comparison between unemployment in the 1970s and in the 1930s (Jahoda 1982). In fact, the work of Jahoda, in particular the Marienthal study, can be considered a principal source of inspiration for our study. Marienthal was a town southeast of Vienna with a population of approximately 1,500. Until 1929, a large textile factory had employed virtually the entire working population. Due to the Depression, however, the factory was closed in 1930 and three quarters of the breadwinners lost their jobs. They had to make do with a quarter of their former wages. Eating habits changed accordingly, and the researchers noted symptoms of malnutrition among the town's children. A third of the children were in poor health, and only 16 percent were in good health. There was no rise in the crime rate among unemployed, but there was an increase in the amount of illegal work done. The perception of time on the part of the unemployed also changed considerably. Time no longer played a role of importance in their lives. The researchers observed that people who had come to adopt a fatalistic view walked to the employment office slowly and walked back home even more slowly. The reactions of the men and their families were described in great detail: 70 percent were resigned to the situation, and 23 percent were "unbroken" and did their best to somehow make ends meet; they continued to go out and look for new jobs. For 7 percent of the families, the situation was intolerable: these families split up; they were desperate; they took refuge in alcohol, crime or total apathy.

A comparison between unemployment in the 1930s and in the 1980s reveals several striking differences. The financial situation is better in the 1980s, social security for the unemployed has improved, there is less social stigmatization, and the unemployed themselves have a somewhat more active attitude. Thus at present the problem of unemployment should be viewed in a different socio-cultural light than in the Marienthal study.

IMAGES OF UNEMPLOYMENT AND
THE RESEARCH METHODS USED

In the literature on long-term unemployment, various pictures are presented of the unemployed and of the psychological and social consequences of being out of work. The first picture is based on statistical information. It corresponds with the well-known stereotypes: the unemployed have a lower educational level, and fewer occupational skills and possibilities, and they are often members of an ethnic minority. This picture is supplemented by data from survey research comparing the unemployed with their working counterparts on a number of points. This comparison demonstrates important differences, which, however, do not provide decisive proof of the existence of a separate culture of unemployment.

The second picture is based on qualitative data regarding the process of becoming and remaining unemployed. These data usually are gathered by way of intensive ethnographic or biographical studies. Marienthal was the first in a long list of studies of this kind, which have come up with a "deterioration thesis," namely, that unemployment sets off a downward spiral of an increasingly worse situation (see also Gordon 1988). These qualitative studies seem to be negative about the possibility of an upward spiral of successful adjustment and return to the world of paid employment.

The third picture, which would do justice to this notion, is the most unclear. A wide range of intermediary services is assumed to exert a positive effect in terms of a return to the world of paid employment, but research indicates that the results are disappointing. The illegal circuit is assumed to offer alternatives for official employment, but very few figures are available; the little available information seems to refute this claim (Pahl 1987, Renooy 1990). In other words, a positive upward spiral of unemployment might be regularly referred to in the literature, but this social process is not described with the same precision as the deterioration process. For a complete depiction of unemployment, it is nonetheless important to include the positive adjustment process.

The difference in the severity of the two negative pictures of unemployment might be linked to the different research methods that were used. A survey among large numbers of respondents, employed and unemployed alike, can never produce as detailed information as a biographical or an ethnographic study of a few unemployed people and their families (see Liebow 1967, Marsden and Duff 1975). A survey gives global views about certain behavior or the opinions of categories of unemployed people without getting detailed insight into how the unemployed live, what problems they are faced with, how they approach these problems, what solutions they try to find and their reasons for choosing these particular solutions.

The social context people live in often is decisive in determining the meaning of their behavior and attitudes. In an intensive, lengthy interview, a researcher can discover and explore the effects of the social environment on behavior and attitudes. A subject like unemployment, surrounded as it is by feelings of shame, requires a more flexible research approach than is feasible in survey research.

Furthermore, some of the "solutions" to the problems of unemployment, such as working illegally or not informing the welfare department of the extra income, are punishable by law, and may be revealed only in longer interviews that allow for a more confidential atmosphere.

Studies such as those by Marsden and Duff (1975) provide good true-to-life descriptions of the trials and tribulations of unemployed people. In these studies, a more or less coherent picture is sketched of how the unemployed live, and the way they feel about work, about not working, and about the alternatives. There are, however, objections to these studies. They confine themselves to small numbers of respondents and hence the generalizability of the findings is questionable. In addition, they sometimes lack theoretical orientation.

In order to arrive at a more complete and realistic picture of the world of the long-term unemployed, a combination of various research methods is desired. First, one should collect detailed information by means of open interviews covering as many aspects as possible. These interviews should be held with a random sample of long-term unemployed large enough to reveal relevant differences between sub-groups and sub-categories. Wherever possible, such qualitative information should be quantified and in turn supplemented by meanings derived from the social context of unemployed. In our study we have tried to combine intensive and qualitative observation methods with quantitative and qualitative processing methods and to apply them for a relatively large group of long-term unemployed people. Our primary aim was to provide a realistic and differentiated description of the world of the long-term unemployed. Since the influence of the social environment was central to the study, we tried to vary this by studying long-term unemployed in three neighborhoods with high percentages of unemployed, each in a different Dutch city: Amsterdam, Rotterdam and Enschede. Altogether we interviewed 271 people (see Appendix II).

FEATURES OF THE LONG-TERM UNEMPLOYED

At the end of June 1987, when our field work was completed, 658,000 people were registered as unemployed in the Netherlands, according to old Dutch definition discussed in Appendix I. A total of 364,000 of them, or 55 percent, had been registered for more than one year and 240,000, or 36 percent, for more than two years. The 271 respondents belonged to the latter category and to the 23-50 age group. In May 1987, the corresponding Dutch population consisted of 182,500 persons.

The first six columns of Table 2.1 show the differences between the features of the total populations of the three locations and the features of the respondents there. The difference in gender can be accounted for by the fact that women were more reluctant than men to participate in the study.

Table 2.1 also provides data on the distribution as to gender, age, ethnic background, educational level and duration of unemployment of the respondents, of the populations at the three locations where they lived, and of the Dutch population as a whole. A comparison of the last two columns shows that these figures, particularly as to gender, ethnic background, level of education and duration of unemployment, differ from those pertaining to the Dutch population as a whole. Some of these differences have to do with the fact that the respondents were from specific urban locations. Thus Table 2.1 shows that in comparison with the Dutch population as a whole, the long-term unemployed at the research locations included relatively large percentages of men and of members of ethnic minorities.

TABLE 2.1 Several Features in Percentages of Long-Term Unemployed Respondents per Location and of the Total Population per Location and in the Netherlands (in numbers for 1987)

City Neighborhood	*Rotterdam* *Nieuwe Westen*		*Amsterdam* *Banne B.* *Overt. Veld*		*Enschede* *Stadsveld* *Pathmos*		*Netherlands*	
	Pop.	*Resp.*	*Pop.*	*Resp.*	*Pop.*	*Resp.*	*Pop.*	*Resp.*
N	*1003*	*90*	*657*	*88*	*410*	*93*	*182,500*	*271*
Sex								
Male	73	80	67	72	83	86	69	79
Female	27	20	33	28	17	14	31	21
Total	100	100	100	100	100	100	100	100
Descent								
Dutch	58	50	72	66	73	79	85	67
Surinam/Antilles	20	31	8	15	2	2	4	16
Mediterranean	17	12	14	15	19	13	7	11
Rest	6	7	6	5	6	6	3	6
Total	100	100	100	100	100	100	100	100
Age								
23-29	32	33	29	31	32	29	34	31
30-39	37	37	37	37	34	33	38	36
40-50	31	30	34	32	34	38	27	33
Total	100	100	100	100	100	100	100	100
Level of Education								
Primary	59	46	53	36	63	49	50	44
Lower Vocational and Lower General Secondary	22	30	25	41	32	44	31	38
Higher	19	24	22	23	5	7	19	18
Total	100	100	100	100	100	100	100	100
Duration of Unemployment								
< 24 months	–	3	–	9	–	8	–	7
24-36 months	31	1	35	15	20	12	30	9
37-48 months	17	11	22	14	22	11	21	12
49-60 months	14	22	14	8	21	23	17	18
61 and longer	38	62	30	54	38	46	32	54
Total	100	100	100	100	100	100	100	100

There were also differences as to educational level and duration of unemployment. The respondents reported a higher level of education and much lengthier periods of unemployment than might have been expected based on the figures of the population they were from.

Table 2.1 shows that there were considerable differences in the composition of the respective populations and research groups. The three locations exhibited clear differences in gender distribution. The Enschede location exhibited a clear predominance of males among the long-term unemployed. As to ethnic background, the unemployed in Rotterdam and to a lesser extent in Amsterdam were multi-racial. In Rotterdam half the long-term unemployed were of foreign descent. This was not the case in Enschede, where they were mainly of Dutch descent. There were barely any age differences, as the average age at all the locations was 35. There were, however, considerable educational differences. The educational level was lowest in Enschede, where 49 percent had no secondary school diploma and there were barely any respondents with higher training of any kind. In Amsterdam the educational level was highest and the Rotterdam location occupied an intermediate position.

The average duration of the most recent period of unemployment of the respondents we studied was five years and three months. Enschede had the shortest average period (56 months), Rotterdam the longest (70 months) and Amsterdam in between (63 months).

It was interesting to note the distribution as to the type of household. Table 2.2 shows a clear difference between Enschede and the other two locations. In Enschede the family household was most common, whereas in Amsterdam and Rotterdam there was a clear predominance of single people.

The research population studied was not representative of the entire long-term unemployed category in the Netherlands. Very long-term unemployed, ethnic groups and men were over-represented in the sample for this study. These differences do not constitute an important obstacle. We were interested in the course of certain processes and mechanisms such as how the long-term unemployed made do with the benefits they received, how they spent their time, the changes in their

TABLE 2.2 Types of Households of Respondents (in percentages)

City Neighborhood	Rotterdam Nieuwe Westen	Amsterdam Banne Buiksloot Overtoomse Veld	Enschede Stadsveld Pathmos	Total
With Partner	11	10	15	12
With Partner and Children	14	24	47	29
Living with Parents	7	10	14	10
One-Parent Family	7	10	0	6
Single	58	42	17	39
Rest	3	3	7	4
Total	100	100	100	100
N	90	88	93	271

social relations, the barriers they were confronted with in their search for work and how they perceived their welfare dependence. The validity of the qualitative descriptions pertaining to these matters was not influenced by quantitative differences between the research group and the population as a whole. As to the extent to which the results of the quantitative analyses in this report can be generalized, however, we would like to note that they were more indicative of tendencies than of exact distributions.

THE CENTRAL ISSUES OF THE STUDY

In the first instance, unemployed people have too little of two things and too much of another. They do not have a job, nor much money, but they have more than enough time. Given this disproportionate distribution of work, money and time, it is interesting to see how a surplus of time influences a shortage of the other two things. Do the ways they spend and perceive time have negative or positive effects on work orientation? Does the combination of a lot of time and little money induce people to pursue alternative sources of income? In this area the social context is important. In an environment where everyone, or almost everyone, continues to encourage an unemployed person to go out and look for work, the reaction to the problem-laden situation may be expected to be different than in a context where no one sees the point of working or where illegal ways of earning money are more widespread. Such environments may be different in various neighborhood cities.

Our study was guided by three research questions. The first question deals with the triad of unemployment problems: money, time and work. Coping with money has to do with being able to live on the benefit received, getting into debt and exploiting alternative legal or illegal sources of income. This issue is discussed in Chapter 4. Coping with time has to do both with how time is spent and how time is perceived; this is covered in Chapter 5. Coping with work has to do with labor market chances and refers to the attitude to the official labor market as well as to participation in the informal labor market. These are the topics of Chapters 3 (labor market) and 6 (labor market behavior). Thus, the first question is: *How do the long-term unemployed deal with money, time and work?*

The second question deals with the dependence of unemployed people on government agencies, particularly the municipal welfare department. Special attention has been given to their perceptions of their rights and obligations. This is covered in Chapter 7. The second question, then, is twofold: *How do long-term unemployed individuals cope with their dependence on government agencies? And, how do long-term unemployed individuals perceive their rights and obligations?*

The third question deals with the influence of the social environment or the neighborhood (Amsterdam, Rotterdam and Enschede) on the perception of unemployment and on the various reactions of unemployed in dealing with time, money and work. See Chapters 8 and 9. The third question is: *What influence does the social environment have on the various reactions in dealing with time, money, work and welfare dependence?*

Since the questions are mainly of a descriptive nature and neither designed nor able to test explanatory hypotheses, the results of this study will serve primarily to clarify and sharpen the picture of the social worlds of the long-term unemployed. Whether this picture can be useful in formulating policy proposals is something that remains to be seen. Policies regarding unemployment depend as well on factors other than the social world of the unemployed, such as economic and political factors affecting the extent and nature of unemployment. It is nonetheless our conviction that a detailed and realistic description of the world of the long-term unemployed can serve a purpose in policy formulation.

This American edition of the Dutch study has a twofold aim. The first is to contribute to international and American debate on unemployment, underclass formation and welfare dependence. Therefore, we open the empirical chapters (4, 5, 6 and 7) with a short overview of some relevant findings, concepts and research questions from the American literature and confront some of them with the findings of our Dutch empirical study. Second, we hope to demonstrate the relevance of cultural theory for the analysis of unemployment, underclass formation and welfare dependency. In an effort to do justice to the intellectual conceptualization that took place in the course of the study, in Chapter 8 we use cultural theory to help us chart the cultural heterogeneity of the social worlds of the long-term unemployed. Only after the study was under way we did realize how useful the group/grid model would be in linking together the various, often contradictory, research results. That is why Chapter 8 was positioned *after* the descriptive chapters on money, time, work and the perception of rights and obligations. Together with Chapter 9, this chapter contains the most important conclusions of our sociological quest in pursuit of the social worlds of the long-term unemployed. In these two chapters we suggest come Dutch answers to questions concerning the formation of an underclass and of a culture of poverty and the perverse effects of social policy.

We have added a chapter on a comparison of the cultural heterogeneity of urban poverty in the United States and the Netherlands. Cultural theory is not only useful for the analysis of unemployment in Dutch inner cities, it can be equally helpful in analyzing poverty and unemployment in the United States. In Chapter 10, we make such an attempt. Let us clearly state that as we based our comparison on secondary analyses of a few ethnographic studies, it is a rather small step. We hope that it might inspire American researchers to use cultural theory in a more substantial and thorough manner for the study of poverty and unemployment.

NOTES

1. See André J.F. Köbben and Jan J. Godschalk, *Een tweedeling van de samenleving?* The Hague: OSA 1985; Frank Coffield, Carol Borril and Sarah Marshall, *Growing Up at the Margins*, Milton Keynes, Philadelphia: Open University Press, 1986; David Fryer and Philip Ullah (eds.), *Unemployed People, Social and Psychological Perspectives*, Milton Keynes Philadelphia: Open University Press, 1987; Stephan Fineman (ed.), *Unemployment, Personal and Social Consequences*, London: Tavistock Publications, 1987; Alan Gordon, *The Crisis of Unemployment*, London: Helm, 1988.

PART TWO

EMPIRICAL STUDY

CHAPTER 3

A Jobless Market

Western society is developing from a manufacturing economic system to a post-industrial, service-centered economic system. In the United States this process has been described by Bluestone and Harrison in their studies *The Deindustrialization of America* (1982) and *The Great American Job Machine* (1986). This process of economic restructuring can partly be recognized in part in the economic developments in the Netherlands in the 1970s and 1980s (Van Zanden and Griffiths 1989). It is characterized by an unprecedented loss of jobs in several traditional industries; an unprecedented growth in other, new industries; and an evenly unprecedented dropout of people from the labor market.

The global economic restructuring has had far-reaching consequences in the United States. Changing market and investment preferences, e.g., transformed consumption patterns, technological innovations and the flexibilization of production, have provoked a process of sectorial shifts. This change has had dramatic repercussions on local and regional levels as well. Series of plant closures have left great parts of local work forces unemployed and have converted formerly prosperous regions into areas in deep crisis, stirring domestic disputes as well as disrupting community life in local communities and urban neighborhoods by poverty and collective hopelessness. Between 1969 and 1976, over 22 million jobs were destroyed, mainly in manufacturing in the United States (Bluestone and Harrison 1982). In the mean time, some 25 million jobs were created, predominantly in the service sector—but these jobs usually were created in other locations, in other regions and under different material (wages) and immaterial conditions. Moreover, both the demand for these new jobs and the organizations in which they were created showed a break with the past. Ever since the 1970s, middle incomes have declined, leaving the wage structure polarized. During the 1980s, the American working class experienced a continuous loss of income. As a consequence of these processes, life in the traditional communities was forcefully removed to suburbs—"bedroom communities"—surrounding the newly booming economic centers, leaving the old town and neighborhoods in social and material decay (Smith 1988). Paradoxically, rapid economic growth, on the other hand, engendered by the "great American job machine" (Bluestone and Harrison 1986), multiplied the concentration of low paid, part-time and short-term service jobs in the cities, thereby generating new patterns of urban social inequality (Smith 1988). Many Americans in the 1990s work more, earn less and have less time off than in preceding decades (Mishel and Frankel 1991).[1]

Due to economic restructuring in the Netherlands, which to a certain extent is similar to that in the United States, many Dutch workers have lost their jobs in manufacturing during the late 1970s and early 1980s. Unlike the situation in the United States, recovery came late. Together with several striking demographic, social and cultural changes in Dutch society, the economic restructuring has left the Netherlands with mass unemployment. High rates of unemployment are still found in peripheral regions that lost their basic industries and in certain urban areas where vulnerable groups are concentrated. Large cities such as Rotterdam and Amsterdam had to face changes in their role as centers of transport, communication and manufacturing. Regions in the south and the east of the country lost their basic industries such as textile mills and mines. The north of the country lost many jobs in the restructuring of manufacturing related to agriculture.

Unlike the American situation, the Dutch group of middle-income earners has remained intact. The polarization of the work force that has occurred in the United States has not taken place in the Netherlands. On the one hand, the proportion of low-income jobs has significantly grown, but on the other hand the proportion of high-paid jobs has declined (Kloosterman and Elfring 1991).

This chapter seeks to describe the labor market context of the study. We start by drawing a sketch of the main developments in the Dutch labor market, referring to the American labor market where necessary. Second, we focus on the labor markets of the three cities where we conducted our study. Third, we position our respondents within the unfolding of the (local) labor market in the recent past and in the near future.

LABOR MARKETS IN TRANSITION

Many people who were unemployed for long periods in the second half of the 1980s had lost their jobs in the first half of the decade, when the recession was at its worst. Companies were reorganized, factories were closed down and a massive number of workers were dismissed. The rapid rise in the unemployment figures did not stop until 1984.

Four processes were responsible for the dramatic economic changes that caused the mass unemployment Dutch society is still facing. First, increased international competition forced several manufacturing industries (e.g., the textile industry) to remove their production to low-wage countries, leaving tens of thousands of unemployed workers behind. Second, a decreased utilization of the production capacity in several other manufacturing branches contributed to the reduction of the total number of people working in manufacturing industries. Third, the introduction of information technology changed production processes and thereby generated a shift in importance from unskilled jobs to jobs for which a higher level of education was demanded. In the meantime, a fourth process became apparent. As in most western countries, the service sector continued to grow. This sector constituted around half of the total number of jobs in the Netherlands in the 1960s, but by the 1980s this figure had grown to nearly 70 percent (Kloosterman and Elfring 1991).

After international economic conditions had improved during the 1980s and sales markets exhibited growth again, the total number of jobs also resumed growth. Between 1987 and 1990, the service industry showed a yearly growth rate of 2.8 percent, with the average growth rate amounting to 2.4 percent. Particularly fast growers were the producer services with a 5.1 percent growth rate, and personal services, with a 4.3 percent growth.[2] The newly created jobs were won predominantly by newcomers in the labor market: school leavers and (re-entering) women. These developments have led to the paradoxical state of affairs in 1990 in which a labor demand of about 100,000 vacant jobs faces a virtually unfit labor surplus of some 315,000 long-term unemployed people.

Both the process of deindustrialization and the growth of the service industry are shown in Table 3.1. The figures reflect the shift of the economic primacy from the industrial to the service sector, which is characteristic for the post-industrial society. The dramatic decline in the number of jobs in manufacturing to was evident in the employment records of many of our study respondents. The construction industry followed this decline and, like the manufacturing industry, failed to return to the prior level. Even during the recession, the service sector continued to develop favorably.

TABLE 3.1 Employment in the Netherlands from 1960 to 1991 (in thousands)

Industry	1960	1965	1970	1975	1980	1985	1987	1992[a]
Agriculture, Fisheries and Mining	498	143	98	78	73	72	80	93
Manufacturing	1,288	1,237	1,145	1,038	1,051	942	976	1,118
Public Utilities	38	42	43	45	46	46	46	45
Construction	388	400	441	380	411	351	328	358
Trade, Catering and Repairs[b]	636	487	662	659	696	743	812	1,077
Traffic, Transport and Communications	289	271	275	279	288	305	329	390
Banking and Insurance				323	415	490	541	711
Other Services[c]	581	1,096	1,269	1,044	1,208	1,459	1,598	2,063
Total	3,718	3,676	3,933	3,933	4,188	4,408	4,710	5,866

[a] Numbers of jobs, including part-time and flexible jobs, provisional figures.
[b] Includes retail and wholesale trade, hotels, restaurants, cafes and maintenance and repair.
[c] Includes government agencies and public health care.

Source: CBS archive data, CBS 1990, 1991 and 1993.

URBAN LABOR MARKETS

Urban labor markets differ from other regional labor markets in a number of respects (Hasluck 1987). The cities we studied served as centers in the fields of trade, transport, communication and manufacturing. This holds true for Rotterdam, the world's largest seaport, where many international companies have offices, and for Amsterdam, where important national and international companies have their headquarters. Many of these companies show a tendency toward trying to work with a greater flexibility, both internally and externally. Internal flexibility often means an upgrading of both jobs and demands in qualifications. External flexibility means that as many peripheral production matters as possible (those not pertaining to central activities) either have been sub-contracted to other companies, which usually are less stable, or are carried out by flexible workers.[3] Thus the access to permanent jobs has become increasingly difficult at these companies. Labor insecurity has increased.

Many of our respondents were qualified to work only in the industries or jobs in which they were last employed. But those industries and jobs were changed drastically or had virtually disappeared. In other industries, the respondents had been replaced by a new generation of better educated workers or by machines. As the specific significance of these and other developments differed in each city, in the next subsection we summarize the developments affecting the three local labor markets.

The percentage of unemployed people who had been out of work for a long period of time was usually higher in the three cities than in the Netherlands as a whole. In 1987, 34 percent of all unemployed people in the Netherlands had been out of work for more than two years. In the three cities we studied, the figures were: 43 percent in Rotterdam, 39 percent in Amsterdam and 44 percent in Enschede. In the Dutch cities, as in American cities, long-term unemployment and poverty are concentrated in the old working-class neighborhoods because many jobs in manufacturing have disappeared and the newly created jobs are subject to the process of suburbanization.

The general labor market situation was most favorable in Amsterdam, which has a more dynamic economy than the other cities (Kloosterman 1991). In Amsterdam, job mobility is greater and there is a wider range of jobs. In general, the unemployed in the large cities had less of a chance of finding another job than the unemployed in other regions. Of the three cities we studied, Amsterdam offered the best opportunities and Rotterdam the poorest.

Rotterdam

Table 3.2 shows that the number of jobs in Rotterdam began to fall in the first half of the 1970s. The peak in this reduction was around 1985, when the total number of employed persons had fallen by a net 100,000 in approximately fifteen years. The job reduction was mainly concentrated in ship building, machine manu-

TABLE 3.2 Employment in Rotterdam from 1960 to 1987 (in thousands)

Industry	1960	1965	1970	1975	1980	1985	1987
Agriculture, Fisheries and Mining	15	13	9	7	3	3	3
Manufacturing	112	116	111	98	77	65	63
Public Utilities	5	5	4	5	4	4	4
Construction	44	48	48	40	31	26	27
Trade, Catering and Repairs[a]	92	103	96	85	81	70	71
Traffic, Transport and Communications	73	81	75	69	64	61	60
Banking and Insurance[b]					43	43	48
Other Services[c]	77	91	119	123	91	94	101
Total	418	457	462	427	394	366	377

[a] Includes retail and wholesale trade, hotels, restaurants, cafes and maintenance and repair.
[b] For the years 1960-1975 included in "other services".
[c] Includes government agencies and public health care.
Source: Van der Meer 1989.

facturing, wholesaling and retailing, repairs and transport industries. There were many former industrial workers among the Rotterdam respondents. Former construction workers were also well represented, as were people who had worked in stores, hotels, restaurants or cafes. The Rotterdam service industry grew from 59 percent in 1960 to 74 percent in 1987, when the Dutch average was 70 percent.

In Rotterdam, many of the unskilled jobs in the traditional industries, particularly in manufacturing and in the harbor, ceased to exist. This situation made redundant people who had neither the education nor the skills to get any other kind of job. This was one of the most important reasons for the persistent and lengthy nature of much of the Rotterdam unemployment.

In only one decade, the number of unemployed people in Rotterdam rose from about 15,000 in 1979 to 52,000 in 1989, amounting to 22 percent of the labor force. Like the unemployment figures in Amsterdam, the Rotterdam figures stabilized at a high level. In recent years, these figures have remained around 22 percent (Ministry of Social Affairs and Employment 1987). In the Rotterdam neighborhood where we conducted the study, the registered unemployment has since risen to more than 30 percent. An urgent problem of urban unemployment is that the longer a person is unemployed, the less of a chance he or she has of ever finding another job (De Neubourg 1990). If we examine the distribution of the unemployed as to the duration of their registration, we see that unemployment has indeed come to be structural. In Rotterdam, 63 percent of the unemployed have been out of work for more than a year.

The Rotterdam labor market differed from the nationwide picture not only with respect to the persistence of unemployment, but in the composition and quality of the Rotterdam working population as well. In spite of the relatively low participation of older people in the Rotterdam labor force, the average educational level was comparatively low. A quarter of the Rotterdam working population had not attended any school beyond elementary school, compared with 16 percent in the Netherlands as a whole. In addition, the relatively one-sided industrial economy in Rotterdam had generated an equally one-sided working population, which was now having a very difficult time keeping pace with the latest developments on the labor market. In recent years, the Rotterdam job machine has, as in the Netherlands as a whole, generated a number of low-paid jobs, especially in the service sector (for example, in stores, hotels, restaurants and cafes) and in the public sector (mainly in health care and education). These new jobs, however, are little consolation for the long-term unemployed, who lack the skills they require and who have certain expectations regarding work and its obligations that are not in keeping with the uncertain and fluctuating nature of jobs in the modern service economy. The groups best fit for those kinds of jobs are housewives and young people who are entering or re-entering the labor market. In the Netherlands, as in the United States, among these groups we see a growing number of multiple jobholders. In addition, often it is suggested that the level and relative security of a welfare benefit discourage people from applying for low-paid or flexible jobs.

Amsterdam

Between 1982 and 1985 in Amsterdam, the number of employees fell in virtually all industries except "other services," including health care, government agencies and cleaning companies. The job reduction was sharpest in manufacturing. During this period, a significant number of our Amsterdam respondents lost their jobs in ship building and the branches related to it. Many others had been employed as installation or construction workers; in stores, hotels, restaurants and cafes; or doing maintenance and repairs. These are notoriously unstable branches of trade. Many of our respondents had worked in catering. The life cycle of many firms in this field is comparatively short, as is the average period of employment. The working conditions are often poor.

The employment records of our respondents made it clear that in Amsterdam and Rotterdam, after being excluded from certain industries, some of the workers had roamed from one field to the other, doing various types of work along the way. In the records of these "labor market nomads," flexible work often played an important role.

In the past few years, Amsterdam's unemployment figures have been fluctuating around 24 percent (Ministry of Social Affairs and Employment 1987). It is striking that although Amsterdam had the highest unemployment figure of all the cities (24 percent in 1989), it did not have a larger share of the long-term unemployed (53 against 58 percent). This Amsterdam figure reflects the somewhat more dynamic nature of the Amsterdam economy referred to earlier. The numerous small companies in the capital, many of which were just getting started, particularly in the service sector and the hotel, restaurant and cafe sector, may indeed have had a relatively short life cycle and were thus able to provide only

TABLE 3.3 Employment in Amsterdam from 1970 to 1987 (in thousands)

Industry	1970[a]	1974	1980	1984	1987
Agriculture, Fisheries and Mining	–	–	–	–	–
Manufacturing	73	55	43	34	29
Public Utilities	5	3	3	3	3
Construction	25	20	15	14	13
Trade, Catering and Repairs[b]	102	86	75	66	62
Traffic, Transport and Communications	22	26	24	21	23
Banking and Insurance	61	62	64	61	73
Other Services[c]	72	53	54	54	99
Total	360	305	278	253	302

[a] Before 1970 no figures available.
[b] Includes retail and wholesale trade, hotels, restaurants, cafes and maintenance and repair.
[c] Includes government agencies and public health care.
Source: Municipality of Amsterdam, Department of Statistics.

a limited extent of continuity, but they did generate opportunities for unskilled workers to now and then get a bit of working experience.

The situation in Amsterdam was thus clearly different than in Rotterdam. In addition, the educational level of the working population was relatively high in Amsterdam. Table 3.3 shows some developments in employment in Amsterdam. In contrast to Enschede and Rotterdam, the Amsterdam service sector has become a smaller part of the local economy, from 71 percent in 1970 to 85 percent in 1987. Most important, however, are the dramatic fluctuations in the total employment; 30 percent decrease between 1970 and 1984, and 20 percent growth in the three years following.

It is interesting to notice that Amsterdam is a national and international center of education. It attracts many students, who after having graduated cannot, or do not want to immediately find a job and stay in Amsterdam. Eventually, when they have found a job, many do leave Amsterdam.

Enschede

Up to the end of the 1960s, the Enschede labor market, largely synonymous with the textile industry, was industrially and economically a virtual mono-culture, comparable with Manchester in the United Kingdom and well-known "motowns" in the United States. In approximately one third of the interviews conducted in Enschede, the textile industry was mentioned, if not as the specific individuals' source of employment, then as the employment of their mothers, fathers or other members of their immediate family. With very few exceptions, however, the textile industry has disappeared from Enschede, although in 1986, it still employed 1,500 people (down from 8,000 in 1974). Today an important employer in manufacturing is a tire factory, where much of the unskilled work is done by machines. For the rest, there are machinery, steel and plastic-processing factories in Enschede. Table 3.4 gives an impression of the shifts in the Enschede labor market.

TABLE 3.4 Employment in Enschede from 1974 to 1987 (in thousands)

Industry	1974[a]	1981	1983	1986
Agriculture, Fisheries and Mining	1	1	1	1
Manufacturing	18	12	12	12
Public Utilities	0.3	0.3	0.3	0.4
Construction	5	4	3	4
Trade, Catering and Repairs[b]	9	8	8	9
Traffic, Transport and Communications	2	2	2	2
Banking and Insurance	2	2	3	3
Other Services[c]	13	17	17	18
Total	50	46	46	49

[a] Before 1974 no figures available.
[b] Includes retail and wholesale trade, hotels, restaurants, cafes and maintenance and repair.
[c] Includes government agencies and public health care.
Source: Municipality of Enschede, Department of Statistics.

Due to the decline of the textile industry and the introduction of automation, many of the workers with little more than an elementary school education lost their jobs. Many of them were either older migrant workers who had come from Mediterranean countries to the Netherlands in the 1960s or older Dutch people with a similarly low level of education. Many of these people had had a comparatively stable employment history, during which they were seldom out of work and had often worked for the same employer for years, but they had since often had an equally stable period of unemployment. The unskilled work they had done in the past was now done either by machines or abroad, in low-wage countries. The educational level of these people was usually too low or their training too specific to enable them to do other kinds of jobs, if and when such jobs could be found. Today, employment in manufacturing has stabilized at a much lower level.

The construction and installation sector was another important branch of industry in Enschede. The last jobs of one quarter of the respondents had been in this sector. The slight revival in construction came too late for most of them. They were already too old and therefore too expensive. In many cases, they had been excluded from the labor process because of physical ailments, though in time they had partially or fully recovered. In practice, however, this did not necessarily mean they were able to go back to their old line of work.

The Enschede unemployment figures fell from 24 percent in 1983 to 18 percent in 1987 (Ministry of Social Affairs and Employment 1987). The increase in the number of jobs could be attributed mainly to the commercial services and other service branches. In the service industry, newcomers were expected to have had a certain extent of education. For young unskilled workers, the only work that was available consisted mainly of temporary or flexible contracts.

The reduction and disappearance of the actual production processes was most evident in Enschede among the former workers in the machine industry and the virtually extinct textile industry. Two thirds of the former industrial workers among the Enschede respondents had been dismissed because there was no longer any work for them or because the factory had been closed. Changes in production methods, especially those involving automation, were the main underlying reason for the disappearance of the jobs in the Enschede rubber manufacturing industry and in the machine manufacturing industry.

ANATOMY OF JOB LOSS

Employment Histories

From the general developments in the local labor markets, we now turn to the employment histories of our respondents in relation to these developments; that is, what kind of work they had done, how they had lost their jobs and what their future chance are on the labor market.

Most respondents (83 percent) had some kind of work experience. The average length of this work experience was 12 years; 8 percent had worked for 25 years or more. Most of the 17 percent of the long-term unemployed who had had little or no work experience lived in Amsterdam and Rotterdam.[4] The people in this group were younger than 30, Dutch and single. They frequently were better educated than the average respondent and more often had had specific vocational training as well. At most, this group had had work experience in some kind of temporary or flexible job in either the private service sector or the public sector. On the average, they had been out of work for more than six years.

Primary and Secondary Jobs

The distinction has been drawn between the primary and the secondary segment of the labor market.[5] In the primary segment are the larger companies with a stable market share, stable jobs and good wages. In the secondary segment are the generally smaller companies with a less stable sales market, less job security and considerably lower wages. The secondary segment includes construction companies, hotels, restaurants, cafes and factories that have not been able to keep up with the latest developments. The work done there is often harmful to the health of the workers. Many of the respondents had either held secondary jobs in primary companies or had held primary or secondary jobs in secondary companies. In the rest of this section, this picture will be filled in and colored.

Former Job Levels and Branches

Table 3.5 shows, the respondents' most recent employment was generally at rather low job levels. In view of their low educational level, this is not surprising. Table 3.5 also shows that 30 percent had worked in manufacturing, another 30 percent in commercial services, 18 percent in the construction sector and another 18 percent in other services. As could be expected, there were striking differences

TABLE 3.5 Levels of Last Jobs in Five Main Industries (in percentages)

Sector (explanation below)	1	2	3	4	5	Total
Unskilled Laborer	63	64	26	37	16	44
Skilled Laborer	21	25	9	18	5	16
Lower Employee	8	2	33	27	50	22
Middle Employee	4	5	14	12	21	10
Higher Employee	–	2	2	3	3	2
Other[a]	4	2	16	3	5	6
Total	100	100	100	100	100	100
N	72	41	43	33	38	227

1 Manufacturing
2 Construction
3 Trade, Catering etc.
4 Banking etc.
5 Other Services

[a] Includes the professions, self employed and assisting members of family.

between the percentage formerly employed in the textile industry and construction in Enschede and the percentage who had worked in stores, hotels, restaurants and cafes in Amsterdam. In a more general sense, the employment history in manufacturing of many of the Rotterdam and Enschede respondents contrasted with the experience in the commercial service sector of many of the Amsterdam respondents. This will be discussed in greater detail in the following section. Table 3.5 also shows that the unskilled jobs were mainly factory and construction work. Low level employees usually worked at hotels, restaurants and cafes or in commercial and other services. The large remaining category who had worked in stores, hotels, restaurants and cafes were mainly people who had had businesses of their own.

How Jobs Were Lost

People Who Were Laid Off

For most of our respondents (83 percent), losing their job was involuntary. The closing down of factories and the introduction of modern work-saving production technology in manufacturing were the main reasons for dismissals, oftentimes in groups. Fluctuations affecting the stores, hotels, restaurants, cafes and maintenance and repair shops many of the Amsterdam and Rotterdam respondents had worked at was the second reason. Their temporary contracts expired, the shops where they worked closed down, the businesses they owned went bankrupt. The third reason was the slump in the construction and installation sector at the beginning of the 1980s. This trend was clearly related to developments in manufacturing. Particularly in Enschede, many respondents had worked in the construction and installation industries.

People Who Quit

Seventeen percent of the respondents had quit their last job; Kloosterman noted a similar percentage (1987). It was usually people under the age of 40 who had quit their jobs. People from Turkey, Morocco and other Mediterranean countries had all been laid off from their last job, but more than a quarter of the Surinamese and Antilleans had quit their jobs. Of the various reasons were mentioned for quitting, some were personal, such as the birth of a child or psychological problems, and some were work-related, such as disappointment with the job or a conflict with the employer. Some people had quit their job quite easily. Often, this had to do with the fact that, compared with those who had been laid off, they had a somewhat higher level of education. This made them more optimistic about their chances in the labor market. Moreover, their assessment of what it would be like to be unemployed was more positive.

WINNERS AND LOSERS

The personal and background characteristics of our respondents resembled those of groups who, according to the findings of De Grip, were bound to be "occupational losers." De Grip listed and analyzed the occupational, job and educational level categories of people who had been "winners or losers" in the job arena in the previous two decades (1986 and 1987). He started by drawing up an inventory of the employment trends in each occupational class.

In the 1970s, the largest percentages of job losses were noted among miners, workers at spinning and weaving mills, supervisory clerical workers, tailors and upholsterers and lathe operators. The educational level of the groups whose position in the labor market had clearly declined was at the lower vocational level, whereas the level of the groups whose position had improved, mainly employees in the public sector, was considerably higher.

In the first half of the 1980s, the losers were found mainly among construction workers (concrete and cement products), furniture makers, masons, carpenters, shoemakers, independent wholesalers and middlemen. The winners were found mainly in the higher and management positions of the market sector. De Grip referred to a management boom and the downward displacement of educational levels.

A comparison of the qualifications and employment history of our respondents with those of the occupational losers De Grip referred to makes it clear that a considerable number of the people we interviewed could already be classified as losers. The results of the study conducted by De Grip during this second period show that at the job level and in the lines of work most of the respondents had been in, the number of jobs continued to decrease. Of the twelve winning lines of work in the period from 1981 to 1985, only three had jobs for people with a low educational level (lower vocational or lower). Only a few of the losing occupations, however, required qualifications above the lower vocational level.

In this perspective, most could be categorized as losers. The majority of the unemployed people of foreign descent were in this category. They were often poorly educated and experienced only at routine work in production functions that had largely ceased to exist, for example in the textile industry, ship building, machine manufacturing and the transport sector. Many of the long-term unemployed had also worked in the construction sector. The type of work involved and the required training and skills had altered during the lengthy slump in the Dutch construction sector so that most of the unemployed construction workers, many of whom were no longer young, were no longer qualified for a job in their former line of work. Moreover, there are more than enough young, comparatively well educated and cheap newcomers available in the labor market. The considerable rise in the number of jobs in stores, hotels, restaurants and cafes did not offer any alternatives for them. In order to save on labor expenses, the jobs there were usually reserved for young people and women, who were often hired on a part-time or flexible basis. For long-term unemployed breadwinners with a family, insecure jobs like that did not offer a realistic alternative for being unemployed with a relatively secure welfare benefit.

Here we should mention two important points of discussion about the un-intended effects of social policy. First, welfare benefits are often said to deter people to opt for paid work. Second, a sufficient welfare system would provide an excuse for not developing an active and activating labor market policy. The first will shortly be addressed to in this chapter and in Chapters 7 and 9. The second will be shortly addressed to in Chapter 10.

Of course we can not refer to the entire category of educated and voluntarily out of work respondents as losers. As will become clear in the sequel of this study, most of them constitute a category of unemployed who have developed an independent way of living without working; cleverly using the possibilities the modern Dutch welfare state offers. A considerable number of them had turned their unfavorable labor market position into quite an easy going life, with not too much to do, and not many obligations. In some cases, they were taking courses and were preparing to eventually re-enter the labor process at a considerably higher job level.

The picture of long-term unemployment outlined here in the light of recent trends in the labor market bears several similarities to the analysis of the Dutch-labor market by Kloosterman and Elfring (1991). First, there is a demand in the service sector for workers and, in view of the high unemployment rate, the supply would seem to be amply sufficient. Second, there is a category of workers, including many of the long-term unemployed, for which there is no demand. In the first case, the jobs are relatively low paid and require a relatively low level of education. The demand is mainly in the service sector and in part, there will continue to be a demand for people with a relatively low educational level. In the second case, Kloosterman and Elfring made it clear that the demand for higher quality workers will also increase in the service-industries. Many of the long-term unemployed have a low level of education, particularly in the large cities. Many of the low-skilled and low-paid jobs that will become available in the service industry will be taken by newcomers on the labor market, youngsters fresh out of school and (married) women returning to work. Thus there is a mismatch between supply and demand, particularly concerning the service industry. The long-term unemployed do not sufficiently meet the demands of service-mindedness; mobility or flexibility. Their former work experience was nearly always monotonous routine work, and they have been trained to do little else. Besides, their expectations of work do not meet the conditions offered. In most cases the labor demand in services concerns part-time or flexible contracts. The prospect offered by such contracts is often too insecure for the long-term unemployed, particularly for the elderly among them, many of whom have social and financial obligations that prevent them from accepting a part-time or flexible job. The low chances of leaving the unemployment situation, particularly for the unemployed in Rotterdam are significant in this connection. There are indications that for some short-term unemployed *flexiwork* can offer opportunities to (re)gain a position in the labor process (Timmer 1991). This pertains mainly to young people who do not have too much obligations yet, and who have ambitions many long-term unemployed have lost. It also pertains to women who try to reenter the labor market. Oftentimes, they have the security of a partner who earns an income and prefer to combine a job with activities at home. Some *flexiworkers* even prefer the independence that flexiwork may offer to the security of a regular job.

Most of the long-term unemployed in this study lost their jobs at the beginning of the 1980s, when the recession was at its worst. In addition to a fall in the entire number of jobs, the change in the kinds of jobs that were available was such that the only kind of work they were qualified for, in view of their low educational level, was gradually disappearing. This clearly made them the losers in the job market. In view of the education and experience of our average respondents and in view of the future trends in the structure of the job market and the composition of the work force, for most of them the job market will continue to be a "jobless market."

NOTES

1. More and more people—recently predominantly women—are forced to have even two or more jobs to meet their financial needs. Among women this phenomenon has grown from 2.7 percent in 1973 to 5.9 percent in 1989. Among men the "multiple jobholding rate" is stable (6.6 percent in 1973, 6.4 percent in 1989). Half of the multiple jobholders does so for reasons of economic hardship. See Lawrence Mishel and David M. Frankel, *The State of Working in America*, 1990-91 Edition, New York: Economic Policy Institute, 1991.

2. The fastest growers among the producer services are the commercial services. Accountants, lawyers, cleaning companies and software houses generated a growth rate of 8.3 percent in the period between 1987 and 1990. Distributive services (mainly retail and wholesale) grew with an average

rate of 3.1 in the same period. The fastest growers among the personal services were catering (8.2 percent) and barbers 3.1 percent. A fast particularly grower in the earlier period 1979-1987 (3.2 percent against an average of 0.6), health care, between 1987 and 1990 showed a growth rate of 1.9 percent, (Robert C. Kloosterman and Tom Elfring, *Werken in Nederland*, Schoonhoven: Academic Service, 1991).

3. Flexible work, or non-standard work, or precarious work, is work done under contracts that do prescribe a steady industrial relation or a certain amount of working hours. Flexible jobs (flexiwork) do not give certainty as to how many hours one has to work, work contents, income or job duration. It may concern: work through commercial temporary work agencies, on-call work, short-term work, home work, free-lance work and all kinds of slightly different variations.

4. This includes people with so little work experience that hardly anything can be said about it (see also Chapter 6).

5. See for instance: Peter B. Doeringer and Michael Piore, *Internal Labor Markets and Manpower Analysis*, Lexington, Massachusetts: Heath 1971; Richard C. Edwards, Michael Reich and David M. Gordon (eds.), *Labor Market Segmentation*, Lexington, Massachusetts/London 1975: D.C. Heath; Richard C. Edwards, *Contested Terrain: The Transformation of the Workplace in the Twentieth Century*, New York: Basic Books 1979; Ivar Berg (ed.), *Sociological Perspectives on Labor Markets*, New York: Academic Press 1981.

CHAPTER 4

Making Ends Meet

As is evident from the strategies they have to employ in order to make ends meet, the long-term unemployed and the poor live under a strict financial regime. In his book *Making Ends Meet*, Caplowitz (1979) distinguished six possible reactions to a lowered income: increase income, restrict expenditures, become more self-sufficient (household production), go bargain hunting, share with others, and apply for consumer credit. Caplowitz noted that self-sufficiency and bargain hunting could be viewed as strategies for the very poorest of the poor; it was so difficult for them to get credit. In the 1980s, the low credit rating of the poor fell even lower. Their limited financial means are reflected in the fact that three quarters of the black residents of Chicago's extreme poverty areas do not have a checking or savings account.[1] If they want to borrow money, they have little choice but to turn to informal loan sharks who charge high interest rates. Caplowitz' observation that "the poor pay more" is just as true today.[2] Currency exchanges (the "banks of the poor") where black residents can cash checks, pay bills and buy money for a fee are one of the few remaining forms of enterprise in the inner city (Wacquant 1992a).

Some ethnographic studies of poverty shed a sharper light than Caplowitz' book does on the income strategies of the poor. The study by Stack (1974), for instance, depicted the extended kinship networks within which women divided up available means. In some low-income communities, sharing appears to be a crucial survival strategy. Another important study into how Aid to Families with Dependent Children (AFDC) recipients make ends meet was carried out by Edin (Edin 1991, Edin and Jencks 1992). Edin conducted an intensive study among 50 AFDC recipients. She convincingly demonstrated that welfare pays too little to entice recipients into a life of passive dependence. She showed that all the women she interviewed supplemented their AFDC and food stamp benefits with at least one or two sources of unreported income: relatives, friends, boyfriends or absent fathers and income from work. In theory, these sources of income should be reported, but in practice they are not reported. Welfare workers often turn a blind eye, since they are familiar with the problems of their clients. The additional income is essential because the AFDC benefit is not enough to live on. What was striking in Edin's study was that seven women had regular jobs, twenty-two had part-time jobs and ten were employed in the informal economy. However, they did not earn enough at these jobs to be able to support themselves independently. Edin calculated that welfare recipients needed approximately twice as much as they received from welfare and food stamps.[3]

Edin's study several various stereotypes: first, that the poor do not work; second that they do not *want* to work; and third, that their behavioral norms deviate widely from those of mainstream society. Her study also implicitly questioned the validity for the United States of Ray Pahl's thesis that being jobless means being workless. According to Pahl, the unemployed lack the skills and the material and social channels to gain access into the informal economy (Pahl 1984 and 1987; see also Renooy 1990). The informal economy reproduces the inequality of the formal economy and contributes toward the further polarization of society. Edin's study illustrated that even though the economic activities they engaged in were not usually very lucrative, American welfare recipients certainly were active in the formal and informal labor markets.

Edin's study suggests a picture of efficient and resourceful women who managed to make ends meet (see also Sidel 1986). The study barely mentions women who were unable to earn an alternative income, yet the category of less inventive welfare mothers has been described.[4] The same holds true for unemployed men. The studies *A Place on the Corner* (Anderson 1978) and *Soulside* (Hannerz' 1969) described poor people who managed to survive in various ways. Some were employed in the formal labor market, others were active in the informal economy, and others were completely marginalized. There were considerable differences in the ways various groups of poor people tried to make ends meet. These differences could be linked to specific features of individuals and the social worlds they were part of.

In their article "The Poverty of Distinction" (1986), Thompson and Wildavsky showed that poor people in America, Great Britain and Israel develop strategies closely related to their social worlds, or their "ways of life." These strategies have their own rationality in specific social contexts and reproduce specific ways of life. According to Thompson and Wildavsky, needs and resources are social constructions. They differentiated between five possible strategies: (1) a *fatalistic strategy*, when poor people are not able to influence their own needs and resources; (2) an *egalitarian strategy*, when resources are controlled by a close community, but needs can be adapted to the resources; (3) a *hierarchical strategy*, when needs are defined by a hierarchical organization; (4) an *autonomous strategy*, when needs and resources are mutually geared; and (5) an *entrepreneurial strategy*, when needs and resources can be maximized.

At first glance, the American observations would not seem to be relevant to our study of the Dutch long-term unemployed, which pertained mainly to men and single people. Moreover, the Netherlands have a well-developed social secur ity system and a less important informal labor market than the United States. It is nonetheless interesting to note how the Dutch unemployed make ends meet. Thus the relation can be addressed between social security systems and strategies of making ends meet. In this chapter, we describe the financial position of the unemployed we interviewed and analyze their strategies for making ends meet. In the concluding section, we draw comparisons with the American literature and review our empirical findings from the point of view of cultural theory.

FINANCIAL POSITION

In this section, the household is the unit of analysis. The financial survey focuses on the following four types of households: single adults, single-parent families, couples without children and couples with children. No distinction has been drawn between married couples and couples who live together.

Through of the Unemployment Insurance Act, people who lose their jobs are entitled to a benefit that equates 70 percent of their last earned wages for a duration of five months to five years, depending on their seniority.[5] In 1989, the Dutch average production worker earned 41,410 guilders; the exchage rate to the dollar being 1.8, this equals $23,005. After the unemployment benefit is exhausted, Dutch unemployed singles and breadwinners are entitled to a benefit under the National Assistance Act, referred to as "welfare,"[6] if necessary until the age of 65, when they are entitled to the General Old Age Pension. For singles the average welfare benefit in 1987 was a monthly income of 1072 guilders ($596), 66 percent of the average income of singles (SCP 1990). A two-parent household with two children was entitled to a welfare benefit of 1854 guilders ($1030), or 50 percent of the average income in this category. In Germany welfare recipients were entitled to the following sums: singles; $420, 41 percent; and households $1005, or 40 percent. The average production worker earned 41,840 German marks ($26,499).

Comparable data for the United States are hard to obtain, since unemployment insurance usually ends after 26 weeks (see also Appendix IV). Unemployment insurance equals to 50 percent of the last wage, with a minimum of $30 a week and a maximum of $210, varying from state to state. In 1989, the American average production worker earned $21,643. Welfare—Aid to Families with Dependent Children (AFDC) or General Assistance (GA)—varies greatly from state to state. A welfare mother with one child in Illinois in 1988 ended up with $399 a month, with $558 if she had two children, with $658 if she had three children, and with $775 if she had four children, including food stamps and Medicaid (Edin and Jencks 1992).

A welfare benefit for a single person living in Washington, D.C. in 1990, amounted to $281, or 9 percent of the average income. A welfare benefit for a two-headed household with two children amounted to $367, or 12 percent of the average income. (For a more extended comparison of American and Dutch incomes and benefits see Appendix IV.)

In addition to the welfare benefit, some households in our study had extra income on the side, derived from the paid employment or benefits of some other member of the household, extra earnings of the respondent or other sources. Furthermore, the households also had access to three other sources of income: the child allowance every parent or parental couple is entitled to, vacation bonuses, and special bonuses given at the end of the year to the lowest income groups.

The average monthly income per person (the income of each household member including vacation bonus, child allowance and annual bonus) amounted to 867 guilders ($482). After the deduction of fixed living expenses (e.g., rent and energy), the remainder amounted to 590 guilders ($328). Table 4.1 shows the differences in household and personal income among the various types of households. As Dutch social security supplies only financial benefits, and no food stamps or housing checks, people have to pay for all their expenses out of this income.

The data presented so far pertain to four types of households: single people, single-parent families, couples without children and couples with children. Some other categories had lower incomes. More than 10 percent of our respondents still lived with their parents. The National Assistance Act entitles them to the same benefit as single people who live with one or more other adults. For those over 23, since July 1, 1987, this amount has been 885 guilders per month ($492).

TABLE 4.1 Monthly Income[a] per Type of Household (in Dutch guilders, N=206)

	Per Household	Per Individual[b]
Couple	1601	897
Couple with Children	1854	392
Single-Parent Family	1394	638
Single Person	1072	1072

[a] The monthly income consists of the benefit, whatever has been formally earned, the other formal sources of income such as child allowance, and the incomes of other members of the household.

[b] This is the actual household income divided through the number of persons in the household. So in fact it is a theoretical individual income. This individual income is used to show the personal spendable income in Table 4.4.

MAKING ENDS MEET

It was not easy to adjust day-to-day expenditures to reduced income, especially in the beginning of the unemployment period. The longer their dependence on welfare, the more the households developed strategies of restricting and rationalizing their expenditures.

If I want a new winter coat, I have to start thinking about it months in advance. There are things I just can't do. I can't go to the movies every week and I can't have a newspaper because

I still have a telephone. Those are choices you have to make (25-year-old woman, single, 3 years unemployed).

Dealing with money in a "calculating" way also means synchronizing the payments that have to be made with the date the welfare check is expected, which leads to a fixed pattern of spending in each time unit.

If you get your money on the nineteenth then you know that on the twentieth it will be on your Post or bank account. So you count the days until the twentieth. On the nineteenth, we finish the last slices of bread. Then the kids can eat everything that is left. Because I know that the next day, I'll be picking up my money. But sometimes I get that frightened feeling: what if it hasn't been transferred to my account? Then I'm in trouble, because I don't even have a bus ticket to get me to Welfare Department (38-year-old Surinamese man, partner and children, 13 years unemployed).

The households spent their income mainly on the primary necessities: rent, gas and electricity, clothes, groceries, the expenses of bringing up children, furniture, and the purchase or repair of durable consumer goods such as a refrigerator or washing machine. Migrant workers often had to support relatives in their native country and had additional travel and telephone expenses.

The basic necessities cost most of our respondents virtually their entire monthly income. There was little or no money left for educational, recreational or social activities and vacations. It was even difficult for them to afford to keep contact with friends, relatives and acquaintances. The costs required could be borne only by a minority of our respondents, single people, people whose friends or relatives helped them out, or people with alternative sources of income. In order to make ends meet, our respondents had to economize on various items. Some of these items are discussed in the following sections.

Economizing on Geographic Mobility

One item our respondents could economize on was traveling, thus reducing their geographic mobility to a minimum. Twenty-eight percent of the households had a car; most had never owned a car. There was a group who once had a car, but sold it or could not replace it. Those who did have a car were planning to use it as long as they could, or they drove an old second-hand car. For some of them, this was cheaper than using public transport. Having a car also gave them a feeling of freedom and independence, and of being a full-fledged member of society.

I have got myself a little car and that's why I don't feel like a total pauper. It makes me feel good (43-year-old woman, single, 6 years unemployed).

The only way migrant workers, predominantly Turks and Moroccans, could visit their relatives in their homeland was by car. Many of them bought a second-hand car for that purpose, often together with a relative or a nearby friend. In the Netherlands, as well as in other European countries, the neighborhoods with high concentrations of Turks and Moroccans are well known for the many mini-buses, being prepared for the yearly trip to the homeland.

Three quarters of our respondents used public transportation. Most of them, however, could barely afford it, and it was an item many respondents cut down on. They used their bicycles or walked, even if distances were considerable. Otherwise they tried to use public transport as economically as possible, that is, by free riding.

That ten guilders public transportation would cost is what I buy my vegetables with. I try to walk everywhere (34-year-old man, single, 5 years unemployed).

I go everywhere by bike. On Saturday and Sunday they don't charge extra for the bike on the Metro (37-year-old woman, single, 20 years unemployed).

Economizing on Contacts with Friends and Relatives

Because many of the respondents had to cut down on travel expenses, it became difficult for them to maintain contact with friends or relatives who lived far away. Social contacts were also reduced because they could no longer afford to buy birthday presents or go to parties. Many kinds of contact involved similar expenditures that were beyond their means but were felt to be expected. Therefore some of the respondents had to stop engaging in certain social activities.

There are certain things you just stop doing. In the beginning, when people asked me if I felt like a game of cards, I would say, "Sure, count me in." But then there came a time when I started thinking: "Five guilders, ten guilders, no I don't really feel like it today." . . . On Sunday usually the whole family gets together at my parents' house. The women sit around having a drink and talking while the men play cards. That is over now. We don't go there anymore (38-year-old Surinamese man, partner and children, 13 years unemployed).

Some respondents did get support from friends and relatives in the form of food, domestic utensils, clothes or free vacation trips—but only one third of them. Sometimes such support was more or less structural. At regular intervals or for certain fixed expenditures, they would receive money from the immediate family or would regularly eat at their place. Most often, the support was incidental and irregular.

We have a very sweet father and a very sweet mother, and every so often they send us a little something. Or they help us out in some other way. Not just with money. They might come over on Saturday and bring along some food, plants or clothes for the children (partner of 38-year-old Surinamese man, partner and children, 13 years unemployed).

Some were helped out by sisters, brothers or parents. Support by parents was most common. A few felt fortunate that they could turn to relatives, but others were uncomfortable about being dependent on them. For larger expenditures, material support by relatives was often given in the form of a loan, which did not always have to be paid back in full.

Sometimes we borrow money from my parents. We decide how much to pay back every month. But after a couple of months they say, "Oh, we don't mind if you just forget about the rest" (32-year-old man, partner and no children, 6 years unemployed).

Economizing on Social Participation

Other items our respondents cut down on were going out, hobbies, sports, clubs and courses. Sometimes they cut out recreational or educational activities altogether, in other cases they reduced the frequency of the expenditures or chose less expensive clubs or activities. Economizing on going out mainly meant they less frequently went to a bar or restaurant or to the movies, even though these activities were important to them for keeping contact with others and making them feel like full members of society.

I'm the kind of person who likes to spend time at a bar. It isn't that I spend all my money there, it's just that I want to be able to talk to people (32-year-old man, single, 6 years unemployed).

Going out less reduced the quality of life. In part, our respondents compensated by looking for cheaper ways to spend their leisure time, like going to a park instead of a bar. Spending money on sports was similarly problematic.

I used to belong to an athletic club and I really liked it. It was easy for me to pay the dues. But that is not the case now. So you even have to economize on your hobby (32-year-old Antillean man, partner and children, 6 years unemployed).

The households also economized on many other smaller items. A subscription to a newspaper or magazine was viewed as a luxury. Even though they could not afford it, as a source of information about the outside world a newspaper or magazine was hard to do without. Therefore some shared subscriptions, although others gave them up.

Economizing on Vacations

Virtually everyone economized on holidays. Like the annual bonus and children's allowance, the vacation bonus was spent on things that could not be paid for out of regular monthly income.

There is no way I can ever go on holidays. How are you supposed to go on vacation if all you have is 600 guilders? I'd be gone for three weeks and every penny I have would be gone too. A nice fix that would be! Not really the kind of thing that would make me feel any better (31-year-old man, single, 5 years unemployed).

I got the yearly 700 guilder vacation bonus this month. For somebody on welfare, it is hard to put 700 guilders aside, because there are so many things you have to buy right away. There is always a kitchen pail or a pair of shoes you need. So a vacation is out of the question (25-year-old man, single, 5 years unemployed).

Only a few of the respondents did manage to get away now and then. Their vacations were paid for by relatives or friends or were limited to short excursions or weekends.

The income strategies of the unemployed often reduce their geographical and social worlds and contribute to the perpetuation of welfare dependence. People who want to get out of a situation of dependence need social contacts. But social contacts cost money and that is exactly what most of them are short of. Welfare recipients often get trapped in a vicious circle of welfare dependence and long-term unemployment (Douglas and Isherwood 1979).

Other strategies beside economizing on goods and social activities, the unemployed also developed other strategies to make ends meet such as saving money, bargain hunting, and buying second-hand.

Saving Money

Another way to finance purchases is by regularly putting some money aside. The National Assistance Act norm amounts included a theoretical margin for such purchases. Twenty-two percent of the households studied were able to save some for special purchases. A similar percentage is found in other studies on minimum income households (Oude Engberink 1984, Engbersen and Van der Veen 1987). Whether or not one managed to save some money had to do with several structural factors, such as the duration of the dependence on welfare and the monthly income per person. The lower the income and the longer the dependence on welfare, the less one saved.

Bargain Hunting

In the strict sense, bargain hunting refers to "time-consuming activities people engage in to do their shopping as cheaply as possible. The shopping is usually done at a wide variety of stores, including large chain stores, and often involves traveling long distances. Price buying mainly costs time. It is done on foot or by bike and fills a large part of the day" (Engbersen and Van der Veen 1987:14). Most of our respondents were price conscious, paid attention to special offers and did their shopping as cheaply as possible.

If I can get margarine cheaper somewhere else, then off I go, even if I have to bicycle half way across the city, you know (49-year-old man of foreign descent, multi-family household, 6 years unemployed).

Buying Second-Hand

Other strategies to cut down on expenditures included buying second-hand items, making or repairing clothes and growing vegetables. Items bought second-hand were clothes, furniture or durable consumer goods such as washing machines, refrigerators or television sets.

The refrigerator broke down. With an advance I got from the welfare people, I bought a little second-hand one for 175 guilders (31-year-old woman of foreign descent, single with child, 3 years unemployed).

Some had a small plot of land where they could grow their own vegetables.

I have a vegetable garden out there where I grow whatever I want, string beans, brown beans, red cabbage, potatoes. In winter I hardly have to buy any vegetables at all (39-year-old man, lives with parents, 6 years unemployed).

ALTERNATIVE WAYS TO AUGMENT THE INCOME

Some respondents did whatever they could to augment their income. Almost 17 percent earned a bit of money on the side with formal work, usually a part-time job and sometimes a temporary full-time job. There were also respondents who added to their monthly income in alternative ways. They engaged in what is termed "calculating" behavior and made "wrongful" or "improper" use of the social security system.

"Calculating behavior" means taking optimal advantage of the opportunities provided by the system, including altering one's own circumstances. For example, people on welfare may divorce in order to receive two benefits for single clients rather than one benefit for a married couple; or they may decide not to live together in order to keep their two separate benefits. This calculating behavior is legal.

Wrongful or improper use of the system involves behavior that goes against the letter and the spirit of the law, though it is not always easy to determine what the spirit of the law is. Wrongful use means actually violating the law for one's financial advantage. Examples include working in the informal economy or studying full time at a university without informing the Welfare Department. Making improper use of social security means violating the spirit rather than the letter of the law. Examples are registering as an evening student in order to receive a benefit but in reality studying full time or somehow avoiding benefit deduction for people who live together in one house.

Working in the Informal Economy

Seventeen percent of our respondents admitted to earning something in the informal economy. Half of these cases did so on a regular basis, in the other half on an occasional basis. For 60 percent who earned something on the side, the extra income did not exceed 200 guilders a month. Five percent earned a sum equal to or above the benefit for single persons. However, these figures should not be taken at face value. The actual extra income might be higher, given that not everyone will easily admit having additional sources of income. However, the figures recorded here, were the highest found in studies like this so far. For those who take on informal work, two factors are important: opportunity and risk perception.

Opportunity

Of the respondents who did not engage in any paid informal work, 38 percent said they simply had no such opportunity. More people mentioned this reason in the Enschede location than in the Rotterdam neighborhood. In Rotterdam, the opportunities were greater and the features of the research population coincided more with the demands in the paid informal work sector.

Opportunities for informal work were determined by three elements: the demand for informal labor, the social networks of the respondents and their skills and training. Demand for informal work is significantly higher in urban environments, due to the anonymity of cities and the greater importance of industries such as catering and cleaning. In Amsterdam and Rotterdam, demand for informal work was significantly higher than in Enschede.

Recent studies in the Netherlands have demonstrated that the size and nature of the social network influence the of unemployed individuals chances to participate in the informal economy (Renooy 1990). Our study confirms this. The ones who did not work informally often said the reason they did not was that they lacked the right contacts. They never "got the chance" to find that kind of work. When they lost their job, they also lost the chance to earn an informal income on the side.

When I had a job, I did that kind of thing pretty often. I would work for the boss all week long, and in the weekend there was always some little extra thing that had to be done. I even did that once for an income tax inspector who wanted the lane repaired in backyard. The line of work I was in gave me plenty of chances to do that (40-year-old man, partner and children, 4 years unemployed).

A large majority got informal work also through relatives and friends. Within the family network, work often was not paid for in money, but in other ways. Work done for people outside the family, but acquired through relatives or friends, was usually paid for in cash.

Through my brother, I once did a job for a company he was working for at the time (45-year-old man, partner no children, 7 years unemployed).

A friend of ours is very busy with her job and all, and there is some work around the house that needs to be done. I do the dishes and the laundry and that kind of thing . . . it's not a lot of money, but it does add up (29-year-old man, partner no children, 5 years unemployed).

Of those with many friends and acquaintances, 13 percent regularly earned something on the side. Of those without friends, only 3 percent worked off the books. There was no correlation, however, between size of the family network and informal work. Within family networks, it is probably more a matter of doing mutual favors. In other words, contacts outside the family are essential.

Regular informal work was done more widely by respondents with a higher education (17 percent) than by those with a high school (8 percent) or elementary school education (2 percent). Those who had worked at a relatively high level were also more apt to work off the books than those who had held lower positions. Furthermore, practical skills and access to necessary tools played a role. Several respondents said they had worked off the books using their former employer's car and tools.

Other studies of the Dutch informal economy have produced comparable results. Renooy (1990) concluded that the supply and demand for informal labor is concentrated in the middle-income category. In a rural working-class area with a high unemployment rate, Renooy found a "surprisingly small informal economy" (1990:121). Since it was so closely linked to the formal economy, long-term unemployed had little access to it. This certainly held true for what Renooy called the "linked" and "semi-linked" informal economy, where activities have a direct or indirect relation to formal companies and formal work. For the "autonomous" informal economy, chiefly consisting of activities in and around the home, social contacts and specific skills were the most important entrance requirements. The best training for informal work was intermediate vocational school. Renooy noted that unemployed people participated less in the informal economy than employed people because of their lack of contacts and insufficient skills. They also were more subject to control than working people and the consequences of discovery were more severe.

Risk Perception

Risk perception was an important factor in explaining whether or not people worked off the books. Of those who did not, 51 percent said it the risk of being caught—their benefit reduced or even stopped altogether—was too high.

I don't have the feeling there is somebody looking over my shoulder all the time, but I also don't think it's safe. If they catch you, you lose everything. I'm already in a hopeless situation, so I don't want to make it any worse (32-year-old man, no-family household, 3 years unemployed).

Respondents with children were afraid that if they were caught, their children would suffer. Fraudulent work thus was less widespread among households with children, even though their financial problems were often the most severe.

Social control in the neighborhood also played a role in the risk perception. The fear of being reported by someone in the neighborhood was greatest in the Enschede area. Almost 65 percent there said they found the risk too great, whereas 45 percent in the other two neighborhoods felt this way. Many people in Enschede were afraid someone would report them to the Welfare Department.

TABLE 4.2 Informal Earnings in Each Location (in percentages, N=251)

	Rotterdam	Amsterdam	Enschede	Total	
yes	19	17	16	17	
• occasional	2	10	13	8	
• regular	16	7	3	9	
no	81	83	84	83	
Total	100	100	100	100	

It means taking much too much of a chance. If they catch you, you are really done for. And there are plenty of people just waiting to double cross you (27-year-old man, lives with parents, 2 years unemployed).

You can't trust anybody, that's what I always say. There are people who get a kick out of seeing someone else in trouble if only out of jealousy (30-year-old man, lives with parents, 5 years unemployed).

The amounts earned through informal work were approximately the same in the three locations. However, in Rotterdam the earnings were predominantly regular whereas in Enschede they were mainly occasional (see Table 4.2).

A Typology of Informal Work

In their informal work, the long-term unemployed respondents can be divided into two types: the entrepreneur and the moonlighter.

The Entrepreneur

The respondents with regular earnings from informal work (9 percent) are referred to here as entrepreneurs. For them, the informal sector was an alternative to the regular labor market. They viewed welfare as a kind of basic income to be supplemented by informal earnings. They valued their freedom and independence which they could not have in the formal labor system.

This group included many people in their twenties or thirties as well as single people. In general, they had a comparatively high level of educational, had an extensive network of friends, did volunteer work, and went out often. Almost half of these respondents felt the advantages of unemployment to be greater than the disadvantages. None were ashamed of being out of a job. They tended to view their freedom and leisure time as advantages and mentioned aimlessness, boredom and lack of social contact less frequently than others. They looked less actively for formal work than others. The large majority of entrepreneurs lived in the Rotterdam area. Social control was relatively weak there and the city environment gave them ample opportunity for finding work in the informal sector.

The Moonlighter

The respondents with occasional earnings from informal work (8 percent) can be called moonlighters. For them, doing paid informal work was mainly a strategy for making ends meet. Most of them had not given up wanting a formal job. This group consisted mainly of people between 30 to 40 years old who did not live alone.

More than 14 percent of these respondents were ashamed of being out of a job and only 10 percent of them felt the advantages of unemployment to be greater than the disadvantages. They did refer to freedom and leisure time as advantages of unemployment, but to a lesser extent than the entrepreneurs. They more frequently referred to boredom, aimlessness and lack of social contact as disadvantages of unemployment. They had a better assessment of their chances of finding formal work than those who did not operate in the informal sector at all. The majority of these respondents lived in Enschede and Amsterdam.

The entrepreneurs and the moonlighters had more in common with each other than with those who did not do any informal work. They were more socially active, had more friends and acquaintances, did more volunteer work, went out more often, and were less bored. They were less prone to feelings of embarrassment and saw more advantages in being unemployed.

Calculating Behavior

Some respondents added to their income by taking a calculating approach to the social security regulations. Nine percent of the households made use of the welfare system in a calculating way. Some people decided not to live with their partners any more. If both of the partners were unemployed and lived apart, they would each be entitled to a separate benefit for a single person, instead of together being entitled to one benefit for a couple.

> I would like to live with my boyfriend but I have a welfare benefit and I don't want to be financially dependent on anybody . . . When I was still getting Unemployment Insurance, we did live together for a while, but when that was over and it was time for welfare, I told my boyfriend it would be better if he moved out. Because I don't like to lie. So he moved out just for the welfare Department. Actually it's more for the sake of appearance than anything else. My boyfriend lives in the neighborhood and he still spends a lot of time here (31-year-old woman, single with child, 3 years unemployed).

Others safeguarded their right to two benefits by living separately only in appearance. They might register under different addresses even though they actually lived together, or they might sign a lease as if one is renting from the other. To the Welfare Department, this would look as if there were two separate households.

> They didn't deduct anything from my benefit because officially I am renting a room here. At least that's what they think. But I don't pay rent to my girlfriend (31-year-old man, single, 12 years unemployed).

Another advantageous arrangement was using welfare as a student loan.[7] The advantages over a regular government scholarship or loan were that the monthly amount was higher and almost none of it had to be paid back.

Three years ago I had a government scholarship. I stopped applying for it because I wanted to get a job and study part-time. But it wasn't so easy. Then I thought to myself: the best thing is to get welfare and go on studying. It makes quite a difference. Because living on a scholarship puts you in debt (30-year-old man, lives with parents, 3 years unemployed).

Strictly speaking, people on welfare are allowed to go to evening school, as long as they remain available for a job in the daytime. Several of our respondents were registered at universities as part-time evening students, but they often attended classes in the daytime as well. Sometimes the Welfare Department knew about this, but the case workers felt that education would considerably improve the client's chances on the labor market.

The calculating unemployed differed from the others in that they were relatively young, had a relatively high level of education, were mainly of Dutch descent, were more frequently women and single, and had been unemployed for relatively short periods of time. Their personal views on work and social rights and the attitudes of the people around them toward unemployment and dependence on welfare, motivated them and allowed them to behave vis-à-vis the social security regulations as they did. They often felt the advantages of unemployment to be greater than the disadvantages. They had less experience with stigmatization than others because their social environment, usually people of their own age with a similar life style, tolerated their behavior. Young people attending courses of some kind usually considered the situation to be temporary. After completing their studies, they would look for a job.

Like the enterprising group described earlier, these calculating respondents were also found mainly in Rotterdam, to a lesser extent in Amsterdam, and hardly at all in Enschede. In an anonymous social environment lacking social control, like the Rotterdam neighborhood, it is easier to work in the informal economy and to set up advantageous arrangements.

DEBTS

Many respondents could not keep their expenditures within the limits of their income: 49 percent of the households had debts, a percentage also found in other recent studies of the financial position of people with a minimum income (Oude Engberink 1987; Engbersen and Van der Veen 1987). The amounts of the debts varied; 46 percent of the cases involved amounts up to 2,000 guilders, 27 percent over 5,000 guilders (see Table 4.3). In many of these cases, the Welfare Department has taken over responsibility and initiative by paying regular expenses like rent, gas, water, electricity, and credits. In practice, such a relation means a bureaucratic invasion into the private life of the individual welfare recipient. This situation primarily concerns the modern poor, people who have been in financial trouble chiefly because of the long duration of their unemployment and have become structurally dependent on welfare state agencies.

TABLE 4.3 Debts in Guilders (in percentages, N=87)

< 1,000	24
1,000-2,000	22
2,000-5,000	27
5,000-10,000	18
> 10,000	9
Total	100

Debts over 2,000 guilders equaled or exceeded a two-months benefit of a single person. More than half the households-in-debt owed amounts they could not hope to pay back within a year. In some households we observed "debt cumulation." More than 26 percent of the households-in-debt owed money to more than one agency, and more than 7 percent owed money to relatives as well as to one or more agencies.[8]

Ways of Going Into Debt

There were five ways of going into debt. The first was taking a bank loan from the Municipal Credit Bank or a similar agency. In general, commercial banks do not give loans to people without a regular income from formal economic activities such as employment and trade. Of the respondents who owed money to commercial banks, these debts dated from when they were still employed. Loans from municipal credit banks are given to pay back existing debts or to finance special purchases. These loans are often paid back by having the Welfare Department deduct a fixed sum from the monthly benefit.

A second way of going into debt was by borrowing money from friends, relatives or acquaintances. Borrowing from relatives usually has the advantage that payment terms are more flexible. In some cases, the debt did not have to be paid back in full. However, it gave some people a feeling of dependence on the people around them.

Third, people got into debt by installment buying from mail order companies. This highlights the predicament of low income people, since the conditions of mail order companies are often unfavorable. Given the interest charged, installment buying meant that "the poorer one was, the more he had to pay" (Caplovitz 1963). Nonetheless, no fewer than 14 percent of the households-in-debt owed money to one or more mail order companies. For households on a minimum income, installment buying is often the only way to purchase expensive and durable consumer items. Often the necessity for such a purchase does not come up until something in the household breaks down or a change in the living situation, for example a divorce or a move, makes it imperative. Then, installment buying can be a solution, though many of the respondents were well aware of the disadvantages.

There are days when we really have to buy something, even though we know we can't. Then we sit down with some mail order catalogues and make calculations so we can just about swing it. But in the end you never come out ahead. Those mail order companies really know what they are doing. It looks so nice when you buy something, and then later you see how much interest you have to pay (38-year-old Surinamese man, partner and children, 13 years unemployed).

The common way of going into debt was by overdrawing on a bank account. Many respondents said they had become accustomed to being in the red on their accounts.

Without my Post Office Giro account, I would really be in trouble. I think that holds true for a lot of people. The Post Office Giro Bank gives you credit. It's like a social agency (50-year-old man, single, 8 years unemployed).

Finally, people got in debt by putting off paying the rent, income tax, radio and television license fees, gas and electricity bills, telephone bills and so forth. Some people did this deliberately, since it did not necessarily involve any significant consequences. For many years, Dutch public utility companies have been quite lenient toward debtors. Until recently, the municipal counsels, the shareholders of these companies, did not want people to be disconnected for reasons of health and sanity. Since the late 1980s, this policy has been changed because many people got into serious financial trouble.

I haven't paid my electricity bill for more than a year, that is 16 times 183 guilders. That's the only way I can manage to get by (44-year-old man, single with child, 8 years unemployed).

The major creditors of the respondents with one debt were the Municipal Credit Bank (26 percent), the Post Office Giro Bank (21 percent), mail order companies (14 percent) and relatives or friends (14 percent).

Reasons for Going into Debt

Whether or not people got into debt was related to the type of household they lived in and the monthly income per person. Table 4.4 shows that households with children were more likely to be in debt than households without children, and single people more frequently than couples without children or respondents who lived with their parents. The household situation determined the income per person, and the lower the income per person, the higher chance there was to be in debt.

People from Turkey, Morocco or some other Mediterranean country (52 percent) or Suriname or the Antilles (71 percent) were more frequently in debt than Dutch respondents (46 percent) or respondents from other countries (31 percent). These immigrant households are often larger than Dutch households, and consequently have lower average incomes per person.

Table 4.4 also shows that the longer the duration of unemployment, the higher the likelihood of debt. After a certain amount of time, there were no more savings to fall back on and expenditures for items that had to be replaced could no longer be postponed.

TABLE 4.4 Likelihood of Debts

	percentage	N
Type of Household		
Single person	48	101
Couple	39	31
Couple with children	63	75
Single-parent family	67	15
Lives with parents	32	28
Other types of household	27	11
Spendable Monthly Income[a]		
< 301	82	11
301 – 500	56	45
501 – 700	52	44
701 – 900	46	54
> 900	29	7
Duration of Unemployment		
Less than 4 year	38	73
4 to 6 years	48	86
6 years or longer	58	93

[a] Monthly income per person in guilders after the deduction of rent, gas and electricity bills and the addition of child allowance, annual bonus and vacation bonus divided into monthly amounts, calculated over the first four types of households.

Table 4.5 shows the debts and debt cumulation at the various research locations. In Rotterdam, more households (60 percent) were in debt than in the other two cities, and debt cumulation was more widespread. With very few exceptions, the debts were to government agencies. However, in almost half the Amsterdam households with debt cumulation, there were also debts to relatives. At the Enschede location, there was very little debt cumulation at all.

Most of the Enschede respondents did not make debts easily. In fact, 56 percent had no debts at all, apprehensive as they were about the extra financial burden paying of debts.

I have never been in the red on my bank account. If all you have is welfare then you'll never ever be able to get out of a situation like that (37-year-old woman, single with child, 8 years unemployed).

I don't have any debts. I wouldn't even think of it. Loans are a scary business. I'd rather save a little while longer. At least, if I can manage to (25-year-old man, lives with parents, 2 years unemployed).

TABLE 4.5 Debts per Location (in percentages, N=261)

	Rotterdam	Amsterdam	Enschede	Total
No debts	41	54	56	51
One debt	33	29	41	34
More than one debt	26	17	3	15
Total	100	100	100	100

In Enschede, there was significantly more social support than in the Amsterdam and Rotterdam neighborhood. This can help explain the comparatively limited importance of debts in Enschede. The social cohesion also meant a closer social surveillance on moonlighting and calculating behavior, and the more traditional ethic was more explicitly negative about debts.

CONCLUSIONS

Financial concerns and problems play an important role in the everyday lives of the long-term unemployed. Not having enough money to make ends meet was the most frequently mentioned (86 percent) disadvantage of unemployment. In the Netherlands, all six reactions identified by Caplowitz were in evidence. One striking difference in the Dutch situation is the relatively limited significance of self-sufficiency and the role of kinship and relatives. This has to do with the urbanization of Dutch society and the socio-cultural process of individualization that has taken place. Only a specific category has access to the informal economy, and the same holds true for the criminal circuit (Renooy 1990).

There are indications that traditional and "hard" strategies are more widespread in the United States than in the Netherlands. By traditional strategies, we mean help provided by relatives and activities that are directed toward self-sufficiency. Particularly in rural regions of the United States, these strategies are in evidence. Opportunities for self-sufficiency are far greater there than in cities, and traditional family structures are still relatively important (Ellwood 1988). In addition, kinship networks play an important role in the black ghettoes. For many women, female kinship networks are the only reliable source of financial support in the event of an emergency (Wacquant 1992a). By "hard" strategies, we mean participation in the informal economy. The American labor market is less formalized and regulated, and welfare benefits and income from formal labor are lower than in the Netherlands, so that the informal economy has come to be much more of a basic component of the economy than in the Netherlands. Also, the differences between the formal and the informal economy are less clearly delineated in the United States. The "hardest" income strategies are the ones used in the criminal and semi-criminal circuit, particularly the drug economy in the large cities.

For the Dutch unemployed going into debt with government and semi-government agencies is the most prevalent way to make ends meet. Such agencies are the Welfare Department, municipal housing companies, and the electricity company. These are state-dependent strategies. The main creditor is the Welfare Department, which in addition to regular benefits provides incidental loans that have to be paid back in monthly installments. Many people are also in debt with post order companies and financing companies. Unlike in the United States, the credit rating of people on welfare in the Netherlands is generally viewed as good enough to allow them to buy on credit or borrow money from companies of this kind. This important difference between the Dutch and American systems plays a role in the different survival strategies of the poor and unemployed. The more generous welfare benefits in the Netherlands and the more responsive and less selective Dutch welfare system have allowed for strategies that are not as "hard" as in the United States and for less reliance on kinship networks because there is less of a necessity for it. To solve their financial problems, the Dutch poor mainly turn to government agencies.

There are, however, differences in income strategies among Dutch unemployed. The social context plays a role in explaining these differences. The most important strategy is to adapt one's needs to the limited resources; this strategy was most common in Enschede. There, the social environment did not tolerate alternative strategies for augmenting income and leaned toward the "egalitarian strategy." Unemployed individuals were in debt and unable to adequately cope with this situation developed a "fatalistic strategy." They could no longer control their financial affairs, which were subsequently taken over by the Welfare Department. An "entrepreneurial strategy" was used by those who worked informally or had a calculating attitude toward the welfare system. They were able to augment their income and maintain a higher level of consumption, for example going out or buying books, records or clothes. Again, the social context is important. In the relatively anonymous Rotterdam neighborhood, informal activities were hardly noticed and, if they were, would often be tolerated.

A "hierarchical strategy" could not be observed. Such a strategy must, by definition, be enforced by the organizations people work for, and this study focused solely on unemployed people who had already been excluded from the labor process for a lengthy period of time. Some unemployed people used a weakened version of an "autonomous strategy." They effectively adapted their spending to their limited income, and some were even able to save a little money. They often viewed the welfare system as a basic income scheme. The very existence of this system actually enabled them to develop this strategy. In Chapter 8, links are drawn between income strategies and social context.

NOTES

1. In "low poverty areas," 34.8 percent of the black residents had a checking account and 35.4 percent had a savings account. In "extreme poverty areas," these figures were 12.2 percent and 17.8 percent (see Loïc J. D. Wacquant and William Julius Wilson, "The Cost of Racial and Class Exclusion in the Inner City," in: William Julius Wilson (ed.), *The Ghetto Underclass: Social Science Perspectives*, The Annals of the American Academy of Political and Social Sciences, Vol. 501, January 1989:8-25). In the Netherlands, practically everybody has a checking account, welfare recipients as well.

2. An interesting study on the effects of pawnbroking and credit on neighborhood and family life is Melanie Tebbutt, *Making Ends Meet, Pawnbroking and Working-Class Credit*, Leicester: Leicester University Press 1983.

3. Edin and Jencks wrote: "We created AFDC half a century ago to prevent single mothers from having to give up their children for economic reasons. . . . What we created, however, was not a system that allowed all single mothers to keep their children but a system that allowed them to keep

their children if they could supplement their welfare check in some way and conceal this fact from the welfare department," Kathryn Edin and Christopher Jencks, "Reforming Welfare," in: Christopher Jencks, *Rethinking Social Policy: Race, Poverty and the Underclass*, Cambridge, MA: Harvard University Press 1992, 204-235.

4. For instance: Alex Kotlowitz, *There Are No Children Here: The Study of Two Boys Growing Up in the Other America*, New York: Anchor Books Doubleday, 1991.

5. For an international overview over social security regulations see the OECD *Employment Outlook 1991*, Paris: OECD, 1991, p. 228 and further.

6. The Unemployment Insurance Act is administered by industrial insurance boards, organized per economic sector, 19 in total. The National Assistance Act is administered by the Municipal Welfare Departments (further referred to as Welfare Department) and largely paid for by the national government.

7. Dutch law allows beneficiaries to study in the evenings, providing that they look for work in daytime. Consequently, some unemployed people are actually part-time students. They study in the evenings, which enables them to continue to receive RWW benefits. However, many studied or did volunteer work related to their study in the daytime. A basic state scholarship amounts to about 600 guilders (depending on the parents' income a student can get an additional loan) and an welfare benefit for a single person to about 1000 guilders. What is more, a student loan has to be paid back later, a welfare benefit has not.

8. These figures have to be read within the context of considerable differences between the Netherlands and the United States concerning debts in general. Unlike the Americans, the Dutch have an average positive saving quote. That is part of the reason why people with low incomes, like unemployed, going into debt is considered a significant problem in the Netherlands. Not including mortgages, the average consumer credit amounted to 8600 guilders ($4800) in 1987 (CBS). (For more information see Appendix IV.)

CHAPTER 5

Dealing with Time

The French sociologist Gurvitch noted the existence of different social times (Gurvitch 1963). He drew a distinction between "macro-social time" and "micro-social time." Macro-social time is linked to the major institutional frameworks of a society, such as the labor market, the school system and the leisure time sector. Micro-social time is linked to the time orientation of specific groups and classes. Social time, which is distinguished from biological and physical time, is a relation between meaningful activities. Social time is also the expression of the social rhythm of social groups (see also Sorokin and Merton 1937).

These concepts can serve as a foothold for describing the time consciousness of various groups of long-term unemployed people. They engage in fewer "meaningful activities," and as a result their time awareness changes and their time horizon shrinks. This process was described in the chapter on "The Meaning of Time" in the Marienthal study (Lazarsfeld-Jahoda and Zeisel 1933). Various American ethnographic studies also have described the social repercussions of the time perspective of the poor. People who have no faith in a future and have been disoriented by the loss of work are not apt to invest in a training course, a working career or a family (Liebow 1967, Macleod 1987). Lauer wrote about this in his study *Temporal Man* (1981): "Without a future orientation and an image of the future, planning has no foundation . . . temporality develops out of the social context in which one exists, and the social context of those in lower strata teaches them in numerous, unmistakable ways that it is best to get what one can while one can. When the future is perceived to offer uncertainty at worst, the rational course of action is to live for the present" (Lauer 1981:117).

Comparing the time orientations of long-term unemployed people with those of teachers in training and in work programs can provide insight into the problematic relation between macro-social and micro-social time. The Austrian sociologist Nowotny (1990) referred to this phenomenon as clashing time cultures *(Zeitkulturen)*. The American sociologist Anderson gave a good example of this in his study on training programs for unemployed youngsters. He described the clash between the content and design of the programs and the street culture of the hard-core unemployed. This gap was illustrated by "the battle for time": "Numerous trainees seem to have difficulty with the middle-class concept of time. From the perspective of the staff, many seem to lack interest in being—or are unable to be—punctual; many seem to take tardiness as normal happenstance, or they may be absent from class much of the time. Instead of an attitude of seriousness, many youths appear to take a cavalier attitude toward the program, appearing simply to be putting in time and thereby expressing a degree of alienation" (Anderson 1990b:222). Anderson felt the teachers ought to be more aware of the clashing time cultures, without losing sight of their teaching aims.

The way the welfare departments and the employment offices cope with their own shortage of time—for example, by restricting access with special consultation hours and giving each client only a limited amount of time—can make their clients feel inferior and powerless. In *Queing and Waiting* (1975), which was based on participant observation in waiting rooms, Schwartz viewed the lengthy periods clients often had to spend waiting as an important feature of the subordinate position of the poor (see Chapter 7).

This chapter deals specifically with how the unemployed perceive and spend time. A central question is the extent to which the temporal disorientation and boredom due to lengthy unemployment, as documented in the literature on the social-psychological effects of unemployment, still take place today. Studies in the 1930s noted that the unemployed had difficulty dealing with the surplus of free time. The literature gives an impression of inactivity, disorientation, lethargy and listlessness.[1] Dutch studies conducted in the 1970s and 1980s concluded that though the unemployed were no longer as inactive and apathetic as in the 1930s, boredom was still rampant and they spent their time, and indeed had to spend their time, in ways different from working people or people with higher incomes (Knulst and Schoonderwoerd 1983, Becker and Vink 1986).

Many studies viewed the unemployed as one homogeneous category. Lazarsfeld-Jahoda and Zeisel (1933) distinguished four types of attitudes on the part of the unemployed, but this typology pertained mainly to their psychological reactions to being unemployed rather than their perception of time and how they spent it. Their conclusions would seem to pertain to all unemployed, but with a gender distinction: women were less plagued by boredom and aimlessness because it was easier for them to fall back on their traditional role as housewife. In recent Dutch studies on how the unemployed perceive and spend their time, researchers similarly either viewed them as one homogeneous category or concluded that it was not feasible to differentiate sub-categories (Becker and Vink 1986). Here, we analyze whether the findings noted in the literature were also valid for the long-term unemployed in the 1980s in the Netherlands.

THE EXPERIENCE OF TIME

Boredom

More than half (57 percent) of the respondents said they were sometimes bored, and 31 percent said they were often bored. Of those who were sometimes or often bored, 86 percent felt the disadvantages of unemployment to be greater than the advantages, whereas 55 percent of those who were seldom or never bored felt that way. The respondents who were sometimes or often bored had no aim or task stimulating them to engage in certain activities or helping them to structure their time.

I am bored a lot of the time. Then I just sit here and I don't have the slightest idea what to do. I just can not cope with all the time I have on my hands. I don't really have any goal, you know. I would like to have a bit more of a pattern in my life. A schedule, so that I have to get up in the morning because I have to go somewhere because someone needs me. That would be a nice feeling (27-year-old man, single, 6 years unemployed).

The difference in the notions of time became particularly evident when a respondent got a job and thus acquired an aim and a structure in his or her daily life. One respondent who got a temporary job via a special program for the unemployed expressed it as follows:

When I was out of work, I never did much. I was bored. I would smoke a lot more, and I never really had much of an appetite. In the middle of the day I would have a bottle of beer. The whole situation was so unhealthy. Nowadays I get on my bicycle in the morning or I get in my car and I go to work. In the afternoon I come home to have lunch and in the evening we have a hot meal. I am really busy. And I really experience the weekend as being something special again (36-year-old man, partner and children, 6 years unemployed).

Shortage of Time

There was nonetheless also a considerable minority (43 percent) who said they were seldom or never bored. Some of them, a quarter of all the respondents, found the advantages of unemployment more important than the disadvantages or thought that they were of equal importance. Many of these respondents felt a job would "cramp their style."

I enjoy my free time so unbelievably intensively. It is such a wonderful feeling to know that whenever I feel like it, I can do whatever I want to. The feeling that you do not depend on a clock. I did my share in the labor process for twenty-five years. With a clock, rush, rush, rush. Now I am active as a folk dancer and I sing in a choir, but I am also hooked on television. Thank God. It saves me a lot of money on theater tickets. And I am also crazy about sleeping. I am a real night person. I usually don't get up before noon. Boy am I good at sleeping. I think it is a very useful activity (45-year-old woman, single, 4 years unemployed).

The category who felt the advantages of unemployment to be more important than the disadvantages had neither the time nor the desire for a job.

When I see other people who have a good job but who don't have much free time, I sometimes think: "Boy, am I lucky. I can do exactly as I please." Of course it is all relative. But my hobbies and the things I think are important to me, those are things I can do and they can't. Then I weigh all this against that well-paid job, and at the moment the scales are tipped this way (24-year-old woman, lives with parents, 2 years unemployed).

Of the respondents who were seldom or never bored, more than half (58 percent) looked for work only now and then, if at all. Of those who were sometimes or often bored, only 39 percent were no longer actively looking for work. Thus the correlation between boredom and looking for work was significant. The relatively "voluntarily" unemployed people felt little need for programs for the unemployed or for courses that were given by the municipality or the Employment Office.

Sense of Time

The way the long-term unemployed think and feel about time cannot be defined solely in terms of boredom. We also examined their sense of time. What was their perception of such time units as hours, days and seasons? Many of the respondents, particularly those who were bored, turned out to have a different sense of time than one would probably find among working people. Due to the absence of a time structure, their consciousness of time units faded.

An hour is exactly the same as a day if you are out of work (33-year-old Moroccan man, partner and children, 7 years unemployed).

For me, there is no such thing as time, no really strict time. For me it always Sunday, you might say (46-year-old man, single, 6 years unemployed).

The difference between weekdays and weekends had also become more vague in the minds of many respondents. Almost half of them (43 percent) stated that there was no longer any difference between the way they spent their time during the weekends and on weekdays.

It is just one long rut. When I had a job, the weekend used to be the end of the week. It meant I would be home for two days, and I enjoyed that. But now everything just goes on and on. The week doesn't have a beginning or an end (42-year-old Mediterranean man, partner and children, 6 years unemployed).

In contrast to their perception of differences between the days of the week or between weekdays and weekends, the unemployed were very aware—probably more than working people—of the differences between summer and winter. A large majority of the respondents (77 percent) spent their time differently in the summer than in the winter. The inexpensive pastimes available to them were mainly outdoors, in public parks, on the beach, in their own backyards, and these activities usually depended on the season. Those respondents who were sometimes or often bored were particularly apt to draw a distinction between summer and winter.

It is summertime now and if the weather is nice I go to the Vondel Park. I see what kind of activities there are. They have a kind of center there and an outdoor theater. I go and take a look (29-year-old man, single, 4 years unemployed).

In the summer it is no problem. I have a little plot of land where I planted a garden and I go there every day. It's only a five minute walk from here. There are cucumbers there that need to be watered every day. In the winter you have to find some way to entertain yourself and that is much more of a problem. Sometimes I feel the walls closing in on me (39-year-old man, lives with parents, 6 years unemployed).

The altered sense of time was also evident from the fact that some of the respondents were not able to clearly state how they spent their time. They could no longer remember the things they had done, since none of their activities were viewed as meaningful.

There are those days when I think at the end of the day: "What did I do that made me so tired?" I did something in the course of the day, sure, but I can't say exactly what. I probably read something, maybe I visited my mother and I rode on my bike somewhere or I walked around downtown. Yeah, I have days like that (25-year-old woman, single, 3 years unemployed).

What did I do yesterday? I got up very early in the morning, at six thirty. For the rest I didn't do anything at all yesterday . . . no, nothing (46-year-old man, partner and children, 4 years unemployed).

The altered sense of time was also evident from the contraction of the time horizon. The unemployed often made very few plans, if any. They said they just lived from one day to the next.

I am the kind of guy who lives from one day to the next. If it isn't there today, it'll be there tomorrow. That is my philosophy of life. I never know what I am going to do next week. Or tomorrow, or even tonight. I'll wait and see what happens. I don't have any plans (27-year-old man, partner, no children, 12 years unemployed).

The Paradox of Doing Nothing
Because There Is Too Much Time

The absence of structure in their days made it difficult for some respondents to know how to spend their time. They did much less with their "leisure time" than when they were employed and had "working time" and "free time." In order for there to be leisure time, it would seem that there also has to be working time.

If you have a job or if you are still at school, you recognize your leisure time. You think to yourself: I have some time off now, I don't have to work, I don't have to study. Let's see how I can use this time. Then you have the idea that you can do something special. But if you are free all the time, if all you have is leisure time, then you don't look at it that way any more (24-year-old man, single, 2 years unemployed).

Faced with a surplus of time, the unemployed were more apt to postpone things since "there is plenty of time to do it tomorrow, isn't there?" They also had trouble starting something new, and it was difficult for them to keep what few appointments they had. They did not get around to carrying out their plans.

Of course there is a big risk that I can postpone a lot of things: I can just as well do it tomorrow. And then the next day I think: ". . . I can do it tomorrow . . ." and I keep thinking that every day. If a bulb doesn't work, I keep on postponing replacing it. By now there are so many of them that have to be replaced, that I can't bear to think of having to change all of them at the same time, it's such a big job (45-year-old man, single, 4 years unemployed).

Respondent was called up by the Employment Office, but then he forgot the date when he was supposed to go there. He has not made a new appointment yet. He is going to do so some time this week (35-year-old Surinamese man, single, 4 years unemployed).

Whether I am going to take a course? If you have to make a decision like that, it takes a couple of months. You take your time, because you have all the time in the world to think about things (29-year-old man, single, 4 years unemployed).

Many of the respondents no longer made any effort to budget their time, since it was not scarce. This is in keeping with the findings of Lazarsfeld-Jahoda and Zeisel: "The realization that free time is limited urges a man to make considered use of it. If he feels he has unlimited time at hand, any effort to use it sensibly appears superfluous. What he might do before lunch can be done equally well after lunch or in the evening, and suddenly the day has passed without it being done at all" (Jahoda et al. 1972:71).

HOW TIME IS SPENT

Just as there were differences in the ways respondents perceived time, there were also differences in the ways they spent time. In this section, we distinguish three categories of unemployed people: those who were passive, those who developed strategies for killing time and those who engaged in activities they themselves viewed as meaningful.

Doing Nothing

First, there were the unemployed who spent their time doing nothing. The following two statements illustrate their life style.

I mainly live on this corner, this spot on the couch. My whole corner is all worn out. Look . . . (stands up and points to a worn-out spot on the upholstery) ha ha ha. So this is where I am all day long. It might sound awful, but it happens to be the truth (45-year-old man, partner and children, 6 years unemployed).

You go to bed as late as possible, two, three o'clock at night, and then you get up as late as you can in the morning so the day is shorter. That is something you do on purpose, especially in the winter (32-year-old man, partner no children, 6 years unemployed).

Some 10 percent of our respondents said they regularly slept in the daytime, and 19 percent did so occasionally. The large majority of the respondents (around

80 percent) got up before ten in the morning. As might have been expected, it was mainly the people who were often or sometimes bored who got up late or at irregular times and sometimes slept in the daytime.

Killing Time

The majority of our respondents tried to keep busy, even if only for the purpose of filling up their time. They did things they didn't really have to do or like doing. Activities—doing odd jobs, household chores, visiting relatives or spending an evening in the local bar—were not engaged in because of their intrinsic value, but simply because they helped kill time. In addition, the respondents went on a lot of walks, bicycle trips and excursions.

Just hanging around and not doing anything special, well, you just do anything to keep busy. You look for some odd job you can do. And if there isn't anything that has to be done, you invent something. As a rule it always amounts to the same thing: running around in circles. And then you go out for a while, you walk your dog. And then after a while you turn around and go home again (31-year-old man, single, 5 years unemployed).

I am on the street every day from eleven o'clock in the morning onwards. I just walk around, because I don't have any friends any more. On the days when there is an outdoor market, I go to the market. Sometimes I go to the library. In the winter I stay home (25-year-old Surinamese man, lives with parents, 5 years unemployed).

Watching television was a popular way of killing time. Almost all our respondents watched television, and two thirds of them did so regularly. This is an important difference of course between the unemployed people of the 1930s and those of today. In the 1930s people who were out of work would hang around the street corner, as Lazarsfeld-Jahoda and Zeisel described, whereas nowadays they sit at home and watch television, closed off from the outside world. It cannot be denied, though, that watching television gives the viewer a glimpse at the rest of the world. However, many of the respondents did not see it that way. To them, watching television was not a source of information or entertainment; it was just a way to kill time. Often the television would be on all day long, even though there was "never anything to see."

You watch television and of course there isn't anything interesting on but you watch anyway. It becomes an obsession. You keep fidgeting with the dials, because you want to spend your evening watching something nice. And then there turns out to be nothing nice to watch (32-year-old man, partner, no children, 6 years unemployed).

I go to bed very late, I catch the very last bit of television. It isn't until there is nothing left on any of the channels that I turn it off (48-year-old woman, single, 8 years unemployed).

The respondents used various strategies to combine a surplus of time with a scarcity of activities. They were never in a rush. As Lazarsfeld-Jahoda and Zeisel noted in their Marienthal study: "they have forgotten how to hurry" (Jahoda et al. 1972:66).

I have come to the point where I really have a lot to do if I can say: Well, I have to go to the store tomorrow to buy batteries for my radio and this afternoon I have to pick up my glasses. Then I don't have to worry any more about how to spend those particular days (44-year-old man, partner and children, 5 years unemployed).

The respondents devoted more time and attention to certain activities and repeated other ones.

If I am bored, I take my hifi set apart, I dust it on the inside and then I put it back together again. Cleaning all those tiny little wires, it's a good half day's work. Why I do that every week? Well, we smoke a lot here in the room and that equipment is very sensitive. If nicotine gets on it, I can hear the difference. If you don't know anything about it, then maybe you don't hear it, but I do (27-year-old man, partner and children, 6 years unemployed).

I go shopping every day. I never buy groceries for the whole week. Whatever I need, I go out and get it every day (43-year-old woman, single, 5 years unemployed).

It was characteristic of the category of unemployed people who killed time that they had very few hobbies, if any. A third of all the respondents had no hobbies at all.

Using Time

Some of the unemployed people said they were never bored and even felt they did not have enough time. They consciously devoted time to activities they deemed meaningful. These activities included hobbies, odd jobs, helping their relatives and neighbors, being active in a club, organization or church, and doing volunteer work.

Hobbies

Two thirds of the respondents had one or more hobbies. Many hobbies popular in the Netherlands were mentioned by one or more of the respondents. Usually they were not full-time activities, and for some people hobbies were more a way, to fill up time than to spend it in a meaningful way. Nevertheless, a considerable minority of respondents spent five days a week on their hobby.

I have a thousand hobbies. I collect science fiction books. I write down what I have and what I don't, and then I take the list and go to the outdoor market where they have second-hand books. I also have the National Hit Parade ever since 1979 on tape. I have some rifles and they require a lot of taking care of. I build model airplanes, I watch the late films on television, I have a big sailboat and a smaller one and I am fixing them up, and I am also fixing up the motorized bike someone gave me. I also read law books and give my friends and acquaintances legal advice (42-year-old man, single, 6 years unemployed).

I grow all kinds of things in my garden. It is a lot of work. You have to get rid of the weeds, for example. Sometimes I am there from early in the morning till late at night. Pretty soon there will be beans, and that keeps me busy. They are already coming, and then I have to string up the plants. Oh, it means I have so much to do (51-year-old man, partner, no children, years of unemployment unknown).

Odd Jobs, Helping Neighbors and Relatives

Doing odd jobs can also be a meaningful way to spend time. A third of our respondents did odd jobs in their own homes, and some of them did not even have time to do all the things they wanted to do.

For the time being, I am still working on my apartment. Not only fixing it up, but also making things. As soon as I am finished with one thing, I think of something else I have wanted to do for a long time. It is a little like the way people are when they are retired. That's the way I see it. I am never bored. When you [the interviewer] called, I wanted to say, "No, don't come now, because I had so much to do" (47-year-old Surinamese man, single, 10 years unemployed).

A quarter of the respondents also did odd jobs for their friends and relatives, and 12 percent did odd jobs for people they did not know, sometimes for money or in exchange for other services. The people in the vicinity often expected the unemployed to help them with odd jobs, since they had plenty of time for it.

Clubs, Organizations and Churches

Forty-one percent were members of a club, organization or church. This percentage was far below the Dutch average of 60 percent (Knulst and Schoonderwoerd 1983). Table 5.1 compares our respondents' membership in social or religious groups with that of short-term unemployed people and working people in a study conducted by Becker and Vink (1986). Table 5.1 shows that as far as athletic and hobby clubs are concerned, there are significant differences between short-term unemployed and working people on the one hand and our category of long-term unemployed people on the other. One explanation for the low participation rate of long-term unemployed people is that these clubs usually cost money. Club, community center and church work usually costs very little, if anything, and the contribution is often voluntary.

TABLE 5.1 Club-Membership of Long-Term Unemployed, Short-Term Unemployed and Working People (in percentages)

Type of Group	long-term unemployed[a]	unemployed[b]	working[b]
Athletic club	18	30	37
Hobby club	6	14	14
Cultural organization	8	7	11
Club and community center work	7	9	7
Religious organization	7	5	7
N	271	375	310

[a] The respondents in this study, average unemployment duration 63 months.
[b] Pertains to a random sample of a total of 1702 respondents, 375 of whom were unemployed. The average duration of the unemployment was 15 months.

Sources: Knulst and Schoonderwoerd 1983; Becker and Vink 1986.

Volunteer Work

The amount of volunteer work done by the long-term unemployed should not be overestimated: 21 percent of the respondents sometimes did volunteer work for an athletic club, church or mosque, school or day care center for children, community center, playground, organization to promote the interests of the unemployed, or some other kind of organization. Most respondents were not interested in doing voluntary work of any kind. They did not like the kind of work involved, or they were in principle against volunteer work. A common notion was that it was useless or at any rate inferior. In their view, the only real work was work you got paid for.

Volunteer work? Well, I want a job, but I want it to earn me some money. That volunteer work does more damage than good. It takes jobs away from people who were earning a living. If you couldn't get it done for free, you would have to pay someone. That's the way it ought to be. Volunteer work . . . I want no part of it (41-year-old man, partner, no children, 6 years unemployed).

I don't think all that work should be done by volunteers and that society should be able to take advantage of the fact that there are certain groups who earn a good salary while other people do the dirty work and are still on Welfare. I don't think it's right (37-year-old man, single, 6 years unemployed).

Effects of Impecuniousness
on How Time is Spent

In a number of ways, the financial position of the long-term unemployed affects their time-spending. First, the limited income forces them to cut down on the costs of leisure activities. Second, the limited income can stimulate them to find new ways of using their free time.

Lack of Money as Obstacle

Many hobbies cost money. Hobbyists have to buy a sailboat, a radio transmitter or fishing gear. Even watching a VCR means renting or buying video tapes. Going to a bar, a discotheque or a football game costs money, too. If you don't have the money, these are things you simply cannot do. Many respondents had to cut down on their hobbies or even give them up altogether.

I am crazy about stereo equipment, video equipment, all that kind of stuff. I have loads of cassettes, records, video tapes. I used to have a good video camera, it was worth a good six thousand guilders, but it was stolen. And now I can't buy a new one. The things I am interested in, I can't do because I don't have the money (31-year-old man, single, 5 years unemployed).

My family was always good at darts. Now I just have a dart board at home; I don't play in the bar any more. People are always buying you drinks, and when it's time for you to pay for a round, you have to say: "I'm sorry, I can't" (25-year-old woman, lives with parents, 5 years unemployed).

Do-it-yourself is less popular among the unemployed than the working population (Becker and Vink 1986). The unemployed might have plenty of time and even the inclination for odd jobs, but they usually don't have the money for the required materials and tools (Pahl 1984). For the same reason, many of the respondents also had to leave the clubs or organizations they had been members of. For a large number of them, being short of money reduced their social participation.

Lack of Money as Stimulus

A lack of money was not always an obstacle to spending time in a meaningful way; it could also stimulate it. Using time in a productive way could provide certain material goods one would be unable to purchase.

Since I was short of money, I started to make my own clothes. I was forced to do so. And after a while I thought: "Wow, that's not bad! Now I make my own clothes and my boyfriend's clothes and I cut people's hair." I don't do it for money, I just do it for the fun of it (23-year-old woman of foreign descent, partner no children, 5 years unemployed).

You have the time to make your own clothes. It isn't just because you have to, no. It becomes a challenge to make something really nice that no one else has (31-year-old woman of foreign descent, single with child, 3 years unemployed).

Gardening was an inexpensive way of producing goods that were a welcome addition to the family groceries. Bargain hunting—looking for the cheapest prices, even if it meant a long walk or bicycle ride—could also take a lot of time, as did walking or bicycling to save the price of a bus ticket.

Others spent their time working "off the books" and thus managed to improve their financial position. We noted in Chapter 4 that at the time of the interviews 17 percent of the "unemployed" respondents were working off the books in one way or another.

One category of respondents used their free time to study. They were not working to earn extra money at the moment, but they were investing their time and energy in themselves, in the hope of improving their chances in the future. For some of the respondents in this category, however, studying was not a way to use the free time provided by unemployment in a meaningful way. It was the other way round: unemployment—particularly the unemployment benefits—was used as a way to study. This was referred to in Chapter 4 as calculating behavior. The respondents in this category did not really think of themselves as being unemployed.

STRUCTURING TIME

Without regular employment outside the home, it was difficult for many respondents to introduce an element of regularity in their activities. There were nonetheless other factors that could help structure time. We distinguished three sources of time structuring: externally imposed structure, self-imposed commitments and self-imposed schedule.

Externally Imposed Structure

Some respondents found it easier than others to give their days a certain structure, since they still maintained ties with the "regular" outside world that imposed some regularity. Respondents with children who went to school or had jobs, or with a partner who had a regular activity outside the home, derived some time structure from them.

After I take my daughter to school in the morning, I clean up the house. Then I go and pick her up for her lunch break. And after she goes back to school for the afternoon, well, that is the hard part of the day, because I have pretty much done everything I have to do. So I go to the shopping mall or the outdoor market. I walk around. It is quite a long time before it is finally three thirty and I can go and pick her up again (26-year-old Surinamese woman, single with child, 5 years unemployed).

He goes to school pretty much every day now, and that sort of gives me the kind of pattern I used to have with weekdays when you have something to do and a weekend when you're free. That's because he goes to school (33-year-old man, partner and children, 2 years unemployed).

Self-Imposed External Commitments

Some respondents made a conscious effort to create external commitments. They did volunteer work, joined clubs or organizations or were active in their local church or mosque. Sometimes their main motivation was a need for regular obligations in their weekly schedule, creating a certain structure in how they spent their time.

Five times a day, I go to the mosque in the neighborhood. I pray for five minutes and then I go home again (41-year-old Moroccan man, partner and children, 8 years unemployed).

There is a big risk of getting into a process where you gradually slide further and further away. I wanted to stop that process, so ever since 1984 I have been doing volunteer work at the Amsterdam Concert Broadcasting Station. Every Monday night it's my turn at the control panel, and two or three times a week there are recordings. Then I'm busy from five to eight, and after that I sit back and listen. And I go to the Concertgebouw for free (33-year-old man, single, 5 years unemployed).

Self-Imposed Schedule

However, many respondents had no external sources on which to base their daily structure and were unable to find any. A few of them tried to create some regularity themselves, for example by making appointments and keeping an appointment book.

I try to do things at regular times. For example, I have my meals at the same time every day. It gives me a feeling of satisfaction (25-year-old man, lives with parents, 1 year unemployed).

Sometimes I get such a depressed feeling. Then I have to do something to cheer myself up so I say now it is time for me to practice. It is hard if you are out of a job. You don't have a boss to tell you what to do, the alarm doesn't go off at nine o'clock. I try to make appointments for rehearsals. Then somebody says, "We had an appointment for nine o'clock, didn't we? So get over here" (28-year-old man, single, 5 years unemployed).

To some unemployed, time structuring meant not only a certain amount of day-to-day regularity, but also an awareness of the future as distinct from the present. They tried to stimulate this by planning things they could look forward to, and the planning itself also filled a certain need.

On the days when people put out the garbage, I would walk around and see what I could find. I picked up any electric appliance I saw, like an old vacuum cleaner. It gave me a nice feeling: "I have something to do tomorrow." I would see if I could repair it or if there were any parts I could use. It wasn't only that it gave me something to do, there was also an element of surprise. Incredible (38-year-old Surinamese man, partner and children, 13 years unemployed).

THE DISTRIBUTION OF BOREDOM

The "burden of boredom" was not evenly distributed over all the long-term unemployed. People with certain individual features were more likely to be bored than others. Table 5.2 summarizes the relation between boredom and a number of individual features.

TABLE 5.2 Boredom and Individual Features (in percentages, N=271)

| Category | Bored: | | | | |
	Often	Sometimes	Seldom/Never	Total	N
Gender					
Male	35	25	40	100	197
Female	20	29	51	100	55
Descent					
Dutch	17	29	54	100	164
Surinam/Antilles	59	19	22	100	41
Mediterranean	68	23	10	100	31
Other	37	19	44	100	16
Level of Education					
Primary School	60	15	25	100	60
LBO/MAVO[a] dropout	28	33	39	100	46
LBO/MAVO	23	35	42	100	97
Higher	13	17	70	100	46
Living Situation					
Lives with partner	41	25	34	100	103
Lives alone	25	27	48	100	149
Duration of Unemployment					
< 3 years	8	39	54	100	39
3-5 years	30	23	48	100	71
5-7 years	42	25	34	100	77
> 7 years	36	25	40	100	56

[a] LBO = Lower Vocational School, MAVO = Lower General Secondary School.

Earlier studies (Lazarsfeld-Jahoda and Zeisel 1933) indicated that on the whole, women had less trouble filling their time than men, because they could fall back on their traditional roles as housewives and mothers. In addition, women have traditionally been more active in volunteer work. Table 5.2 shows that in our study women were indeed less frequently bored than the males.It is questionable, however, whether the traditional explanation for this difference is still valid. In our study, the category of female respondents consisted mainly of single women with a nontraditional mentality whose aims in life were not centered around domestic chores in the household. They were less frequently bored because on the average, they were more active and more enterprising than the male respondents. Traditionally oriented women who feel their task in life is to be a housewife are less likely to be registered as looking for a job. This category can be referred to as the "invisibly" unemployed.

The respondents born outside the Netherlands, particularly in Turkey or Morocco, had more difficulty dealing with having nothing to do than those of Dutch descent.

Another relevant individual feature was the level of education. Table 5.2 shows that the higher their educational level was, the less bored the unemployed were. Certain aspects of their working histories were related to the amount of schooling they had had. The respondents who were often bored had started to work at a relatively early age and had more frequently done unskilled work, mainly in factories or in the construction industry. The traditionally unskilled factory workers were most apt to be bored. The unemployed who were seldom or never bored were mainly people who had not started to work until after the age of eighteen, people who had done skilled or white collar work, often on a temporary basis, people who had had their work experience in the commercial service sector, or people with a comparatively high education but with little or no work experience.

Finally, there was a relation between the duration of unemployment and boredom. Many of the respondents said they had been most bored during the first few months after they lost their job. The contrast with a working life was the greatest during that initial period (see Sinfield 1981). Only gradually did some of them manage to adjust to having a surplus of time. However, the longer the duration of their unemployment, the more apt the respondents were to be bored. Only in the "more than seven years" unemployed category did we observe a decrease in boredom compared to the "five to seven years" category, though they were still more bored than the "three to five years" category. This could perhaps be explained by differences in the composition of the various unemployment-duration categories. Many of the younger, better educated female respondents who belonged to the "less than three years" category were still going to school, and in a certain sense some of them were voluntarily unemployed in order to complete their studies. They were less apt to be bored. Similarly, the "more than seven years category" included relatively many voluntarily unemployed who had found new ways of organizing their lives and using their time.

SOCIAL CONTEXTS AND
DEALING WITH TIME

Unemployed people who lived with a partner, whether they were married or not, were far more likely to be bored than those who lived alone (see Table 5.2). Family life apparently failed to provide them with adequate ways to spend their time after they lost their jobs. This was particularly true of men with families in which traditional role patterns were still dominant.

There are days I just seem to be getting in my wife's way all the time when she's vacuuming and doing things like that. Or I interfere with something. That causes friction. The more time I spend out of the house, the more normal it is. Because normally a man shouldn't be home (44-year-old man, partner and children, 5 years unemployed).

In many families, tensions were caused by the respondents' unemployment, tensions that in several instances even contributed to a breakup. However, in the course of time most of the families managed to find a new modus vivendi.

It goes wrong in a lot of families if Dad is hanging around the house all day. But not here. I act just as if I have a busy schedule. I say: "Don't mind me, do whatever you would if I were not here." I have my own room, so if she wants to do some housework, I can just close the door (25-year-old man, partner, no children, 3 years unemployed).

Traditional role patterns generally prevented the male respondents from being more than marginally active in the household, even though the amount of time they spent doing housework was more than before they lost their job. The surplus of "free time" was spent on more "manly" chores around the house like carpentry, painting and other odd jobs. Changes in the traditional role pattern occurred only if and when their wives got a paying job and the male respondents were left to do the housework and take care of the children. However, this occurred only sporadically. Unemployed women who lived with a partner had far less trouble finding something meaningful to do with their time. They had their housework to do and their children to take care of. This did not necessarily mean they liked this role.

Relatives served an important function in spending time. Respondents did various chores for their relatives, such as odd jobs and shopping; even if this did not earn them any extra income. Chatting, playing cards, and having a cup of coffee with relatives were common ways of spending time.

Every Friday afternoon I take my youngest daughter and we go shopping for my mother-in-law, who is in a home for the aged. So that takes care of one afternoon a week (40-year-old Antillean man, partner and children, 4 years unemployed).

. . . and then there are all your relatives who always want you to do things for them. There is always a room that has to be wallpapered or painted, or they want you to put in wall-to-wall carpet. So of course you do it all. You're the family handyman. You're home all day anyway. So you have plenty of time (31-year-old man, partner, no children, 1 year unemployed).

The respondents with a large circle of friends were considerably less likely to be bored than those with fewer social contacts. Dropping in to visit someone, playing cards, going shopping together, or going out for an evening were all examples of the things they did with friends and acquaintances. Moreover, social contacts could serve to structure their time. Another advantage was that such activities with friends and acquaintances did not necessarily have to cost much money. Given the norm of reciprocity, however, now and then the respondents were expected to foot the bill. If they were unable to do so, it could become difficult to continue the relationship.

The fact that they didn't have to go to work every day led some unemployed to spend more time in the immediate vicinity. In contrast to what one might expect, however, most of them did not spend more time with their neighbors. It was only in scattered parts of the Enschede location and to a lesser extent in the Rotterdam location (only one street or just a part of it) that the respondents spent a great deal of time with their neighbors. Most unemployed were not at all happy with the altered composition of the neighborhood population. This was particularly the case in Rotterdam and Amsterdam.

Nowadays a lot of the people here in the neighborhood are old. And a lot of them are Turkish. I can't say I am enthusiastic about that. Because of all the things I have been through, I have learned to discriminate. I never used to discriminate, but if you see what a privileged position the minorities are in compared to ordinary, normal people, then I say: "They ought to kick them all out" (44-year-old man, single with child, 8 years unemployed).

It's a mess here. The foreigners just put their garbage out any time. Even if it's Easter. Though every Dutchman knows the Sanitation Department has the day off. And all that noise their kids make. They don't do anything to shut them up. And if you say something about it, they curse you out (31-year-old man, partner no children, 1 year unemployed).

It is no coincidence that these quotations are so full of ethnic slurs. In describing "the neighborhood," the respondents viewed "the foreigners" as the most visible symbol of the transformation of a homogeneous community into a heterogeneous conglomerate of life styles.

To summarize, social contexts significantly affected how the unemployed spent their time. In Enschede the immediate family and relatives were particularly important, though some respondents did maintain intensive contact with their neighbors. In Rotterdam, the immediate family was of much less importance. There, the circle of friends played a more substantial role. In this sense, Amsterdam was in between the other two locations.

CONCLUSIONS

There are similarities between how the unemployed people in Marienthal in the 1930s spent their time and how our respondents spent theirs in Amsterdam, Rotterdam and Enschede in the 1980s. In both cases, many unemployed had problems dealing with a surplus of time.

And yet there were also clear differences. The domain of "free time" has mushroomed in the interim. In the post-war years, the working week and the entire working year have been shortened. People have longer weekends and longer vacations, which have taught them to deal with leisure time. In addition, the unemployed of the 1980s have more ways to spend their time. This has been made possible by the greater general prosperity and social security and by technological and industrial developments. Financial deprivation is no longer as dramatic as in Marienthal, where at best the unemployed had to make do with benefits equalling a quarter of their former factory wages, which had not been generous to begin with.

Today entire industries cater to leisure time demands and technological progress has led to new forms of entertainment. The time the jobless used to spend hanging around the street corner is now spent watching television. Almost a fifth of our respondents (19 percent) had a VCR and almost a third (28 percent) had a car. The car and public transport have greatly increased the geographic mobility of modern-day unemployed people, compared to their counterparts of the 1930s. But, as described in Chapter 4, the unemployed still have to live under a strict financial regime that forces them to cut down on mobility spending.

The most important difference between our respondents and those in Marienthal is that, regarding how they think and feel about their time and how they actually spend and structure it, the long-term unemployed of the 1980s do not constitute one homogeneous category. Roughly speaking, a distinction can be made between the respondents who were often or sometimes bored (57 percent) and those who were seldom or never bored (43 percent). As noted in this chapter, boredom was related to a number of other variables. The bored respondents exhibited many of the characteristics generally attributed to unemployed people in the literature. This category includes males with a low level of education have started working at a relatively young age doing mainly unskilled factory work; respondents from Turkey, Morocco or other foreign countries; and breadwinners and heads of relatively large households. These long-term unemployed individuals exhibit no desire to use the social frameworks available to help them spend and structure their time in a meaningful way, such as volunteer work or club-activities. They feel the disadvantages of unemployment to be greater than the advantages. They estimate their chances of finding a new job as poor, though they still relatively frequently go out and look for a job. They get up late or at irregular times, sometimes sleep in the daytime to pass the time, and feel there is no difference between a weekday and the weekend, though they do see a big difference between the summer and the winter.

In addition to these "traditional" passive long-term unemployed, there is also a category of active and enterprising people who are seldom or never bored. This category includes relatively large numbers of women, single people, people with a higher level of education, and relatively few people of foreign descent. They started working at a late age and have done skilled work or white collar work on a temporary basis. They are frequently active in clubs, get up early in the morning or at any rate at regular times, and feel that there is a clear difference between a weekday and the weekend, but not between the summer and the winter. They feel that the advantages of unemployment are more important than the disadvantages or that the two are equally important. They estimate their chances of finding a job as anywhere from reasonable to good, though they do not go to much trouble to find one.

The diversity in the ways our respondents dealt with their time corresponds with the results of some German, British and Belgian studies. These studies also present a heterogeneous picture, with the patterns exhibited by the unemployed situated on a continuum from active to passive behavior. In Gurvitch's terms, we can speak of a "plurality of different social times" among the unemployed.[2]

NOTES

1. Marie Lazarsfeld-Jahoda and Hans Zeisel 1933, *Die Arbeitslosen von Marienthal: Ein soziographischer Versuch über die Wirkungen langdauernder Arbeitslosigkeit*, Leipzig: Verlag von S. Hirzel; Edward Wight Bakke, *The Unemployed Man: A Social Study*, London: Nisbet, 1933. M. Komarovsky, *The Unemployed Man and His Family*, New York: Dreyden Press 1940.

2. The term "plurality of social times" was coined by Gurvitch. See also Dieter Frölich, *The Use of Time During Unemployment: A Case Study Carried Out in West Germany*, Assen: Van Gorcum, 1983; David Fryer and Stephan McKenna, "The Laying Off of Hands – Unemployment and the Experience of Time," in: Stephan Fineman (ed.), *Unemployment, Personal and Social Consequences*, London: Tavistock Publications, 1987; Mark Elchardus and Ignace Glorieux, "De ontwrichting van het levensritme: de effecten van werk en werkloosheid," Paper prepared for the Flemish-Dutch Conference for Sociologists and Anthropologists, 7 en 8 April 1988, UFSIA, Antwerpen.

CHAPTER 6

Looking for a Job

Mark Granovetter stressed in his study *Getting a Job* (1974) the importance of "weak social ties." He stated that people with whom one does not have particularly close ties, such as acquaintances or fellow members of clubs, can be especially important in finding a new job. These weak ties can bridge social boundaries and provide the unemployed with more and different information than they get from their own social group. Having weak social ties of this kind is an important form of social capital (Bourdieu 1986). The significance of the network approach, which is an important sociological supplement to economic job search theories, is exhibited in contemporary studies on the ghetto poor. They live in areas with large concentrations of unemployed people and largely operate within closed homogeneous social networks. On the basis of their Chicago study, Wilson and Wacquant wrote: "Our data indicate that not only do residents of extreme-poverty areas have fewer social ties but also that they tend to have ties of lesser social worth, as measured by the social position of their partners, parents, siblings, and best friends, for instance. In short, they possess lower volumes of social capital. . . If they have a best friend, furthermore, he or she is less likely to work, less educated, and twice as likely to be on aid" (Wacquant and Wilson 1989:22-24).[1] The specific social network of the ghetto poor, and particularly the lack of access to formal job networks, perpetuates their weak labor market position.

Contemporary ghetto studies also confirm the relevance of traditional job search theories: the costs of finding a job outside the ghetto—material costs due to poor or non-existent public transportation as well as social costs due to constant rejection or the everyday practices of employer discrimination—are too high. Employer discrimination practices have been described by Kirschenman and Neckerman (1991), who noted that white employers are frequently unwilling to hire black coworkers.

The unemployed are not only confronted with the selection procedures of employers, but also with those of the agencies created to help them find jobs. A recurrent theme in numerous evaluation studies on work programs is that precisely the groups that are in the weakest position are barely reached, if at all.

A process of "creaming" takes place; that is, the most suitable candidates are helped first and best. The selection procedures unemployed people are confronted with if and when they come into contact with work programs to reinforce their feelings of resignation and powerlessness (Lipsky 1984).

The difficulty they have in gaining access to informal job networks, the negative experiences during the job search and the double exclusion by employers and work programs alike can make certain groups even more apt to turn away from the formal labor market.[2] Ethnographic studies such as those by Liebow (1987) and Anderson (1978) have documented this process in detail. On the grounds of their quantitative study on labor force activity, Tienda and Stier suggested that "discouragement may be pervasive in Chicago's inner-city neighborhood" (Tienda and Stier 1991:152). The most important finding of their study was that the majority of the respondents did want a job. Only 16 percent were not looking for a job, and this category consisted mainly of female heads of households who were not able to work due to poor health or family responsibilities. Tienda and Stier did not make any reference to youngsters who were active in the drugs circuit and therefore had no desire for a formal job. Their study produced a differentiated picture, but failed to provide much insight into the underlying factors affecting differences in labor market behavior.

Similarly, there is little systematic information in the American literature about the willingness of the unemployed to make sacrifices in accepting a job. This chapter deals with this aspect of job-searching behavior among Dutch long-term unemployed. We also examine the search frequency and the search channels that were used. In the Netherlands, less use is made of informal channels than in the United States. A third of Dutch unemployed individuals looking for a job manage to find one through social contacts, whereas this is true of almost 60 percent in the United States.[3] There are more intermediary agencies in the Netherlands than in the United States. This is why we also focus attention here on the role of the Employment Office and the various work and training programs.

The efforts the unemployed make to try finding a job are central in this chapter. Whether or not these efforts are successful depends on various factors. Some are located among the unemployed themselves, such as how they look for and apply for jobs and their willingness to accept a less attractive job. However, possible re-entry in the labor market also depended on the availability of jobs and the selection procedures of employers. In effect, re-entry into the labor market depends largely on features that are difficult or impossible for the unemployed to influence, such as age, work experience, educational level and so forth. We did not examine our respondents' objective chances of finding a job, but concentrated on their experiences with selection procedures on the demand side. These experiences can be so disheartening that at a certain point unemployed people give up trying. This can make people resigned to their fate, but it can also make them develop new strategies to find a job.

TABLE 6.1 Looking for a Job (in percentages, N=264)

	percentages
Often (weekly)	20
Regularly (monthly through various channels)	30
Once in a while (monthly through one channel)	17
Rarely/never	33
Total	100

TABLE 6.2 Use of Channels for Finding Work (at least once a month) (in percentages, N=264)

Channel	*percentages*[a]
Advertisements	48
Social Network	31
Employment Office Files	28
Call on Firms	25
Temporary Employment Agency	14

[a] It was possible to use more than one channel.

LOOKING AND APPLYING FOR A JOB

Table 6.1 indicates significant differences in the job-seeking behavior of our respondents. A fifth of them regularly looked for work. A third of them rarely or never did so. The figures in Table 6.1 are supported by other Dutch studies (Kloosterman 1987).

The channels for finding work that were the easiest to use were indeed the most frequently used, as Table 6.2 shows. Forty-eight percent looked over newspaper advertisements at least once a month; 31 percent asked their relatives, friends and acquaintances at least once a month, 28 percent consulted the files of the District Employment Office (further referred to as the Employment Office); 25 percent called on firms; 14 percent inquired and registered at temporary employment agencies; and a few occasionally visited organized "job markets," consulted Employment Office officials or inserted advertisements themselves. The most frequently used channel, personnel advertisements, is a rather vague instrument for judging the intensity of job-seeking behavior. Many claimed to regularly buy and read the newspaper just to see if there were any openings; others casually glanced over the advertisements while reading the paper.

Informal social relations seemed to be particularly important for younger people. These relations were often not only a source of information, but also a source of advice, stimulation and social control. The unemployed frequently came to experience these relations as so irksome and meddlesome that they tended to avoid the subject of their unemployment altogether. Granovetter (1973) and Flap and Tazelaar (1988) have argued that contact with people one does not have close ties with, such as acquaintances or fellow members of clubs, are especially important in finding a new job. Our study shows, however, that the importance of contacts of this kind for re-entry into the labor market remains limited, at least for the long-term unemployed. Family relations, especially the closer ones, usually remained intact throughout the period of unemployment, but the networks of friends and acquaintances tended to shrink. Of our respondents, 30 percent said they had no friends and almost 60 percent did not belong to any club or association. They felt that the chance of finding a job through a friend was small if your friends and acquaintances are also out of work, since "if you have work, you can get work." Almost a quarter of our respondents mainly had friends who were also unemployed. Furthermore, friends with a job often did not work in the sector the respondent was qualified for. Finally, the subject of "work" would have to come up in conversations and meetings. For various reasons, talking about work and unemployment was not a popular pastime. And even if it were, friends would have to be willing to provide information.

> I don't get tips from friends, no. The guys who have work won't tell you about vacancies. They wouldn't want to jeopardize their own job. And I can understand that. If you are better than them, they might be the ones who are sacked first if new lay-offs are necessary. And you will certainly do your best, since you have been unemployed for so long (26-year-old man, lives with parents, years of unemployment unknown).

The channels requiring the most effort were used relatively often by the respondents of foreign descent. They were among the most active job-seekers. It was not unusual for them to consult relatives about possible vacancies and to use their house as a base, even if these relatives lived far away by Dutch standards. Respondents of foreign descent were also the most tenacious visitors of shops and factories in search of work.

> The translating son of our respondent said that his father went out to look for work two or three days a week: "They leave at eight in the morning and look till about ten. They ask everywhere. No work. Then they go outside Amsterdam. No jobs either. They go to every factory, sail factories, a lumberyard, a leather factory, a chocolate factory, a sugar refinery" (48-year-old Moroccan man, partner and children, 5 years unemployed).

As expected, the longer they had been unemployed, the less intensively respondents tended to look for a job. Sixty-three percent of the respondents admitted that their efforts were less intensive at the time of the interview than in the past. Nevertheless, almost a quarter (23 percent) said they still looked with the same intensity, and 3 percent said they were looking more intensively than in the past (and 11 percent had never really looked at all).

Table 6.3 shows that the respondents who had been unemployed for long periods of time did not necessarily search any less intensively than those who had been unemployed for shorter periods, although there was a general tendency of decreasing intensity over time.[4]

TABLE 6.3 Job-seeking Intensity and Duration of Unemployment (in percentages, N=264)

Duration of Unemployment (in years)	2-3	3-4	4-5	5-6	6-7	7-8	≥8	Total
Percentage who had looked for a job in the past month	79	63	64	61	74	74	58	67

Our study shows that the long-term unemployed are a heterogeneous group made up of two main subgroups, each of which each reacts quite differently to unemployment. The first group—about 45 percent of our respondents—remained dutiful and tenaciously continued to look for a job, even in the face of repeated rejection.

I haven't given up hope yet. I keep trying. If I had to think I would never get anything anymore (41-year-old man, partner no children, 6 years unemployed)

I have the feeling that someday I am going to find myself some kind of job. Maybe it's very naive, but I think I am going to be lucky and there are always going to be jobs around, I am convinced of that. Maybe it won't happen soon and I am not all that ambitious, but in the end it is going to work out (33-year-old man, single, 7 years unemployed).

Given the limited chances of success, such behavior sometimes became almost ritualistic. It was especially common among respondents of foreign descent. Their social environment still valued a traditional work ethic. By continuing to look for a job, they could maintain their self-respect and morale and that of their family. For them, looking for work was also a way of spending time. Ritualistic job-seeking behavior was also stimulated by the obligation to look for work, a formal precondition for receiving a welfare benefit; unemployed people have to register at the Employment Office when they apply for a welfare benefit.

Every half year you have to fill in a form at the Welfare Department. I think they require that you apply at least three times. So I apply like mad. For any advertised position, no matter what. I don't care if they require a high school diploma. They only want that piece of paper that shows that I applied (26-year-old Surinamese woman, single with child, 5 years unemployed).

The other category of respondents had reduced or even completely stopped their job-seeking efforts (55 percent). This category consisted of at least two subgroups. One subgroup had made this decision for negative reasons (25 percent). They were resigned to their fate and no longer saw possibilities. Some of these respondents had agreed informally with the Welfare Department case workers that they would no longer have to search and apply, given their poor chances.

The other subgroup had stopped looking for more positive reasons (30 percent). They had found other activities to give meaning to their lives: hobbies, volunteer work, studying, or working in the informal economy. Eight percent were studying at the time of the interview: law, history, sociology, psychology, art, French, music, high school courses and so forth. Like working people, people with an unemployment or welfare benefit are allowed to attend courses or study part-time in the evenings, but in the daytime they have to be available for work. In practice, however, taking courses was often not an evening activity but a full-time activity. They took courses supported by a welfare benefit rather than a government scholarship or loan because benefits are higher and do not have to be paid back later. As long as their studies had not been completed, they were not likely to look for work.

Seventeen percent of this subgroup had become active in the informal economy (10 percent structurally, 7 percent occasionally). A few considered this a possible channel for finding regular work: one could demonstrate one's capabilities and it might provide useful connections. For most of these respondents, however, informal work was not a means for finding regular work but an alternative for it. Together with the welfare benefit, it provided at least as much income as a regular job and often more, and the immaterial benefits of work such as social contacts could also certainly be acquired in the informal circuit. This subgroup, largely made up of people who were single, young and relatively well educated, could live much more easily with unemployment than others. A large majority of them lived in the inner city of Rotterdam, where there was less social control and more opportunities for informal activities than in the other locations.

THE WILLINGNESS TO ACCEPT JOBS

This section deals with the willingness of unemployed people to make concessions in order to obtain a job. How great was our respondents' willingness to make concessions in order to find work? About a fifth of our respondents were willing to accept any kind of work (see Table 6.4). Around 50 percent of the respondents, were willing to accept work only on certain terms, and a sizeable minority were not willing to make any concessions at all. Willingness to compromise on one point did not necessarily imply a similar willingness on other points. For example, of the respondents willing to make concessions on the point of job content, 32 percent did not want to accept lower wages, and of those willing to accept wage concessions, 38 percent would not accept lower jobs than they felt qualified for. None of the respondents were willing to compromise on all the points, however, nor were there any who were unwilling to compromise on any point at all. There was always some willingness on their part.

TABLE 6.4 Willingness to Make Concessions to Find Work (in percentages, N=264)

	willing unconditionally	*willing under conditions*	*not willing*
Moving to another city	14	42	44
Long traveling times	20	56	23
Temporary work	23	34	43
Lower wage level	13	55	32
Job content and working conditions	22	40	38
Part-time work	23	50	27

Moving and Commuting

A fifth of the respondents were willing to accept long traveling times to a possible new work site, no matter what the conditions were. Respondents were quite critical on the point of moving. The reasons given most often for not being willing to move were attachment to the city and neighborhood and fear of losing contact and losing the support of relatives and friends who lived close by.

I won't move. I was born and raised here. I have lived on this street for thirty years. Not for a million guilders would I go (31-year-old man, partner and children, 7 years unemployed).

If I moved I would lose the support of all the people who are close to me. Would my brother still come by every other day? (26-year-old Surinamese woman, single with child, 5 years unemployed)

Another argument against moving was the limited mobility of the spouse or children. The respondents did not want to take their children away from their school and environment, there was a sick mother who had to be cared for, or the spouse had a job in the neighborhood (29 percent of the partners had a job, in three-quarters of the cases a permanent [part-time] one). Furthermore, moving expenses were cited, especially by respondents who owned a house (almost 10 percent). In the eastern city of Enschede, people did not want to have to move to the west of the country (the region of Amsterdam, Rotterdam, The Hague and Utrecht), even though some of them believed that was where jobs were to be found. They felt the west of the country was too noisy, too crowded and too dirty. If respondents were prepared to move, it was only under the condition of being offered a permanent job. That is, a job had to be there first. They would not move to another area of the country just to look for work.

This limited mobility was less evident in earlier periods of high unemployment. From the late nineteenth century to the 1940s, moving in search of a job was quite common. Unemployed farmhands moved in large numbers from the agrarian southwest to the shipyards and factories in the Rotterdam region, peat diggers in the middle of the country traveled by the thousands to industrial cities in the east to work in the textile mills, and Frisians from the north moved to Amsterdam to look for work in any number of trades. In the postwar years, many poor Dutchmen, some of whom had never before ventured more than a few kilometers from their village, emigrated to Canada, Australia, New Zealand and South Africa in search of work and a better life. However, there are now very few emigration possibilities, and most municipal housing and welfare departments do not allow unemployed people drawing on welfare to move into their region. Apart from that, the social security system now provides people with alternatives and with more freedom to choose. Through newspapers and television, unemployed people are far better informed about their chances on the labor market than they were in the 1930s. They know that unemployment is high in other parts of the country as well.

Although relatively few respondents were prepared to move, many were willing to accept longer commuting times. However, this too had its limitations. Most of them wanted to remain in their own region, at most fifty kilometers from their home. Furthermore, they expected their prospective employer to pay the traveling expenses.

Temporary and Flexible Work

The unwillingness to accept temporary work was second highest, although unconditional willingness to accept temporary work was high as well. Of our respondents, 43 percent refused to accept any temporary work through employment agencies, 34 percent would consider it only under certain conditions, and 23 percent would accept it without a second thought. Five percent actually had a temporary or flexible job at the time. The contrast between willingness and unwillingness can be accounted for by the respondents' work experience and level of education. Elderly, poorly educated people who had had routine factory jobs were far less willing to accept the uncertainty of temporary work than young, better educated people.

As the firing of personnel is legally quite complicated, employers have become used to hiring temporary labor through commercial employment agencies and under all kinds of "atypical" contracts (e.g., call on contracts, free-lance contracts and outwork). Temporary employment agencies employ workers and rent them out to employers. This allows employers to dismiss temporary workers at their convenience. Research has shown that temporary and flexible work may lead to permanent employment. According to a labor market survey, 55 percent of temporary and flexible employees had a regular or steady job after a year and a half (OSA 1988). However, our respondents did not use this channel any more than average. One reason was that most of the factors that prevent long-term unemployed people from finding a permanent job—age, lack of skills, etc.—also limited their access to temporary and flexible work. There were a few, however, who liked having a temporary job, as it could be easily combined with studying, traveling abroad or raising children. In their case, the Welfare Department provided an additional income via welfare.

The negative opinions about temporary work stemmed partly from past experience. Many respondents mentioned low wages, the lack of job security, and poor working conditions as problems. Others, who did register with temporary employment agencies, complained about never hearing from them.

I am registered everywhere. How many employment agencies do you think there are here in the inner city of Amsterdam where I live? Do I ever hear anything from them? Never, not a word. Why bother going there? What's the use? (31-year-old man, single, 5 years unemployed).

Another problem the unemployed had with temporary or flexible work was that it complicated their relations with the Welfare Department. Getting a temporary or flexible job meant changes in their registration at the Welfare Department. They had to sign out and, after the job was over, sign up again. Given the workload of the Welfare Departments, these procedures were prone to errors and could take months. In the meantime, recipients might not get their checks. Due to their fear of the risks, most respondents preferred not to change their welfare status in any way, especially since most temporary and flexible work is limited to six months or less, which is too short to acquire the rights to the higher unemployment benefits. Furthermore, as many respondents were in debt to the Welfare Department, any income from temporary work would be directly claimed, thus leaving the respondent no better off. So it was not only the availability of welfare that reduced the willingness to accept temporary work, but also the bureaucratic procedures involved.

Wage Level

Table 6.4 shows that a little over 10 percent of the respondents would accept work at any wage. One-third were unwilling to make concessions as to wages. They would work only if it paid them at least what they had formerly earned or wages comparable to what other people earned.

What I consider a reasonable wage? Well, really, the wages I earned at my former job. It took years to get up to that level. When I became unemployed, my income fell rather drastically. Now I don't feel like working again for so many years to get back to that level. I'll only go back to work for the wages I earned last (46-year-old man, single, 6 years unemployed).

The remaining 55 percent were willing to accept lower wages under certain conditions. That usually meant they wanted to earn a wage not too much lower than their former wages or higher than the legal minimum wage (in 1987 around 1600 guilders a month).

I could have had jobs for the minimum wage. But I said: "Forget it, I'm not crazy." That's ridiculous. For working from early in the morning till late in the evening. I have worked for quite a few years, but someone who is 23 and has never worked before gets the same wage. That's not right (38-year-old man, single, 4 years unemployed).

A reasonable amount. Given my last salary of 1700 guilders I would consider something between 1500 and 1700 guilders reasonable. I would certainly like to do something, but not for 1200 guilders (48-year-old man, single, 11 years unemployed).

Most of the respondents expected to at least earn more than their welfare benefit. Too small a difference between their wages and welfare benefits might even mean a decrease in net income, since a wage-earner could lose secondary benefits such as rent subsidy or certain tax deductions.

I would like to take care of the elderly in some way. Not for the same amount as my Welfare benefit, but for the minimum wage, yes, I would do it (37-year-old man, single, 6 years unemployed).

Of the 87 percent who were not willing to accept work at any wage, one-third expected at least 100 to 200 guilders more than welfare and two-thirds expected 300 guilders or more. Thus, in the opinion of the vast majority of our respondents, welfare had become a basic social right. Any effort on their part would justify a wage significantly higher than welfare. A few respondents would even be willing to work for a wage as low as their welfare, but they would make demands regarding the job content and working conditions.

Job Content and Working Conditions

Desires about job content were often formulated in terms of past working experience or vocational training. The respondents wanted to get back to similar jobs, which constituted part of their self-image. That desire legitimized refusing work they considered less attractive.

I want to stay in health care, where I have worked all my life. I don't feel like working as a maid or in the hospital kitchen. No, I can do much more than that (26-year-old Surinamese woman, single with child, 5 years unemployed).

I invested time and money in getting my papers for carpentry and masonry. So I want to stick with these trades (27-year-old man, lives with parents, 2 years unemployed).

Some of the respondents did not want to go back to the jobs they had formerly held. Several had actually quit their jobs because they disliked them, saw no future in their prospects in the labor market, or tried to get more attractive work by taking courses. For others, hobbies and volunteer work led to a reorientation to work. They would prefer to see these activities transformed into paid employment.

R. works as a volunteer at a radio station. He hopes for a paid position there. "Something I have always wanted, to earn my living with classical music" (33-year-old man, single, 5 years unemployed).

The chance of getting paid work in this kind of field is not great. Some respondents, however, had found their identity in these activities, considered them useful contributions to society, and were not willing to return to whatever former jobs they may have had. They hardly ever looked for work.

Qualifications as to job content and working conditions were most often phrased in negative terms. Respondents refused to do heavy, dirty, monotonous or unhealthy work: cleaning, hauling, working with toxic chemicals, assembly line work, and factory work in sectors with a notorious reputation, such as the meat processing or rubber industries. For some of them, the idea of being cooped up indoors or having to work in hierarchical relations was plainly terrifying.

I hate working on an assembly line or having to work fast, doing the same tedious task over and over. I may not have learned much at school, but that kind of work, no, I'm sorry . . . (25-year-old man, lives with parents, 2 years unemployed).

I can't stand working for a boss. I can't have people telling me "do this, do that." And certainly not now, after having been out of work for more than fifteen years (30-year-old man, partner and children, 14 years unemployed).

Many of those who knew what they did not want were not quite so clear about what they did want. This group was composed mainly of younger people with little work experience and a low or very general education. They moved about in the labor market without any apparent direction in mind.

R. is registered for "clerical work," though it does not appeal to her. What then? "I really don't know. I have never worked. I don't know what working is like. There is nothing special that could make me say: 'Gee, that's what I'd like to do'" (24-year-old woman, partner no children, 3 years unemployed).

Fewer than 25 percent of our respondents did not make any demands as to job content. They maintained that their unemployment condition was not due to unwillingness on their part. However, they either had other demands (high wages, a permanent job) or mentioned factors that made it impossible for them to find work: poor health, no diplomas, too old, and the absolute lack of openings for unskilled workers.

Part-Time Work

Table 6.4 shows that relatively few respondents (27 percent) refused to accept any part-time work at all. However, 50 percent would do it only under certain conditions. An important condition was that it had to benefit them financially. Usually this condition could not be met with completely, as the Welfare Department tended to deduct the income from part-time work from their benefit. Welfare recipients are allowed to earn an extra income of up to 200 guilders a month for a period of two years. After that, the extra income is fully deducted from the benefit.

I do some part-time work, 75 guilders a week. However, the Welfare Department deducts all of it. So it does not help me. It only got me a lot of trouble and it costs money in connection with rent subsidy and so on. It was intended as a bridge towards real work, but at my age it turned out to be impossible to find work in my own field (40-year-old man, partner and children, 7 years unemployed).

The respondents who kept a part-time job did so for the social contacts it provided. Furthermore, part-time work had the advantage over temporary work that respondents did not completely lose their benefits. Hence, it entailed somewhat fewer bureaucratic problems and risks.

Differences among Respondents
and between Locations

There were significant differences in the willingness to compromise were related to the respondents' personal characteristics and their surroundings. Men were more willing to make concessions than women, older people more than younger ones, married people more than singles, Turks and Moroccans more than Dutch and other foreign-born respondents, and poorly educated more than well educated respondents.

The respondents who were willing to make concessions on the points of job content, temporary work and traveling times looked for work more frequently than those who were not. However, they were also the ones who considered their chances of finding work poor because of their limited qualifications and the gradual disappearance of unskilled work. Respondents who were less willing to make concessions and who looked for work less frequently were more often among the last two or three selected applicants for a job. Notwithstanding their unwillingness to make concessions, their chances were better. This group had also more often refused to take jobs that were offered to them. Thus the two categories remained unemployed: one due to their unwillingness to accept jobs, the other due to their inability to find jobs.

The more traditionally oriented unemployed, who were willing to make concessions to find a job, could be located in the Enschede neighborhood more than in Amsterdam or Rotterdam. This has several reasons: the Enschede respondents were older, more often married with children, and less well educated. Relatives and neighbors in the traditional working class Enschede neighborhood tended to impose a traditional work ethic upon the unemployed.

THE WORK ETHIC

The differences in job-seeking efforts were related to differences in work ethic. Many of the respondents who kept on looking for work still had a traditional work ethic. To them, working was a self-evident duty, and being out of work was unnatural and even immoral. They were ashamed of being out of work and not being able to look after their family.

I think you ought to work for a living. You have to do something for society. I still have that feeling. If I could get a job I would certainly take it. I know people of over thirty who have never worked in their whole life. That's terrible! You ought to have worked in your life. You have to learn discipline, and to bear responsibility. You can't play around your whole life (31-year-old woman, single with child, 3 years unemployed).

As stated before, this type of work ethic was dominant in the Enschede neighborhood more than in the other two neighborhoods, partly because of the social pressure of relatives and neighbors. The role of the family can indeed be directly corrective. The significance of the neighbors as social controllers is often present in the perception of the long-term unemployed.

What shall I say? They keep an eye on you. On what you're doing all day. And: "How can he afford to do this or that?" (38-year-old man of foreign descent, partner and children, 3 years unemployed).

Some of the usually younger respondents had quite a deviant work ethic. Instead of a duty to work, they felt they had a right to life and to an income provided by society.

People should be able to choose for themselves to work or not. That's why I'm in favor of a basic income scheme (27-years-old woman, single, 6 years unemployed).

These were mostly respondents who did not look for a job intensively or at all. They were quite content with their lives and a few were even satisfied with the lower income they had as a result.

I don't mind being out of work. Nor do I complain about not having enough money (23-year-old woman of foreign descent, partner no children, 5 years unemployed).

The majority of our respondents, however, could not be classified in either of these two general categories of "traditional work ethic" and "alternative work ethic." They did not talk in a general and abstract way about work, but focused on concrete aspects of work, unemployment, and welfare. They seemed to agree that they had a certain duty to work, but only insofar as it did not detract from what they saw as their "rights" to suitable work and to a difference between wages and benefits. One might perhaps speak of a utilitarian work ethic, generated by a feeling of dependence and the discouraging experiences in the course of years of looking for a job. To them a job did not mean just an abstract duty; it meant an end to financial hardship, boredom, aimlessness and non-participation in society. However, they would not accept just any job. The job had to meet certain requirements regarding wages earned, job content, labor relations and so forth. Welfare liberated them somewhat from the necessity to work and allowed them to claim new rights; the right to do decent and useful work, to fulfill themselves and to develop on the job, to develop social contacts, and to participate in the consumption of the goods and services provided by modern society.

LABOR MARKET EXPERIENCES

Many respondents justified their failure to look for jobs by referring to their poor chances on the labor market. They stated that there were no jobs, that employers were too choosy, or that they themselves were too old or did not have the right qualifications. Their earlier experiences confirmed these convictions.

Almost 80 percent of the respondents cited the absolute shortage of jobs as a cause of their unemployment. They often meant a lack of unskilled work, the type of work they were qualified for. The respondents in Enschede, the "Dutch Manchester," which has witnessed the almost complete disappearance of its large cotton industry, frequently cited this factor. Given the high rate of unemployment, employers could select prospective personnel more critically and could afford to leave out workers who were not relatively cheap and/or productive.

Most of the respondents (81 percent) thought they were too old for employers, even though their average age was only 35. Even people in their thirties and late twenties had of this opinion. These categories mentioned different age levels beneath which they considered it possible to find work, curiously enough usually a few years below their own age.

I have looked for work everywhere, really. But I am too old for everything. Above 45, then you are too old. They prefer younger people (49-year-old woman, single, 15 years unemployed).

Have a look in the paper. What does it say? Everything is for 23, 25 years old (39-year-old man, single, 9 years unemployed).

Once in a while I look through the papers, but even at 20 you're already too old. It's all 18, 19 years old that they want (25-year-old woman, lives with parents, 5 years unemployed).

"Too old" meant "too expensive." In the Netherlands, people under 23 do not have a right to the legal minimum wage. There is a lower minimum wage for them, increasing somewhat from the ages of 17 to 23. Furthermore, they often don't fall under pension plans. Several respondents mentioned other age-related reasons: health ("I think they are afraid that women my age will get menopause problems"), the lack of a "young and modern" appearance (for work in shops), and the lack of flexibility ("Look, a young boy they can still fool"). Many respondents believed they already knew from the newspapers that there was no place for them in the labor market. Others had been told so more or less explicitly on the phone by an employer when inquiring about a position.

In addition to age, the lack of formal education was often mentioned. Almost a quarter of our respondents had only primary school (the older ones and the Turks and Moroccans), and one-fifth had an unfinished lower level of general or vocational secondary training (many younger people). Thus, almost half of our respondents were qualified only for unskilled work, a type of work that has gradually disappeared in recent years. However, even in unskilled jobs the poorly educated are forced out by others with diplomas.

I call a company and the guy asks: "Do you have a diploma?" I say: "What kind of diploma, for cleaning windows?" I got crazy. For everything they want a diploma, a diploma (30-year-old Turkish man, partner and children, 5 years unemployed).

Furthermore, the lack of work experience was sometimes an obstacle. Eight percent of the respondents had no work experience whatsoever. They were caught in the classical vicious circle of unemployed school-leavers: no job, no work experience, no job. Others did have some work experience, but it was outdated or for jobs and industries that had disappeared.

Look, there is a large gap in my work experience. In the past, work designs were made quite differently, without computers, word processors. That experience I don't have (39-year-old man, single, 3 years unemployed).

Being out of work is a handicap in itself, a stigma, as various research findings indicate. Van Ours et al. (1987) noted that the unemployed, even if they have the right education and experience, are not considered eligible in 30 percent of the cases. The experience of many of our respondents confirmed this.

If you've been out of work for a while, it gets more difficult. They get the idea that you don't want to work (25-year-old man, lives with parents, 7 years unemployed).

Some admit, however, that they too do not consider themselves immediately employable, even if their education and experience would fit.

It would take me two to four weeks to get back into a work rhythm (29-year-old man of foreign descent, partner and children, 6 years unemployed).

More than half the foreign born respondents considered their foreign origin a problem in finding work. It was not necessarily the result of racism, but could also be the consequence of functional requirements. Many of the Turks and Moroccans barely spoke Dutch. With the introduction of more modern machinery, the mastery of the Dutch language has increased in importance, even for some unskilled jobs.

They don't need me any more at the RDM [shipyard]. The foreman used to understand me. One word from me was all it would take. It's not like that anymore. Now you have to speak Dutch (47-year-old Turkish man, multi-family household, 4 years unemployed).

It even went so far that first they asked you to send in a photograph. Then I thought: "That's probably a civilized form of discrimination. They want to have a look at the color" (38-year-old Surinamese man, partner and children, 13 years unemployed).

About a quarter of the respondents also referred to health problems as an obstacle, since these problems limited them to certain kinds of acceptable work (e.g., in the case of back aches). Epilepsy or a psychiatric past might not hinder their working but nevertheless stigmatized them.

Finally, 8 percent of the respondents admitted they had a criminal record, which was another obstacle. For these various reasons, the majority of our respondents felt their chances of finding work were low (44 percent) or even non-existent (24 percent). Only 8 percent were really optimistic, and 24 percent considered their chances reasonably good. Of course, the group of pessimists mainly consisted of older and poorly educated people, members of minority groups and people who have been out of work for extremely long periods of time. Many of them did not even have the experience of almost getting a job. About one-third of the respondents gave a positive answer; they were mainly women, younger, better educated single people of Dutch origin.

EFFORTS TO INCREASE THE CHANCES
OF FINDING WORK

Most of our respondents tended to lay the blame for their unemployment on others (selective employers), on society (no jobs) or on characteristics they could not change, such as their age or ethnic background. In doing so, they referred to their own job-seeking experiences. Although there was of course a large measure of truth in this, one might wonder what the unemployed were willing to do to increase their value on the labor market and change some of their own objective characteristics. Did they pursue whatever opportunities were available for training or job experience?

The Dutch government has provided various "intermediary facilities" between the unemployed and the labor market. Some of these have been organized by the central government (Ministry of Social Affairs and Employment) or regional employment offices, others by various local governments or private agencies. The intermediary facilities consist mainly of vocational training and work experience programs. The labor market measures that were taken in 1988 and 1989, when the unemployment figures were 682,000 and 645,000, are summed up in Table 6.5. The differences between the number of unemployed people and the number of positions available illustrates the discrepancy between the expectations and the goals of the labor market policy and the means that were actually at hand.

At the time of the interview, 4 percent of the respondents were attending some form of vocational training and 19 percent had done so in the past. These figures are low considering that 80 percent of the respondents viewed their poor education as one of the major reasons why they could not find work. About 35 percent said they were not willing to attend any kind of school. The other 65 percent were willing in principle, but often only under the condition that there was a realistic prospect of a job afterwards; 42 percent did not even know about the possibilities for training and education. The intermediary facilities were unknown to large segments of the population they were designed for (see Wong et al. 1988). Rather than going out and getting the necessary information, some respondents expected government agencies to approach and inform them of the possibilities.

They talk a lot about helping the long-term unemployed, but we never get anything in the mailbox. If the Employment Office gets so much money from the government for re-training, we ought to get a notice (49-year-old man of foreign descent, multi-family household, 6 years unemployed).

TABLE 6.5 Unemployment Schemes (in Numbers of Positions, 1988 and 1989, in thousands)

	1988		1989	
	goal	actuality	goal	actuality
Total number of wage expense subsidies and work experience positions	35	25 to 30	40 to 45	30.5
including Vermeend/Moor[a]	12	8	9	4
Total number of vocational training positions	150	150	155	150

[a] Work place subsidy program for the private sector.

Source: Ministry of Social Affairs and Employment 1989 and 1990.

The respondents gave several reasons for their non-attendance. First, many of them felt they were unable to attend courses. The Dutchmen among them said they "could not learn" and preferred working "with their hands." The respondents of foreign descent referred to their limited knowledge of the Dutch language.

> More schooling is not for me. I only had six grades of elementary school and my marks were awful. I can't read or write well. If you can't do that, there isn't much you can do (32-year-old man, partner and children, 7 years unemployed).

Others felt they were too old to go to school again. It wasn't just their feeling that they could not learn anymore; they were afraid that even another diploma would not be much of a help. They would still be rejected because of their age.

> Even if you have diplomas, you won't find work. I might be wrong, but I think they prefer 17 and 18 year olds. What should I expect at the age of 41? (41-year-old woman, single, 4 years unemployed).

Finally, many believed that more education would not help them, even though they considered their poor schooling a major explanation for their unemployment.

> My father-in-law has diplomas, but there was no work for him. So now he sits at home with all his diplomas. I don't mind learning again, but when I'm done with it I want to work. Otherwise it's a waste of time (34-year-old Surinamese man, partner and children, 5 years unemployed).

Only a very few felt there was an intrinsic value in education. They studied because they considered it a useful pastime, liked the social contacts, or expected to learn skills that could also be useful around the home.

> It gets you out of the house. And it's nice, you belong to a group. You can also see what you can and what you can't do. Often I could already do all those things [woodworking] and other people had to start at the beginning. There is a real difference (23-year-old man, partner, no children, 3 years unemployed).

Working Experience

In the hope that it might aid them in finding a permanent job, the Dutch government has created several plans to provide the unemployed with working experience. One of the recent ones was the Vermeend-Moor Bill, named after two Social Democratic Members of Parliament. For four years, employers do not have to pay any social insurance premiums for a long-term unemployed person who is hired for at least six months. Only a few respondents in our study had experience with plans of this kind to provide working experience. Many, however, had their doubts about such plans and referred to possible counterproductive effects.

> I went to see a company where they hired people under the Vermeend-Moor plan. I asked them: "What are my chances of finding a permanent job here?" The man replied: "Well, if we hired

you on a permanent basis we would lose our subsidy." "Look," I said, "Forget it. That's ridiculous" (25-year-old man, lives with parents, 2 years unemployed).

Other plans allowed the long-term unemployed to keep their benefit while working as volunteers, but gave them little or no guarantee of a job. Many such "work projects" were created by social and cultural institutions and municipalities in need of cheap labor. Only rarely did any of our respondents participate in such projects. Many of these projects were not focused on the older and poorly educated unemployed. In addition, many respondents were opposed to the very idea of working without getting paid more than their benefit. There was a great deal of opposition to such ideas as the American workfare.

In practice, very few companies took advantage of the opportunities to hire cheap labor through government subsidy programs (see Table 6.5). Several empirical studies have shown that many unemployment programs have considerable unintended consequences. The "creaming of the unemployed" is one of them (Engbersen 1990).

Help from Government Agencies

The Dutch welfare state has government agencies with the sole task of aiding the unemployed in finding work, the Employment Offices. However, most of our long-term unemployed respondents had infrequent contact with these agencies. Their relation could be characterized as a "paper relation." In order to be eligible for a welfare benefit, the unemployed are required to remain available for work and to exhibit some willingness to look for work. In practice, this means sending back a form to the Employment Office four times a year listing when and where they applied for work. In addition, the Welfare Department requires a monthly form of the same kind. According to law, the Welfare Department is entitled to penalize welfare recipients who have not made frequent enough efforts to find a job. In practice, this is hardly ever done. The street-level bureaucrats in the Welfare Department know very well that most of their clients have very little chance of returning to the labor market (see Lipsky 1980, Engbersen 1990).

For the vast majority of our respondents, sending back the forms was their only contact with the Employment Office. In principle, there should be more contact. The Employment Office should help the unemployed find work. However, this hardly ever happened. For one thing, the Employment Offices tended to concentrate on the unemployed who were easiest to place, thus excluding most of the long-term unemployed. They did so in an effort to improve their reputation among employers and thus increase their effectiveness as a mediator in the labor market. This process was referred to earlier as the "creaming of the unemployed."

It should be noted here that the situation in the labor market practically paralyzed such agencies as the Employment Offices. At the time, a labor supply surplus of about 600,000 people was facing a labor demand of only 100,000 jobs.

Many of the unemployed had nonetheless expected more active help from the Employment Offices. They were disappointed when this help was not forthcoming.

The agencies, such as the Employment Office, could do a little more. But they don't do anything at all! I can't imagine that they don't have a single job for me, since the commercial employment agency does have some jobs once in a while. . . It's just as if the Employment Office is only a bookkeeping system (32-year-old man, partner and children, 7 years unemployed).

At first I still had to come to the Employment Office to talk about work. I miss that now. They ought to make that compulsory again. Now it's too easy. You only have to throw the card in the mailbox. You can't talk any more about how everything is or about how to establish contacts with bosses. You can't write anything like that on such a small card (34-year-old man, single, 5 years unemployed).

Many of the respondents expected the initiative to come from the Employment Office ("Why don't they ever send you any information?") and could not deal with the self-service policy of the Employment Offices.

As far as I'm concerned they might as well close the Employment Office. It has no function at all. People who are difficult to place—and that includes me—ought to get more help. But they don't even know what that is! They tell you: "Yes sir, but you'll have to look for yourself." I did it, but what if I can't find anything? Look, there comes a moment when you really need help. But it is as if all the agency does is register you! (32-year-old man, lives with parents, 6 years unemployed)

CONCLUSIONS

The Dutch welfare state has, in a way, liberated people from dependence on all-powerful employers and the willingness of employers to hire them as the only way to make a living; that is, from dependence on the discretion of powerful "capitalists." Yet, in doing so, the welfare state seems to have created a new form of dependence on street-level bureaucracies for income, labor market information, housing and so forth. By introducing social rights, especially the right to a decent living for everyone through the creation of a social security system and welfare benefits, people have been provided with an alternative for dependence on paid employment. Even without work, they can have an income, albeit a relatively low one. Of course, Dutch welfare recipients do have the formal obligation to apply for jobs regularly, but it is no longer necessary to accept any kind of work under any condition. This opportunity to critically evaluate job offers has been a form of emancipation. As is apparent from our study, people take advantage of this choice. They are sometimes critical of job offers, and some of them prefer a low welfare income to a job they dislike. It is also true that the availability of alternatives seems to have reduced the incentive to look for work. This explains in part the difference in the duration of American and Dutch unemployment. In Chapter 1 we noted that more than half the Dutch unemployed have been out of a job for over a year. In the United States, this is true of less than 6 percent.

Dutch unemployed are under less pressure to accept whatever job they can get at any cost. In addition, the growing number of part-time and flexible jobs in the service sector is often not interesting for unemployed heads of households, since income earned this way would be less than the welfare income.

Some Dutch unemployed people are confronted with more or less the same problems that Edin (1991) described in her study of AFDC recipients. Despite all the disadvantages, a welfare benefit, and the various arrangements linked with it, does provide more security than an uncertain part-time job with poor working conditions. However, for many long-term unemployed there were no real alternatives in the labor market. Since they had no chance of getting any job whatsoever, living on a welfare benefit was the only option. An exacerbating aspect of contemporary urban unemployment is the impossibility for many people to find any job, so that they tend to become permanently dependent on the state. Many are of foreign descent, poorly educated and experienced only in the simplest factory work.[5] Most live in the inner cities of the large Dutch metropolises where the unemployment rate is extremely high (up to 35 percent). The closed homogeneous networks they are part of do not provide them with any relevant contacts for getting jobs.

The respondents in this study had been unemployed for an average of more than five years. About half of them still frequently looked for a job. The other half did so only once in a while or had given up altogether. The qualitative and quantitative gap between supply and demand on the labor market gave these people few opportunities to find a job after having been without one for so many years. Their perception of the labor market as a jobless market was reflected in their efforts to look for work. It is, however, difficult to generalize. The long-term unemployed do not constitute a homogeneous group, and their reaction to unemployment, the intensity of their jobseeking behavior, and their willingness to compromise as to former or ideal jobs and wages differ a great deal. Several categories of unemployed people can be distinguished, as will be done in Chapter 8. Here we will note that there are certainly people whom welfare benefits have made lethargic, but also many who have exhibited initiative and used the opportunities and facilities provided by the welfare state to their own advantage in an often creative (although sometimes not quite legal) way.

Another relevant finding is that the complexity of the system of institutions "guarding" and "guiding" the labor market and the unemployed often obstructs rather than stimulates active labor market behavior on the part of the long-term unemployed.[6] The Dutch welfare system stimulates non-participation through a system that combines relatively generous benefits with easy access. At the end of the 1980s, there was still no "active labor market policy" to reintegrate unemployed people into the labor market. Thus the Dutch regime, capable as it might be of compensating for unemployment, was not able to conduct an effective employment strategy. In this respect, the Netherlands clearly differs from a country like Sweden, where greater facilities have been made available for efforts to provide for full employment (Therborn 1986).

In the early 1990s, there has been more and more of a call for an activating labor market policy. Measures designed to steer the unemployed to the labor market are expanded. In addition, the Dutch welfare state has put on a "grimmer" face. Unemployed individuals are more obliged to accept whatever jobs are offered, and to invest time and energy in vocational training or work experience programs. If they do not do their best or exhibit adequate willingness, their welfare benefits might be reduced or stopped altogether.

NOTES

1. Granovetter wrote: "Especially important to recognize, moreover, is the self-maintaining aspect of personal contact systems. Blacks are at a disadvantage in using informal channels of job information not because they have failed to 'develop an informal structure' suitable to the need, but because they are presently under-represented in the structure of employment itself" Mark S. Granovetter, *Getting a Job: A Study of Contacts and Careers*, Cambridge, Mass: Harvard University Press, 1974, 133.

2. See Sarah Buckland and Susanne MacGregor, "Discouraged Workers? The Long-term Unemployed and the Search for Work" in: Stephen Fineman (ed.), *Unemployment, Personal and Social Consequences*, London/New York: Tavistock Publications, 1987.

3. These figures have been taken from Flap and Tazelaar (1985). Granovetter wrote that studies on blue-collar workers showed that 60 to 90 percent of jobs were found informally, principally through friends and relatives, and by direct application Mark S. Granovetter, *Getting a Job: A Study of Contacts and Careers*, Cambridge, Mass: Harvard University Press, 1974.

4. Compare Robert C. Kloosterman, *Achteraan in de rij: een onderzoek naar de factoren die (her)intreding van langdurig werklozen belemmeren*, The Hague: OSA, 1987.

5. On January 1, 1988, 13 percent of the Dutch population was unemployed, but for people of Turkish or Moroccan descent the rate was over 40 percent. The unemployment rate among people of Surinamese and Antillean descent was about 25 percent.

6. These findings are in keeping with those of American studies on the effectiveness of work programs and employment placement services. The hard core unemployed often fail to be reached or they get a job in the secondary segment of the job market, which only serves to perpetuate their poverty and insecure situation. See Yeheskel Hasenfeld, "The Role of Employment Placement Services in Maintaining Poverty" in: *Social Service Review*, December 1975, 569-587.

CHAPTER 7

The Perception of Rights and Obligations

In *Beyond Entitlement, the Social Obligations of Citizenship* (1986), Lawrence Mead explained that in the case of welfare recipients, the equilibrium between rights and obligations was off balance. Based on communitarian notions of citizenship (Burke and Tocqueville), Mead argued that parallel to the right to a welfare benefit, the obligation to look for a job had been inadequately developed. Mead's point of view was that citizens have social obligations to the community whose public means they benefit from. There is, or should be, a reciprocal relation between citizens and the state. Mead used his conception of citizenship to criticize the permissiveness of the welfare state and to support his argument in favor of workfare programs. The right to a welfare benefit should be linked to the willingness to work, regardless of the quality of the job. In Mead's opinion, workfare is a form of public education, and education and work are public activities that can be expected of all the competent members of a society "for their own good and society's" (Mead 1989:166).

To a European reader, Mead's analysis might seem exaggerated. Compared to European welfare states, social rights are in the American welfare state weakly developed. Large groups of citizens, including families without children and the "working poor," can make little or no claim to a welfare benefit (see also Ellwood 1988). The third stage of the process of citizenship-building described by T. H. Marshall, the guarantee of social rights so that everyone can function as a competent citizen, has only been instituted to a limited extent in the United States (Marmor et al. 1990). Mead's analysis focused only on the obligations of citizens and did not pay attention to the public obligations of the government to its citizens. Critics of Mead argued that a society that is incapable of providing adequate schools, reasonable housing and decent health care for all its citizens loses the moral authority to impose obligations. As Katz put it: "Unless it provides the prerequisites of competence, society lacks a moral title to obligation" (Katz 1989:164-165).

Doubts have been raised about the notion that people regard welfare as something they automatically have a right to. The legal rights movement may have contributed to a view of welfare as a right by the general public and local officials (Sossin 1986). The stigma linked to welfare has never disappeared, however. This is evident not only from the public discussion on the underclass, in which the AFDC mother often serves as the modern symbol of the undeserving poor (Katz 1989, Gans 1991), but also from studies like the one conducted by Popkin (1990) on the experiences of AFDC recipients. Most of them perceived receiving welfare as an unpleasant and stigmatizing experience. Popkin noted feelings of depression, shame and having let one's own children down. She also observed a group of respondents who did not seem to have any trouble accepting welfare dependence.

Various authors have criticized the unfair and unequal treatment of the poor by welfare departments and other street-level bureaucracies. In *Street-Level Bureaucracy* (1980), Lipsky described the actions of officials whose job it was to implement social policies. The working conditions of the street-level bureaucrats were characterized by time pressure, rapidly changing instructions, a chronic shortage of funds and personnel, contradictory organizational aims and unclear quality evaluations. Under the pressure of these working conditions, the goals and rules were adjusted to suit day-to-day practice. These adjustments, which often conflicted with officials rules and goals, were often to the disadvantage of the weakest groups who were the most dependent on official agencies. Lipsky stressed that clients did not receive equal treatment. Due to the large number of clients and the limited possibilities, choices had to be made, usually to the advantage of the people in the more favorable position to begin with. When extra assistance was considered, the hard-core poor or long-term unemployed were ignored or written off as hopeless, so that their situation was perpetuated and feelings of dependence and powerlessness were intensified. Handler and Hasenfeld observed that the normative policing practices of street-level bureaucrats in distinguishing between the "deserving" and the "undeserving" were morally degrading and contributed toward stigmatizing welfare (Handler and Hasenfeld 1991).

In the early 1990s in the Netherlands, a discussion took place comparable to that in the United States on the equilibrium between rights and obligations. The view is widespread that in the development of the Dutch welfare state, obligations have been neglected compared to rights, and the agencies that implement social policies contribute to the perpetuation of welfare dependence. The permissiveness of the Dutch system is viewed as one of the causes of the growth in number of welfare clients. This is why a "tougher" welfare state is now being proposed, with more emphasis on the obligations of the people who receive benefits. Under the penalty of losing their benefits, they should be compelled to accept whatever jobs they can get, to take vocational training courses, or to do unpaid work just to get some work experience. Others refute such views with the argument that it is wrong to impose obligations at a time when there are not enough jobs available. Besides, the government does not have the funds required for creating any serious alternatives to welfare benefits. Still others believe that forcing people to work is not an acceptable idea. In Dahrendorf's footsteps, there has been widespread criticism of the workfare concept. It is apt to turn work into forced labor, opponents say, so that the employment contract loses its fundamentally voluntary nature (Dahrendorf 1988).

This chapter describes how unemployed people in the Netherlands perceived their rights and obligations and experienced their welfare dependence in 1987, on the eve of the process of the "hardening" of the Dutch welfare state. We also studied the perception by the unemployed of national politicians and other representatives of the state they are dependent upon. The question arises whether the Dutch system leads to a different perception of dependence than has been described in the American literature. The Dutch welfare system is more universal, more generous and less disciplinary. Receiving welfare is less stigmatized than in America (Engbersen and Van der Veen 1991).

WELFARE DEPENDENCE AND WELFARE INDEPENDENCE

The welfare state has two opposing faces. On the one hand, it provides people on welfare with a certain degree of freedom. The minimum income they receive allows them the choice to refuse work they feel is unsuitable and to refuse to move to another region where more jobs might be available. On the other hand, that same welfare state has created new forms of social dependence and social inequality. The dependence relation typical of the capitalist society of the past —the dependence of labor on capital—has been partially replaced by a new fundamental dependence relation: that of welfare recipients on the state and its agencies, such as the Municipal Welfare Department—a dependence of citizens on bureaucracy.

An occasional respondent was aware of these two sides of the welfare state ("You feel you are dependent, but of course you are glad the system exists"), but in the interviews most of them emphasized either one side or the other. There was a category of respondents who were happy with a welfare benefit and emphasized the independence it gave them. They felt that the alternative, working for a living, meant greater dependence.

To me, being in some kind of organization would be like being in a straightjacket. You work like a horse for maybe 1500 guilders a month and it costs you your freedom. Welfare gives you much more freedom (32-year-old man, single, 6 years unemployed).

Most people who work don't like their jobs. Every day they have to do what their boss tells them. As for me, I like having my freedom and my money. I can do as I please (24-year-old woman, partner, no children, 3 years unemployed).

Diametrically opposed were respondents who stressed the dependence Welfare entailed, which they did not like. They did not view their benefits as a way to avoid dependence. In fact, for some being on welfare made them even more dependent, not only on the Welfare Department, but also on relatives and acquaintances because benefits were not high enough to pay for all of their expenses.

You feel terribly dependent and if you have always been self-reliant, it's a hard situation to get used to. It causes tensions in the family at home, and in every aspect of your life. Your hands are always tied, you always have to do what people tell you (40-year-old man, partner and children, 7 years unemployed).

They give you money, but it isn't enough. After you pay your rent and your gas and electricity bill, you have two hundred guilders left to last you the rest of the month. That's why I sometimes feel so dependent. If I want to buy something, I don't have any money. I have to go to my mother and she lends or gives it to me (25-year-old Surinamese man, single, 3 years unemployed).

The feeling of dependence led to anxiety about the future, about possible political decisions to cut down on welfare benefits, and about arbitrary decisions on the part of the Welfare Department.

You are dependent. If they decide somewhere that I don't get it any more, what then? (48-year-old man, partner and children, 4 years unemployed)

The Welfare State can't survive forever. Soon hardly anyone will have a job and everyone will be on Welfare. Then it will all be much too expensive (32-year-old man, single, 6 years unemployed).

RIGHTS AND OBLIGATIONS

This section deals with three themes related to how the long-term unemployed view their rights and obligations: their perception of welfare as a favor granted to them or as something they are entitled to, the ways they try to justify being on welfare and their awareness of the obligations the benefits entail.

A Favor or a Right?

Some respondents who felt dependent perceived their benefits as a favor granted to them, a kind of charity. They sometimes even felt guilty about it. One respondent went so far as to spend the benefit on people who "deserved it" rather than on herself.

When I first started getting Welfare, I would buy presents for a lot of people because I didn't feel I had a right to that money. I thought: "What in the world am I supposed to do with it? I didn't earn it, did I? I ought to spend it on people who work" (24-year-old woman, lives with parents, 2 years unemployed).

You feel so horribly dependent and if you have always been independent it's a hard thing to accept. Even though you have a right to it, you feel it is a kind of charity (40-year-old man, partner and children, 7 years unemployed).

Most respondents, however, felt the welfare was something they were entitled to, and those who viewed it as a source of independence could certainly be classified in this category. Some of these respondents considered their benefits so much of a right that they found it unfair that any money they earned was deducted. Such a deduction of money earned on the side is based on the assumption of the National Assistance Act that people should in principle earn their own living, and only when their earnings remain under a certain minimum level are they entitled to a supplementary benefit. Various respondents nonetheless viewed their benefits as a kind of "basic income" they should be allowed to supplement by working.

> If you want to work, you are punished for it. I work part-time, but the Welfare Department deducts my whole salary from my benefit. The Welfare Department has me registered in the computer as someone who has been working on the side for three years and you can only keep part of it for two years. So of course I am not going to work to support the State. The mentality they promote is: "Stay lazy, you might as well stay in bed because at the end of the month you'll be getting your check anyway" (36-year-old man, partner and children, 6 years unemployed).

> A while back I earned two hundred guilders with some wallpapering. If I told the Welfare Department they would take 75 percent of it. That is ridiculous. I would be crazy to work a whole week for fifty guilders (31-year-old man, partner and children, 6 years unemployed).

The respondents who felt dependent and viewed Welfare as a favor were often ashamed of it. The following comments illustrate the feelings of this category of 19 percent of the respondents.

> I am a bit ashamed of the position I'm in. Every time I have to go to the Welfare Department to hand in the form, first I make sure no one I know is around (23-year-old man, partner, no children, 3 years unemployed).

> If someone asks me what I do, I say I take care of the kids, I don't say I'm unemployed. I feel embarrassed about it (42-year-old man, partner and children, 4 years unemployed).

Most respondents (81 percent) said they were not ashamed of being unemployed. An important element in this perception was that they were no longer the only one out of a job. Many of them referred to the enormous number of unemployed in the Netherlands.

> You don't have to be ashamed, because nine out of ten of the people you meet are out of work. It didn't used to be that way. You would have a new girlfriend. You went to meet her parents and they would think: "What are you doing with him, he hasn't even got a job. You better break up with him." But nowadays they say: "Your boyfriend has a job! Wow!" (30-year-old man, partner and children, 14 years unemployed).

> There are eight hundred thousand people out of work in the Netherlands. There is a whole army of us (41-year-old man, single, 10 years unemployed).

Justifications

Almost all respondents, whether they viewed their benefit as a favor or as a right, felt obliged to justify it in some way or the other. They used a variety of justifications, from "classical" to "modern" ones. Classical justifications were given mainly by respondents plagued by feelings of dependence; modern ones by respondents who stressed the independence of their position.

Classical Justifications

The most common justification for being on welfare was that one had worked for years and paid the premiums working had entitled one to. The National Assistance Act was not seen as welfare (financed out of tax income), but as a kind of unemployment insurance. (In reality, the National Assistance Act provides a general benefit that is paid out of public funds.) Some respondents even felt that the benefit they received was much too low for the work they had done. This classical justification was most frequently found in the Enschede neighborhood, where a more traditional ethic of work and income was found; modern justifications were found more frequently in the more individualistic culture of the inner-city neighborhoods in Amsterdam and Rotterdam.

I worked for thirty years and I paid the premiums. So I don't have to be ashamed of being on welfare now. It is not that society is paying for me. I did it myself (46-year-old man, single, 6 years unemployed).

They step all over you. I paid unemployment insurance premiums for years and now that I need it I don't get a cent. I'm stuck with a Welfare benefit I can't do a thing with. They trick us old people out of what we deserve (51-year-old man, partner no children, years of unemployment unknown).

These respondents often felt that anyone who had not worked and paid premiums should not be entitled to welfare. They considered themselves to be different from the "undeserving unemployed." They were the "respectable" unemployed who had earned their benefit.

A variation on the "benefits for work" theme was expressed by respondents who had never had a job. They promised to work in the future to "make up for" what society was giving them now. This promise implied that they were doing their best to find a job. Training courses were also viewed as an activity that justified being on welfare. The respondents in question were investing in themselves, hoping that it would later help them get a job.

I know for sure that once I have a good job, I will be more than willing to pay it all back. I don't have the slightest objection to that (26-year-old woman, single, 6 years unemployed).

I am finishing off my secondary school (four-year course) just to show them I am doing my best. Then they can't say I am just a lazy good for nothing. Maybe it will help (43-year-old woman, single, 6 years unemployed).

A second classical justification was that it was not one's own fault to be unemployed. Respondents pointed out that factories had closed or that specific kinds of work were no longer being done. They also drew attention to their poor health or disability.

It isn't my fault Schuttersveld [a textile factory] closed down and that there are no jobs in this region (37-year-old man, single, 6 years unemployed).

Can I help it that I have a bad hip and a bad back? It isn't my fault, it isn't anybody's fault. You can't blame me for being on Welfare (32-year-old man, lives with parents, 10 years unemployed).

Modern Justifications

Modern arguments were presented mainly by respondents who were using welfare to freely choose their own life style. First, there were the respondents who spent their time doing unpaid work. They viewed this work as a justification for being on welfare. They felt they were doing something useful in return for the benefit they received.

You really work unbelievably hard in those bands I am in and at that non-profit video foundation. From early in the morning until early the next morning: loading the equipment into the truck, driving there, unloading everything, setting it up, doing the sound check, hanging up the screens, then the performance itself and then it takes you another two hours to take it all apart and drive back to town. So that benefit is completely justified. A civil servant gets a salary for doing some paper work and we do this. I see my benefit as my salary. I don't feel guilty. I'm not taking advantage of anybody. We work hard and do plenty of good things (34-year-old man, single, 8 years unemployed).

Second, there were respondents who felt entitled to their benefit because they had "the right to live." Some of them referred to the fact that they were raising children.

It is just something you have a right to, that's how I think of it (38-year-old man, single, 1 year unemployed).

You have to live your life. In this country, you can't do that without money. Maybe you could in a warm country, but here you have got the winter (33-year-old Surinamese woman, single with child, 12 years unemployed).

You have a right to welfare, especially if you have children (48-year-old man of foreign descent, partner and children, 4 years unemployed).

Finally, the alternatives public money could be spent on, such as defense, were used to justify being on welfare.

The benefit I get means one less piece of a tank (39-year-old man, single, 3 years unemployed).

Obligations

Rights, such as the right to a welfare benefit, also imply obligations. Benefit receivers are required to look for a job or to provide private information. They have to fill in forms about the jobs they apply for, when they will be out of town, the income earned by their partner, and what they have earned on the side. They have to accept restrictions regarding taking classing in the daytime and doing volunteer work and accept having a close check kept on them. These obligations are manifestations of the dependence of welfare recipients. To what extent did our respondents accept these obligations?

First, there was a category who accepted the obligations and found them to be self-evident. This category included many people who felt dependent on welfare. Some were even of the opinion that there were not enough obligations. In their view, the unemployed—*all* of the unemployed—ought to work for their money and should be given a broom, a rake or a pair of shears in their hands. This was in keeping with their conception of welfare as a right that should be earned. In this conception, vocational training also should be compulsory.

Look, if the national or the city authorities were to say that everyone who is on Welfare gets a broom and has to go out and sweep the streets, then I would think they were absolutely right. You don't have to give people money for doing nothing. I don't feel it is necessary to spend my whole life living in luxury at the expense of the state. Nowadays the city is an impossible place to live. And we are just the ones to remedy the situation. In the Depression, they had the people who were out of a job plant the Amsterdam Woods. That was a good investment (45-year-old man, partner and children, 6 years unemployed).

I think it's a good idea to reduce benefits if people refuse occupational retraining. Let them go ahead and do that (46-year-old man, partner and children, 4 years unemployed).

These respondents also felt an even closer check should be kept to make sure everyone on welfare adhered to all the rules and obligations.

When you are sitting in the waiting room at the Welfare Department, you hear people talking to each other about what they are going to say so they can gyp the Department out of as much money as they can. They say: "Yeah, you ought to say you don't live with me yet." And: "You don't have to tell them about that job" (25-year-old man, single, 3 years unemployed).

A second category, and quite a large one, consisted of respondents who complained about the rules and obligations but still felt they had to be complied with. Like the first category, these respondents felt dependent on welfare, but they had trouble accepting some of the obligations, such as the obligations to provide information about their private lives and to keep applying for jobs.

I don't like the idea that I have to keep the Welfare Department informed about all the details of my life. I want to be independent, I don't want to have other people know about everything I do. You aren't free any more (37-year-old man, single, 6 years unemployed).

The only privacy I have left is in my bedroom and if they had the chance they would also like to know what is going on there. Whenever you go to the Welfare Department, they have you fill in a whole list of questions. "Do you still have any debts, do you still have this, do you still have that?" So what I say is: "What if I did have some debts, would you pay them for me? It's none of your business." (48-year-old man, partner and children, 4 years unemployed).

Being dependent on the Welfare Department is a very disagreeable thing. It puts you under a certain pressure to keep applying for jobs, but if you have tried again and again and all you keep hearing is: sorry, better luck next time, then there is nothing you can do. But that pressure is still there (38-year-old man, single, 1 year unemployed).

A third did not let the obligations bother them in the least. They barely paid any attention to their obligations or had little trouble fulfilling them, since the obligations did not interfere much with their way of life. Many of these respondents were people who viewed their benefit as a source of independence. Finally, there were other "independent" respondents who tried to circumvent one or more of the rules and obligations, such as going to school on welfare, living with someone who was working, or working off the books (see Chapter 4).

EXPERIENCES WITH THE
WELFARE DEPARTMENT

In actual practice, the agency that enforces the obligations of the unemployed is the Welfare Department, the "street level bureaucracy" that represents the welfare state (Lipsky 1980). This is why the perception of obligations and rules is so closely related to how the Welfare Department puts them into effect. Therefore, many people project their feelings of dependence on the Welfare Department.

More than half the respondents had no clear assessment of the Welfare Department. But of those who did, most had a negative one (see Table 7.1). The most negative assessments were expressed by the Amsterdam respondents. Only 5 percent of them had anything positive to say about the Welfare Department. The Enschede respondents were the most satisfied. These figures confirmed the results of other studies, which indicated large differences in the ways various Welfare Departments implemented the social security system (Engbersen 1990, Van der Veen 1990).

Neutral assessments were made mainly by respondents whose relation with the Welfare Department was more or less a formality. This did not mean that they had no contact with the official bureaucracy, but that the contact was of a written nature. In this "anonymous" contact, there was very little personal interaction, if any, between the client and the Welfare Department. Such relations were particularly frequent in Rotterdam. Many of the respondents who felt the Welfare Department "didn't bother them in the least" were in the category who viewed welfare as a source of independence.

I never had any problems. I was there once. Every so often you have to fill in a form for a reexamination of your case, and then there is a card you have to send in every month. For me it is a kind of charade. We are all putting on some kind of act, aren't we? (27-year-old man, single, 5 years unemployed).

TABLE 7.1 Assessments of the Welfare Department (in percentages, N=233)

	Rotterdam	Amsterdam	Enschede	Total
Negative	24	34	25	28
Positive	13	5	25	14
Neutral	57	47	43	49
Fluctuating	6	14	7	9
Total	100	100	100	100

Negative assessments were made by respondents who had feelings of dependence. There was a relation between such feelings and negative assessment. Negative experiences with the Welfare Department served to reinforce dependency feelings. On the other hand, people with such feelings were probably likely to interpret certain experiences in a negative way. They saw the Welfare Department primarily as an opponent, an agency that had power over them, controlled them and did not trust them.

I think it's disgusting. You want to know how they treat you? As if you are the scum of the earth. One of those bums who lives off other people. That's the way it feels to me. They once asked me to come in because I happen to have a car. They wanted to know how I got it. Or sometimes they want to know how much money you have in the bank. Like they are your official guardians or something (42-year-old woman, single with child, 3 years unemployed).

Sometimes I get the idea they are checking up on me. The day after I send in the form, I always get a call with the weirdest questions. And I wonder why in the world they are calling. To see if I'm home? To see if I really live at that number? (25-year-old man, single, 3 years unemployed)

Finally, there were respondents with a positive assessment of the Welfare Department. They were conscious of their dependence on the agency, but it had given them welcome help during hard times. They had been helped by a debt settlement project or a one-time benefit, by a supplementary rent subsidy or an extra amount to pay their moving expenses.

The Welfare Department is fantastic. They helped get an enormous burden off our shoulders. We owed ten thousand guilders and they settled the debt. It was a loan I had taken out when I still had a job. None of those endless questions about why did you do this and why did you do that. I had to come in twice to fill in the forms and that was it (46-year-old man, partner and children, 3 years unemployed).

A negative general assessment of the Welfare Department was often backed by detailed criticism. This criticism is relevant because it indicates the problems clients had with the Welfare Department. Even many of the respondents with a neutral or fluctuating assessment of the Welfare Department expressed criticism on certain points. The reader might get the impression from the following criticisms that all the respondents did was complain. However, it is important to bear in mind that approximately 40 percent had no complaints at all.

Inaccessibility

Most of the complaints pertained to the typical non-responsiveness of a bureaucracy, particularly an overworked and understaffed one. The most frequent complaints were about inaccessibility: it was hard to reach the people who worked there, one had to wait a long time and when one finally did get to talk to someone, they were in a rush, especially in Amsterdam.

I was once there for two days at a stretch. From nine in the morning to five in the afternoon, and it still wasn't my turn. The next day I was there from nine to four. Then it was finally my turn and five minutes later I was out the door again (30-year-old man, partner and children, 14 years unemployed).

It is hard for me to get a baby-sitter for my daughter. If I have to go to the Welfare Department, I sit there with a little kid all day long, from nine to five. That is how crowded it is. You just have to wait your turn. It's a nightmare (26-year-old Surinamese woman, single with child, 5 years unemployed).

There were also complaints about all the paperwork and the red tape, typical for a public bureaucracy that has to account for every action in writing. This makes the whole process quite inaccessible for people who are not accustomed to bureaucratic procedures. The fact that they often fail to see the point of having to write down the same information again and again only makes it worse.

Furthermore, it seems difficult to find the person at the Welfare Department who is responsible for any given matter. The result is that clients often feel they are being sent on a wild goose chase. This perception was also evident from the respondents' experiences with how difficult it was for altered information to "penetrate" the Welfare Department and how long it often took for errors to be corrected.

From 1984 to 1986, I was registered at my mother's address. Despite the fact that I must have told the Welfare Department dozens of times, that address was never changed. That seems to be a very difficult thing to do (28-year-old man, partner no children, years of unemployment unknown).

Last month they deducted 620 guilders from my check because I have a job now, but I only earn 560 guilders so they shouldn't have deducted that much. I did all that work and it just cost me. I have already been there twice to try and correct it (49-year-old woman, single, 15 years unemployed).

Impersonal Approach

The inaccessibility was partly due to the fact that the Welfare Department staff had no time for a more personal approach. Almost all respondents felt they were being treated like a number instead of a person. The Welfare Department keeps its records by number, but the clients couldn't understand that. They found it too impersonal.

Whenever I call, the first thing they ask is: What is your case number? They just see you as a number (25-year-old man, single, 3 years unemployed).

You come in, you sit down, you have to wait, then they put you in a cubicle, they have got ten of them, with a door and a light on top of it. So you sit down at a kind of counter. And all that time you have just been a number. No name, just a number (25-year-old man, single, 5 years unemployed).

The talks between the client and the case worker were perceived as being too short. This was particularly true of the half-yearly checks. These checks were initially carried out once a year in writing, but pressure from the national authorities made the Welfare Departments increase the frequency to twice a year and made personal contact with the client mandatory. The case worker often has no more than ten minutes for each client. The respondents viewed the conversation that took place there as a meaningless ritual. The impersonal aspect was reinforced by the fact that many respondents spoke to a different case worker every time they came in.

They help maybe a hundred people every five minutes there. And every time they ask the same questions. Have you applied for any jobs? They should be familiar with my situation by now, shouldn't they? It's unbelievable the amount of paper work they do there. Why don't they just have a good talk with whoever happens to be interested. The group of people who would rather spend their time fishing, they can just cross them out and deal with them later (37-year-old man, lives with parents, 6 years unemployed).

I have had four different case workers and they each start all over again with exactly the same questions (37-year-old man, lives with parents, 6 years unemployed).

Lack of Understanding

The inaccessibility of the Welfare Department was also due to the lack of mutual understanding between clients and case workers.

I once went there, to the Welfare Department, but I couldn't really follow what they said to me (38-year-old Surinamese man, partner and children, 13 years unemployed).

If you ask them a simple question, it's as if you're talking to a wall or asking something very complicated. But what you are asking isn't hard at all (38-year-old man, single, 1 year unemployed).

They just don't understand you. It is as if you are speaking a different language, as if you are speaking Spanish to a Dutchman (30-year-old woman of foreign descent, partner, no children, 4 years unemployed).

The Welfare Department has to interpret the position of each unemployed client in terms of official concepts stipulated in laws and rules. Case workers consequently answer questions in those terms. However, many respondents were unfamiliar with the terms and had no understanding of the rule context.

Powerlessness and Inequality

Inaccessibility, impersonality and lack of understanding amplify the feeling of powerlessness the welfare recipient already has. The power relation between the client and the Welfare Department is by definition an asymmetrical one. The client wants something the department has, but has little or nothing to give the Welfare Department in return. The department is the party that stipulates the conditions for a welfare benefit and the rules for interpersonal contact and communication. It decides how much time is spent on each client and how long they will have to wait (Lipsky 1980, Hasenfeld et al. 1987). The one-sided dependence and powerlessness is evident in many ways.

> You have the feeling those people have some kind of power over you. Nothing you say counts. You can't do anything, you can't leave, you have to keep applying for jobs, you can't go abroad for a couple of weeks. You have to stay home because someone might call to offer you a job (28-year-old man, single, 5 years unemployed).

> If there is something they want to ask you about and you don't react when they tell you to come to the office, you can be sure something will happen to your income. You have to be at their beck and call (30-year-old man, lives with parents, 3 years unemployed).

The power position of the Welfare Department was also evident from the fact that in case of a difference of opinion—for example, about whether a client met with the requirements, whether a form was filled out right, or whether a card was sent in on time—the matter was decided by the Welfare Department. The long waiting periods about which so many complained were also seen as a symbol of inequality between a Welfare Department and its clients (Schwartz 1975). From a position they perceived as subservient, clients were hesitant to question any decisions made by the Welfare Department. In the Netherlands, very few people ever appeal Welfare Department decisions. Of the approximately 100,000 decisions made by the Rotterdam Welfare Department in 1987, only 1,900 cases were appealed (Engbersen 1990).

> Once the Welfare Department has made a decision about something, it is very hard to change it (25-year-old man, single, 3 years unemployed).

> If there is something you don't agree with and you try to do something about it via the normal legal way, then the simple fact that you are on Welfare makes you feel you are the weaker party. You are sure people think: "He is on Welfare, he couldn't be right" (40-year-old man, partner and children, 7 years unemployed).

The power inequality was also reflected in the personal relations between clients and case workers. Many respondents were aware of a status difference as soon as they entered the Welfare Department building.

> As soon as you go in the door, you are the person who is on Welfare. The person at the desk has a job. That is one difference you notice immediately (25-year-old man, single, 5 years unemployed).

> The people at the windows there think they are so smart. They think: "She could get a job, she just doesn't want to." They treat you like you are inferior (26-year-old Surinamese woman, single with child, 5 years unemployed).

Legal Equality, Legal Security and Arbitrary Treatment

The purpose of a public bureaucracy is not only to be efficient and effective, but also to guarantee equality before the law and legal security. However, the subjective perception of many respondents was one of arbitrary treatment. This was due in part to the discretionary authority case workers had, which could give clients a feeling of being treated unfairly.

My mother was sick for three years before she died. My sister and I took turns taking care of her and going to see her in the hospital. My sister, who is also out of a job, had her travel expenses paid without any problems. Within a month, she had 1200 guilders transferred to her account. With me they were much stricter—I am in the same city but a different district. I had to show them my train tickets, which I didn't have any more. I went to the railway company to see if they would write me a receipt. I had to show them my mother's death certificate. That really made me mad. Even with all those papers, all I got was 450 guilders (27-year-old woman, single, 6 years unemployed).

Overload, inaccessibility, lack of understanding and inequality produced, notwithstanding the ideal of legal equality and security, a subjectively experienced reality of arbitrary treatment. For reasons unclear or incomprehensible to the client, benefits would be reduced or stopped altogether and promises made by case workers would not be realized. Such experiences made the respondents afraid of new forms of arbitrary treatment.

You look forward to the day you get your money. I think everybody does that, whether you get a salary or Welfare. We get our money every month on the twentieth. We eat every last bit of food on the nineteenth. The kids can finish off whatever is left, because you know there will be money coming in the next day. But the fear is always there. If it hasn't been transferred to your account, then you're stuck, because you don't even have bus fare to get to the Welfare Department. There is good reason to be afraid, because sometimes for some incomprehensible reason, they don't give it to you (38-year-old Surinamese man, partner and children, 13 years unemployed).

Survival of the Fittest

In such an organization one had to defend one's own interests. And, as in society as a whole, those respondents who were most enterprising, resourceful, smart, well informed and assertive were best able to promote their own interests. In an effort to adjust, respondents lacking in these traits sometimes managed to develop them.

It's a full-time job just to watch your own money (30-year-old woman of foreign descent, partner no children, 4 years unemployed).

It gives you a kind of training, it makes you smarter, shrewder, tougher, you don't care about anyone else. That didn't happen to me, but it did to other people. They get divorced just to get more money, and if they get caught and they are broke, they start doing other things, much more extreme things. Things they never thought they would ever do (38-year-old Surinamese man, partner and children, 13 years unemployed).

Respondents who viewed welfare as a source of independence were most likely to have these skills or to acquire them. In their dealings with the Welfare Department, this category actually needed these traits the least, since they had relatively few problems with it.

A Vicious Circle of Dependence

Some unemployed individuals were of the opinion that the way the Welfare Department dealt with its rules and clients unwittingly led to a continuation of their dependence. Since clients had to ask permission for everything they wanted to do, they stopped taking any initiative at all. In particular, the restrictions pertaining to volunteer work or odd jobs were viewed as an obstacle to self-fulfillment.

The Welfare Department says I can't do anything. No gardening, no nothing. So what am I supposed to do all day? Sit around the house with my hands in my lap, that's what (31-year-old man, partner and children, 7 years unemployed).

I once happened to mention I worked for a hospital radio program, it just slipped out. It isn't volunteer work in the sense that you do it during the hours you are supposed to be available for work. You do it in the evenings and in the weekends. But the Welfare Department case worker still said, "I'll jot that down, you never know." I thought it was ridiculous. Not only don't I get paid for it, it even costs me something (29-year-old man, single, 6 years unemployed).

Not only the rules but also the bureaucratic procedures and the red tape kept clients from taking any initiative. If they told the Welfare Department they had a temporary job for a couple of weeks, it could lead to serious problems. It seemed very easy to be taken out of the system, but very difficult to be put back in and receive one's benefit on time after having worked for a while.

My boyfriend works for an employment agency, but every time they don't have any more work for him there, it takes six weeks before he gets his benefit. That's why I'm not so anxious to work for one of those agencies (27-year-old woman, single, 4 years unemployed).

This summer I don't want a vacation job. It would just mean problems again with the Welfare Department. Last year I worked for the Post Office for about 250 guilders a week. After that I didn't get any money from the Welfare Department for a good six months. They said I had earned too much and there was all that paper work that had to be done. That's how long it takes (23-year-old Turkish man, partner and children, 3 years unemployed).

Part-time work could also lead to problems. This was one of the reasons enterprising respondents felt they had little choice but to ignore the rules and work off the books. Less enterprising respondents were discouraged from accepting temporary work, which could be a stepping stone to a permanent job. Certain rules and bureaucratic bottlenecks were contributory factors in the perpetuation of the dependence of the long-term unemployed on the Welfare Department (Engbersen 1990).

CONFIDENCE IN POLITICIANS AND THEIR LEGITIMACY

No matter how much of a difference of opinion there might have been among our respondents on many topics, there was a total consensus on one point: they had little or no confidence in politicians. This is why many of them were so uninterested in politics in general, though they were aware that the conditions of their own lives were shaped by political decisions.

Respondents already felt they had little influence on the policy implementing agency, and they felt even less influential in the political decision-making process. The political power center was much farther away from them. Politicians served the function of identifiable parties who could be held responsible for the respondents' situation. Politicians also played a role in how the respondents defined their own low position in society. These self-definitions were discernible in several recurrent comments.

You can grumble all you want about those big shots at the Ministry of Social Affairs, where they keep so much money for themselves. But when push comes to shove, there is nothing you can do about it (25-year-old man, lives with parents, 2 years unemployed).

We are the simple people and whatever they decide, we have to like it (45-year-old woman, single, 4 years unemployed).

Like always, it's the big guys deciding what happens to the little guys (24-year-old woman, lives with parents, 2 years unemployed).

These self-images illustrate the marginal social position of the long-term unemployed. The undertone was that they did not count. Table 7.2 shows how little faith they had in politics in general. Only 6 percent of the respondents had a positive attitude toward national politics. Fewer respondents had a negative attitude to municipal politics, but they were less interested and less involved in politics at that level. National politics do in fact play a more important role in the lives of people on welfare. It is in Parliament that the legal measures are taken that they are dependent on.

TABLE 7.2 Attitudes to Politics (in percentages, N=253)

	National Politics	Municipal Politics
Negative	59	23
Positive	6	7
Fluctuating	8	5
Neutral	5	9
No Opinion	22	55
Total	100	100

Although the social distance between the world of politics and the world of the long-term unemployed is enormous, the individual politicians were well known to our respondents. In a certain sense, they were even "members of the family." Day in and day out, they were right there in the living room on television, and no one watches more television than the unemployed. Most respondents thus had clear opinions about individual politicians. The heated criticism concerned the "heartlessness" of politicians, but more often it was the alleged corruption, extravagant salaries, padded expense accounts and expensive limousines that the respondents resented most. Recent political scandals were referred to again and again, and 14 percent of the respondents spontaneously mentioned real or alleged subsidy swindles.

They are a bunch of scoundrels. Take Van Aardenne for example [former Dutch Minister of Economic Affairs], who took off with all those millions. And the other Ministers were in on it. They divided it up among themselves. Those guys know where the real money is. Afterwards they threw a big party. In a hotel with fancy call girls and one bottle of champagne after the other (44-year-old man, partner and children, 8 years unemployed).

Ruding [former Dutch Minister of Finance] makes barroom jokes about people who are out of work, only he makes them in the Cabinet and they call it policy (29-year-old man, partner, no children, 5 years unemployed).

Lubbers [Dutch Prime Minister] is a racketeer. He went to Kuwait and came back with a nice fat contract for his brother [who runs an international construction company]. They're hypocrites (48-year-old man, single, 2 years unemployed).

Scandals like these served to confirm what everybody already thought: the members of the elite, the people with power in society and in politics, take advantage of their position to promote their own private interests. Prominent politicians were the personification of this distrusted elite. Alleged corruption and stereotyping reinforced "us-them" thinking, emphasizing the distinction between "ordinary people" and the political elite.

You never hear them say: "Now it's time to cut down on our own expenses." No, it's always the poor slobs they want to save some money on (30-year-old man, partner and children, 14 years unemployed).

There is no justice. Did you ever see a Cabinet Minister out of a job? Yeah, but his salary keeps coming in! (27-year-old man, lives with parents, 2 years unemployed).

The predominantly negative judgement about politicians was not solely related to the fact that they were viewed as representatives of the elite. Simply by being politicians they were no good. They lied, fooled and manipulated ordinary people. Some respondents were certain that politicians did not understand the unemployed and consequently were not qualified to serve as representatives of the people; politicians did not know anything about what it was like to be out of work and could not understand their problems. It was one-way traffic: the unemployed knew the politicians and their ideas, but the politicians did not know anything about the unemployed.

They ought to put all those political people and their whole families on Welfare for a few months. Then they'd see whether it was enough or not. They'd be in sad shape. They'd have to give up so many things they think are normal, like going on vacation twice a year (42-year-old Mediterranean man, partner and children, 6 years unemployed).

They ought to listen more to what people say. They have no idea what kind of problems there are in a neighborhood like this. They don't know what a quart of milk costs or how much it costs to bring up a child (27-year-old man, single, 5 years unemployed).

CONCLUSIONS

The dependence on the state that long-term unemployment entails is perceived in a wide range of ways. In this chapter, we have described how our respondents viewed their rights and obligations, their feelings of shame, their experiences with the Welfare Department and their views on politicians. We can distinguish two ideal-types of long-term unemployed people. In the next chapter, we shall give more detailed descriptions of these two categories.

First, there was a category who felt very dependent on the benefit they received and were bothered by this feeling. They tended to view the benefit as something they should be grateful for and not as something they had a right to. They were ashamed of being dependent on welfare. They justified their often lengthy dependence on the state by a number of classical arguments, such as "I worked for it for years" and "I do my best to find a job." These respondents took their obligations as a Welfare Department client seriously. Some of them even felt there were too few obligations. According to them, the unemployed ought to be put to work on projects that serve a useful purpose. Others complained about the enormous number of rules and regulations and about how unreasonable some of them were, such as the rule that they had to keep the Welfare Department informed about the details of their life and the regulations regarding odd jobs and volunteer work. Many of them perceived a great discrepancy between their own obligations and the efforts made by politicians to alleviate unemployment and welfare problems. However, much as the obligations bothered them, they did not ignore them.

The second category of respondents were not bothered in the least by feelings of dependence. Instead, they viewed welfare as a source of independence. They perceived their benefit as something they had a right to and were not ashamed of it, even though they too had their ways of justifying their situation. They met with their obligations as long as these did not interfere with their lives or did not "cramp their style." It was in this category that we found respondents who had managed to manipulate the welfare system or who worked off the books. These respondents knew how to avoid having too much contact with the Welfare

Department. With no feelings of guilt or dependence to disturb them, they easily went on living as they liked, making every effort to keep their relation with the Welfare Department down to a mere formality.

Very little has been written about this second category in the American and international literature on the social and psychological consequences of unemployment and welfare dependence. It is a category of people who have redefined the rights and obligations linked to Welfare in such a way that they can function in a relatively independent manner. For a number of reasons, this category is interesting. First, it does not fit the notion that welfare dependence always entails feelings of shame and failure. Second, some people in this category view and use welfare as a basic income that enables them to do as they please with their lives. It is no coincidence that this category has hardly, if ever, been described in the literature. It is the product of a welfare state where the level of benefits is relatively high and where there is no active and activating labor market policy, so that people can remain dependent on welfare benefits for lengthy periods of time. Only a limited number of European welfare states meet both conditions; for example Belgium, Germany and France (see Therborn 1986 and Pierson 1991). In the Netherlands, the proponents of a basic income scheme have used our findings to demonstrate the necessity of such a scheme. They view some types of unemployed people—in particular the autonomous type described in Chapter 8—as members of a vanguard paving the way to a post-industrial society where jobless citizens engage in meaningful activities without any loss of identity. In view of the recent intensification of work and schooling obligations, this vanguard will not have many followers in the near future.

PART THREE

ANALYSIS AND COMPARISONS

Cultures of Unemployment

In the Netherlands, the patterns and configurations of long-term unemployment have been multifarious. A far less homogeneous description could be written of the long-term unemployed in Rotterdam, Amsterdam and Enschede than of the unemployed residents of the Austrian town of Marienthal at the start of the 1930s (Lazarsfeld-Jahoda and Zeisel 1933). Differences have been noted earlier in the ways unemployed individuals cope with work, time, money and welfare dependency. Generally speaking, the main difference is between the "traditional" unemployed, who have a hard time accepting a life without work and maintain a rather passive attitude toward their unemployed condition, and the "modern" unemployed, who become masters of their own fate in a far more active fashion. But this division is too simplistic and overlooks the subtleties and sub-categories that have been distinguished as well.

In this chapter, we coordinate the various findings using a formalized sociological typology of various groups within the long-term unemployed population. This typology does justice to the wide range of ways the unemployed cope with the triad of unemployment problems (work, time and money) described in the previous chapters.[1] An effort is then made to explain the behavioral reactions and strategies of the various unemployed types on the basis of the culture they are part of. The group/grid model described by the anthropologist Mary Douglas (1970, 1978) and its supplementation and application by Wildavsky (1987) and Thompson et al. (1990) served as our source of inspiration and guide. This model enabled us to draw links between the social environment of various types of long-term unemployed people, their strategies and their justifications for them.

Based on the research findings, in the closing section we draw some policy conclusions and address the theme of a recently emerging underclass in the Dutch welfare state.

SIX TYPES OF LONG-TERM UNEMPLOYED PEOPLE

In his classic essay *Social Structure and Anomie*, Merton distinguished five types of individual adaptation to anomic situations: conformism, innovation, ritualism, retreatism and rebellion (1957). These behavioral reactions were structured around the distinction between the cultural goals embedded in a society and the institutionalized means to attain these goals. In his essays on anomie, Merton approached success as a cultural goal worth striving for, a goal pervading every aspect of American culture, but one that was not within everyone's reach. The behavioral reactions Merton distinguished were individual adaptations to the field of tension between the cultural goals that existed in a society and the chances specific groups had—or did not have—to attain them.

In Western societies, work and consumption can be viewed as central cultural goals. Receiving training and looking for a job are the institutionalized means to attain these goals. The long-term unemployed are faced with the problem of having to formulate alternatives for work and consumption. Merton's conceptual apparatus can be used to classify the various adaptations and alternatives formulated by the long-term unemployed. With the help of Merton's types of individual adaptation, six types of long-term unemployed people can be specified. In three cases, the names correspond with the behavior reactions Merton described (conformism, ritualism and retreatism). The enterprising and the calculating types exhibit the behavioral reaction referred to by Merton as innovation. The behavioral reactions of the autonomous, however, have very little to do with rebellion. This category was somewhat expanded to include unemployed groups who attached less importance to the goals of work or consumption and were not unhappy living on the benefits they received.

Before we sketch the various types, there are several points that should be clarified. First, in categorizing our unemployed respondents, the only aspects taken into consideration were their behavior on the labor market, their expectations of the labor market and their informal work-related and income-related strategies. Second, each respondent was categorized as the type he or she bore the greatest similarity to. In social reality, however, intermediary types can also be observed. Third, the types of unemployed individuals that were distinguished are not personality types. The six types are based on the behavioral reactions the long-term unemployed develop. These behavioral reactions are closely related to personal qualities and skills and to the culture the long-term unemployed are part of. However, changes can take place over time because the circumstances of their personal lives and the social opportunities they are presented with are subject to change. During the analysis of the research material, Merton's classification based on the goals/means model seemed to be the best way to classify the different ways people coped with unemployment. The typology was not formulated beforehand; it was developed, established and confirmed in the course of the research. The personal features of the six types of unemployed people are shown in Table VI. (All tables to this chapter—except Table 8.1—are in Appendix V).

The *conformists* continued to strive for the goals of paid employment and a higher consumption level in the generally accepted ways. They applied for jobs, went to the Employment Office and sometimes attended courses to acquire additional skills. The conformists were only occasionally or not at all active in the informal economy and did not make improper use of the social security system.

The conformists were mainly male respondents who were not above the age of 40 and whose educational level was low to average. Some of them had part-time jobs and almost all of them had had some working experience. The conformists were over-represented among the long-term unemployed who had been out of work for relatively short periods of time. Half the conformists lived in a family situation. More than a third (36 percent) of the respondents belonged to this category.

The *ritualists* had given up any hope of a job and a higher consumption level, but they still adhered to society's generally institutionalized customs and pre-scribed rules. This was most clearly illustrated by the fact that they regularly went to the Employment Office and continued to apply for jobs, though they had little hope of ever getting one. The ritualists barely participated in the in-formal economy and did not make improper use of the social security system.

The ritualists were mainly older male respondents who had been out of work for long periods of time. Their educational level was low and they had had working experience. A number of them received partial disability benefits. Half the ritualists lived in a family situation. The ritualists included relatively large numbers of people of foreign descent. Less than a tenth (9 percent) of the re-spondents belonged to this category.

The *retreatists* no longer aspired to a job and a higher consumption level. They no longer made use of the appropriate means and channels for attaining these goals (Employment Office, job applications, training courses, work projects). The retreatists no longer saw any prospects for themselves in the labor market and were resigned to their situation. Like the conformists and the ritualists, the retreatists made little or no use of illegal or informal strategies to acquire extra income.

This category also were mainly older male respondents who had been out of work for long periods of time. Their educational level was low and they had had working experience. Some of them received partial disability benefits. Half the retreatists lived in a family situation. The retreatists included large numbers of people of foreign descent, particularly of Turkish or Moroccan descent. A quarter (25 percent) of the respondents were retreatists.

The goals of the *enterprising* were still a job and a higher consumption level, but unlike the conformists they tried to attain these goals by informal methods, working in the informal economy. Some of them also continued to strive for regular employment. The enterprising had a more instrumental view of work than conformists or ritualists. In their opinion, the main purpose of work, whether formal or informal was to attain a higher income level.

The enterprising category consisted mainly of relatively young male respon-dents who had been out of work for lengthy periods of time. Their educational level was generally average to high and they had had working experience. A large portion of the enterprising category consisted of single people, and there were very few people of foreign descent. A tenth (10 percent) of the respondents belonged to this category.

The *calculating* made very little use of the formal channels and methods for getting a job and attaining a higher consumption level. It was not their aim to find a job soon. They had no compunctions about making improper use of the social security system. The students in this category continued to view working as their goal for the future. Welfare simply provided them with a higher monthly income than students had to live on.[2] For the others, the goal of attaining a certain consumption level was more important than getting a job. Unlike the enterprising, the calculating were barely active in the informal economy.

The calculating respondents were mainly young, well-educated people who had been out of work for less than six years. The group included relatively large numbers of women. Some of them had not had any working experience. Most of them lived alone. The calculating category included very few people of foreign descent. Less than a tenth (9 percent) of the respondents belonged to this category.

The *autonomous* attached far less importance to the goals of work and consumption than other categories. Some of them went so far as to reject these goals. They were the cultural rebels who did not even want to consider a formal job or make use in any way of the formal channels for finding work. They barely made any effort to seek employment and felt little need to do so. They wanted to do their own thing (volunteer work, study, a hobby). The autonomous managed to adjust their needs to their limited financial means. They were not active in the informal economy and did not make improper use of the social security system. Many of them felt welfare was enough to live on.

Older respondents comprised half the autonomous category, which included relatively large numbers of women. The autonomous had a low to average educational, level and, with the exception of a number of the younger respondents in this category, they had had working experience. Many of the autonomous lived alone, and very few of them were of foreign descent. A tenth (10 percent) of the respondents belonged to this category.

The conformists and the retreatists were the largest categories. Together with the ritualists and the enterprising, they constituted the four classic groups that recur so often in the literature on long-term unemployment. In part they coincided with the groups described by Lazarsfeld-Jahoda and Zeisel in their Marienthal study (1933). There were similarities between the "unbroken" group in Marienthal and the conformists and enterprising at our locations (Jahoda 1972). There were also similarities between the "resigned" group in Marienthal and the ritualists and retreatists among our respondents. The two other types were the "modern" unemployed, who either viewed welfare as sufficient income (the autonomous) or managed to get an extra income by taking undue advantage of the social security system (the calculating). Both of these types, which can exist only within the contemporary social security system, were thus non-existent in Marienthal.

TABLE 8.1 Distribution of the Types of Long-Term Unemployed Respondents over the Various Locations (in percentages, N=221)

	Conform- ists	Ritual- ists	Retreat- ists	Enter- prising	Calcu- lating	Auto- nomous	Total %	N
Rotterdam	21	13	22	17	17	11	100	72
Amsterdam	38	5	28	9	8	13	100	79
Enschede	50	10	26	6	3	6	100	70
Total	36	9	25	10	9	10	100	221

The distribution of the various types of unemployed people over the locations exhibited striking differences (Table 8.1). In Enschede, the conformists, the ritualists and the retreatists accounted for 86 percent, in Amsterdam 71 percent and in Rotterdam only 56 percent of the respondents. The relatively large numbers of calculating and enterprising respondents in Rotterdam were also striking.

The differences between the locations could be explained partly the features of the various populations (Appendix III). The Enschede respondents were largely poorly educated, on the average they had been out of work for the shortest period of time, and most of them lived in a family situation. Respondents with these features tended to exhibit conformist and retreatist behavior.

In Rotterdam, half the respondents were of foreign descent, and on the average the Rotterdam respondents had been out of work the longest. Almost half of these respondents were single, and relatively large numbers of them were reasonably educated. Respondents with these features exhibited mainly enterprising and calculating behavior.

Amsterdam occupied an intermediate position regarding the respondents' ethnic background, household situation and duration of unemployment, though the average educational level was high. Relatively large numbers of women were interviewed in Amsterdam. The intermediate position of Amsterdam was also evident in the behavioral reactions: the conformist, enterprising and calculating reactions were between the Enschede and the Rotterdam levels. Autonomous behavioral reactions, particularly on the part of women, were relatively common in Amsterdam.

The specific features of the respondents provided an initial explanation for the prevalence of certain types at the three locations. Well-educated single people had specific social skills that gave them more of an opportunity to participate in the informal economy and better enabled them to approach the social security system in a calculating way. Enterprising and calculating behavior thus was more common among respondents with these features. Older, poorly educated respondents of foreign descent had much less of an opportunity to participate in either the official or the informal labor market. Thus retreatism was quite an understandable reaction on their part.

Greater insight into other behavioral reactions can be gained by examining specific features of the long-term unemployed. Yet these features do not sufficiently explain why the situation of long-term unemployment led certain groups to adopt a specific behavioral reaction and why there were such great differences between the three locations. The various behavioral reactions cannot be understood without addressing another question: Which social environments stimulated the development of the various behavioral reactions? Mary Douglas' theory enables us to explain Merton's typology. Merton designed a classification model for the various behavioral reactions, but failed to adequately account for why certain individuals reacted in an innovative manner and others in a ritualist or conformist way. By analyzing the cultures the long-term unemployed were part of, the differing strategies can be explained.

We use the concept of culture in much the same way as Douglas (1978), Wildavsky (1987) and Thompson et al. (1990). Culture pertains to the social environment in which people function, but it also pertains to the symbols, ideas and convictions that regulate and justify their actions and serve as a basis and justification for their social relations. Drawing Douglas' grid/group model, we shall try to draw a link between the social environment of the types of long-term unemployed people, the strategies they develop and their justifications and motivations for these strategies.[3]

CULTURAL THEORY

In his presidential address to the American Political Science Association, Wildavsky (1987) transformed Douglas' group/grid model into four models of culture: egalitarian, hierarchical, individualistic and fatalistic culture (Wildavsky 1987:6). A fifth model could be added as well; the model of an autonomous culture. There are individuals who can live their lives relatively autonomously. They are only slightly subject to group coercion and to the norms and rules imposed by other individuals or institutions. In the social environment of the autonomous individual, there is a withdrawal cosmology, a culture characterized by withdrawal from the mainstream of society. This autonomous culture can be situated at the point where group and grid intersect.[4]

In *Cultural Theory* (1990), Thompson, Ellis and Wildavsky present a more detailed theory based on Douglas' group/grid model.[5] The terminology has been adapted somewhat. They distinguished three interrelated concepts, cultural biases, social relations and ways of life: "Cultural biases refer to shared values and beliefs. Social relations are defined as patterns of interpersonal relations. When we wish to speak of a viable combination of social relations and cultural bias we speak of a way of life" (Thompson et al. 1990:1). Thompson et al. emphasize that there are only five viable ways of life: hierarchy, egalitarianism, fatalism, individualism and autonomy. They illustrate these five ways of life with five archetypical social beings (see Figure 8.1): a high-caste Hindu villager, a member of a self-sufficient Western commune, a self-made Victorian manufacturer, a nonunionized weaver and a hermit (for example a marginal farmer). The high-caste Hindu is a member of a confined group and acts on the basis of a hierarchic

FIGURE 8.1 Five Ways of Life

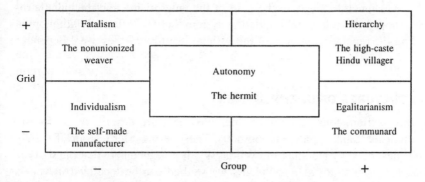

Source: Thompson et al. 1990:8.

system of rules (strong group, strong grid). The commune member functions within a close-knit group where egalitarian rules are dominant (strong group, weak grid). The Victorian manufacturer is a self-made man, an individualist who creates his own networks and follows his own rules side by side with the rules of the free market (weak group, weak grid). The nonunionized weaver has an isolated position in society and has to follow the rules set down by his employer (weak group, strong grid). The hermit is in a position to retreat from the coercive social environment other social beings are caught up in (Thompson 1982).

These five archetypes are, of course, atypical for a mainstream member of modern society. Besides, it is questionable if hermits exist in societies like the Netherlands, with an obvious scarcity of land. However, we will try to show that there is also a place for "ordinary people" in the group/grid diagram.

Cultural theory is used in the following section to interpret and explain the behavioral reactions of the various types of unemployed individuals. There are reciprocal relations between social organization forms, cultural biases and the social practices of the unemployed. The various types of unemployed individuals can be viewed as the bearers of the different cultures described by Douglas and Thompson et al. (We have opted for the more commonly used term "culture" rather than "ways of life.")

We have divided the grid dimension into external rules or regulations, especially the formal rules dictated by official institutions, and the informal or self-made rules that evolved spontaneously in everyday life. Analogous to the work of Moore, who specializes in the anthropology of law, we drew a distinction between *external rules* and *internal rules* (Moore 1983). This distinction enabled us to approach the grid with more precision. We observed that on the whole, all of the long-term unemployed were equally subject to the external rules of official institutions, particularly the Welfare Department, but there were differences in the extent to which these rules affected their social life. In the case of the retreatists, considerable pressure was exerted by external official rules, but this was much less true in the case of the enterprising and the calculating. These groups had an internal regulation system that was relatively autonomous regarding the regulation system of the official institutions they were dependent on.

FOUR CULTURES OF UNEMPLOYMENT

In this section, four cultures of unemployment are described: conformist, individualistic, fatalistic and autonomous. These terms refer to four of the five cultures described by Douglas and Wildavsky. It is argued here that the six types of long-term unemployed respondents we studied can be localized in various squares of the group/grid model.[6]

The conformists and the ritualists lived in a social environment with a strong group and a weak grid (see Figure 8.2). We refer here to a conformist rather than an egalitarian culture of unemployment in order to stress the dominance of the traditional work ethic. The enterprising and the calculating operated in an individualistic culture of unemployment and the retreatists in a fatalistic culture of unemployment. The social environment of the autonomous exhibited similarities with the environment of the hermit described by Douglas and Thompson et al. They managed to lead relatively autonomous lives centered around what Douglas called a withdrawal cosmology. However, they cannot be viewed as typical hermits because in order to put their autonomous way of life into effect, they were dependent on the social security system. The autonomous did nonetheless withdraw as much as possible from the demands of a labor-oriented society and managed to live in a relatively autonomous fashion. Since their way of life and social environment differ on essential points from those of the other types of unemployed individuals, we devote special attention here to this relatively autonomous culture of unemployment. It is erroneous to view the autonomous culture as a specific sub-variety of the individualistic culture.

FIGURE 8.2 Cultures of Unemployment and the Six Types of Unemployed

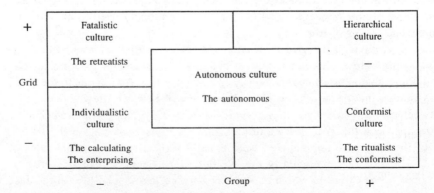

A hierarchical culture was not observed in the course of our study. In view of their name, the ritualists would seem to be best suited for this square, but they were not localized in it because they were not part of a social environment with a hierarchical structure. They were strongly influenced by the imperatives of the bureaucratic welfare system, but they themselves were part of an egalitarian workers' culture. It is not easy to find a hierarchic culture of any kind among the unemployed or the poor. In our Western world, hierarchic cultures are mainly reserved for specific working organizations. This is why it is no coincidence that in their study on strategy behavior on the part of the poor, Thompson and Wildavsky described only one very specific example of a hierarchic culture, a religious community (1986).

To what extent, one might wonder, are the various types and cultures solely linked to unemployment? Is it possible to describe "types of employed people" and "cultures of employment"? The classification models applied here can also be used to interpret and explain the behavior of people employed in working organizations. The behavior of employees in working organizations can also be classified as conformist, retreatist, enterprising, calculating or autonomous. And these behavioral reactions can be more easily comprehended if they are linked to the organizational structure and culture of the work site. The group/grid model already has a number of applications in this connection.[7] In this study, however, we confine ourselves to the world of the unemployed.

The long-term unemployed respondents were localized in the various squares of the group/grid model on the basis of ideal types. As the results showed, not all of the retreatists lived in an isolated way and not all of the conformists were integrated into a close-knit group. In deciding which type a respondent was, we focused on his or her labor market behavior, labor market expectations and informal work and income strategies. In the further examination of the various types and of the environment they lived in, attention was devoted to other aspects as well. The strategies discussed here not only pertain to work and money, but to time as well. In order to gain more insight into their justifications for their behavior, we focussed on five elements that largely shaped the cultural bias of the long-term unemployed: work ethic, time perception, risk perception, dependence and responsibility. Risk perception involved the extent to which the unemployed took into account the risk that participation in the informal economy entailed. Responsibility referred to the persons or agencies the unemployed held responsible for the situation they were in. In the discussion of the four cultures of unemployment, we refer to Tables VII, VIII and IX (Appendix V) and to the research results in Chapters 4, 5, 6, and 7.

A Conformist Culture of Unemployment

The conformists and ritualists were part of a social environment with a relatively strong group and a weak grid dimension. Enschede had the most close-knit social networks, this was particularly true for the Pathmos neighborhood. The following statement was made by one of the respondents there.

It is a communicative neighborhood, yes people like to talk to each other. We spend a lot of time sitting outside, when the weather is warm. Then we open the doors, open the windows, we play cards on the street and someone collects some money and they go get some beer. And then we just sit around talking until one or two o'clock at night, at least if it is warm enough. That is something we all really enjoy, yes. But it is not as nice now as it used to be. Now that the neighborhood had been renovated, there is much less of all this (31-year-old man, partner and children, 7 years unemployed).

More than the other locations, Pathmos was a traditional working-class neighborhood with very little cultural stratification, egalitarian social interaction and a large extent of social control. Communities of this kind have been described in Dutch literature by Haveman (1952) and Simonse (1971). A higher standard of living, growing geographic mobility, the altered labor market and the influx of people of foreign descent have combined to change the nature of the homogeneous working-class community. Nonetheless, there are still neighborhoods and streets where the social structure is homogeneous, where social commitment is still relatively strong and where family ties still play an important role. Pathmos is an example of this kind of neighborhood. The conformists and ritualists, who constituted 60 percent of the research group in Enschede, exhibited the greatest extent of neighborhood bonding.

The grid dimension of the social environment of the conformists and ritualists was relatively weak. There were no great status differences. Within the group they were part of, the principle of reciprocity played an important role. People helped each other and received help in return. An internal regulation system could be observed that served to inhibit excessive independence. As members of a relatively strong group, the conformists and ritualists had been able to attain a certain extent of autonomy in regard to the official institutions.

In the Amsterdam and Rotterdam locations, there were also remnants of former working-class communities, pockets similar to those observed in Enschede. In Rotterdam, we noted that people of foreign descent had developed close-knit social networks in which relatives and neighbors played an important role.

Job-Seeking Behavior and Work Ethic

The conformists and ritualists held a rather traditional view of work. They felt it was their duty to work. Thus a jobless life presented certain problems. They had strong feelings of aimlessness and of being left out. Their traditional work ethic made the conformists and ritualists willing to make greater efforts to find another job. In comparison with the other types, they were also more willing to go out and actively look for a job, to accept heavy labor and or to commute long distances. They were also willing to accept lower wages than the other types, with the exception of the autonomous (Table VII).

In Chapter 6, we described the efforts that unemployed people made to find a job. The conformists and ritualists were among the respondents who frequently tried to find a job and whose demands regarding a new job were modest (Tables 6.1 and 6.4). The job-seeking behavior of the conformists and ritualists was influenced by the specific social relations they were involved in. First, there was a certain amount of pressure from their families to continue looking for a job. Having a job was part of the role of the male breadwinner.

> It was frustrating for me, that all my relatives kept saying: "That's a nice job, why don't you try and get it." And they wouldn't let up. Sometimes I think it was more important to them that I found a job than it was to me. They used to keep calling me every day when there was some kind of job I had applied for, and they would ask: "Did you hear anything yet?" If it was up to them, not a day would go by without me applying for a job, and what they really wanted was for me to do it three, four, five, six, seven times a day. Then at least they would have the idea I was doing something with my life (25-year old man, partner, no children, 3 years unemployed).

The neighborhood also exerted a certain amount of social pressure to look for a job.

> In the beginning, they had a lot of trouble getting used to the idea. They thought I was some kind of parasite, taking advantage of the system. Just out of curiosity, they would sometimes say: "Don't you work any more?" And you get tired of saying "There aren't any jobs and there is no way I can find a job." For a long time, I didn't tell anyone, I gave everyone the impression I had a job. Yes, it is one of those really old-fashioned neighborhoods. Everybody looks down on you if you are out of work, but now they know that I have had an operation and that there isn't anything I can do about it (41-year-old man, partner and children, 6 years unemployed).

The social pressure exerted by relatives and neighbors makes it understandable that the conformists and ritualists were more likely to be ashamed of the fact that they were out of work than the enterprising, the calculating and the autonomous. The ritualists were particularly prone to feelings of embarrassment. In part, this is what accounted for their ritualist behavior. For the benefit of their friends and relatives, they would continue to carry out the application rites of the labor market without really believing in them any more.

Making Ends Meet and Risk Perception

The conformists and ritualists applied the egalitarian strategy described in Chapter 4 (Thompson et al. 1990). They made every effort to adapt their needs to their limited resources. Some of the strategies the conformists used to make ends meet were individual ones. However, there was also the extra support or financial assistance they received from their family or, to a lesser extent, from the neighborhood. In most cases, family and neighborhood help was given on a reciprocal basis. The assistance relations of the conformists and ritualists made it clear that the more homogeneous and closely knit the social networks were, the greater the priority of reciprocal help over help based on financial remuneration. Close-knit group relations necessitate altruism, whereas loose group relations tend to invite egocentrism (Thompson and Wildavsky 1986).

In their effort to make ends meet, the conformists and ritualists also went into debt. The average monthly income per person was relatively low in the households of the conformists and ritualists (Table VII). The fact that the percentage of people in debt was relatively lower than among the other types can be explained by the close-knit group relations. People could rely on each other and there was also the social correction in the event of excessive conspicuous consumption. Debt accumulation was relatively limited among the conformists and ritualists. Most of them were in debt to only one creditor, whom they were paying off in regular installments (Table 4.5).

The social life the conformists and ritualists participated in was a public life with a large extent of social control. This social control was expressed in their risk perception regarding informal work: many of them said they would not work off the books because it involved too much of a risk (Table VIII). The homogeneous, egalitarian structure did not allow people to distinguish themselves from others by earning an extra income in any illegal way. Anyone who did so was rejected and excluded from the community.

> There is no point in even trying that here, any work that isn't completely legal. They will just go and report you for it to the authorities. That happened to people who live down the block and it also happened to someone who lives next door to me. They always make such a big deal of it. That guy is always making a commotion, they report every little thing (31-year-old man, partner and children, 6 years unemployed).

Dealing with Time and Time Perception

The conformists had a relatively integrated social position. They spent a great deal of time with their relatives and the other people who lived in the neighborhood, and 45 percent of them were active in some club or organization (Table VII). The ritualists led a more isolated life. Their social circles were more limited. Only 32 percent were in any kind of club or organization. This was in part due to the feelings of shame and embarrassment, which were stronger among them. Both the conformists and the ritualists continued to have a hard time coping with a jobless life. They belonged to the group described in Chapter 5 as the traditionally passive unemployed who are often bored and have not developed any meaningful alternatives for work.

The time perspective of the conformists and ritualists was an extrapolation of the past (See Douglas 1978). Most of them had had a working past that would hardly give rise to expectations of upward mobility. The job levels they had worked at were low. The short-term perspective was rooted in a common working past, during which they had learned that career planning and looking toward the future were not feasible options for them. The result was a short-term attitude toward the future in which people were not likely to give up what little security they had.

Dependence and Responsibility

The conformists and ritualists belonged to the group described in Chapter 7 as unemployed people who had a difficult time accepting the fact that they were dependent on welfare. They did feel they had a right to the benefits they were receiving, but they were still embarrassed about being dependent on welfare. The loss of independence was felt to be the greatest problem.

> You feel you are totally dependent. It creates a lot of tension at home and in everything you do or don't do all day long. You always have to rely on other people and you are dependent on them. Even though you have a right to the money you get, it feels like you are getting charity (40-year-old man, partner and children, 7 years unemployed).

The ritualists and conformists did everything they could to keep from becoming dependent. They did not want to allow the external rules of the authorities to dominate their social life. The internal rule system of the group they belonged to served as a barrier against over-dependence on the authorities. A dominant value of the conformists and ritualists was: Try and take care of yourself, solve your own problems. This is why the majority of the conformists and ritualists had a neutral relation with the Welfare Department (Table 7.1). It was interesting to note that this internal rule system functioned in a *harmonious relation* with the external regulation system of the authorities. The strong emphasis on being an upstanding, respectable citizen who was self-reliant kept people from violating the external rules.

> I would not even think of it. It is stealing from society and that is wrong. No matter how you look at it, it is not right (25-year-old man, partner, no children, 3 years unemployed).

> I am against it and I really feel very strongly about that. It is against my principles. It is not something I would ever do. If I did, I would lose the right to criticize other people who did it (42-year-old woman, single, 3 years unemployed).

The relatively closed nature of the group the conformists and ritualists belonged to led to a sharp us/them perspective (Hoggart 1957). This us/them perspective was clear from their views on politics and on foreigners. Their views were examples of "blaming the system" and "scapegoating." Chapter 7 gives a small sample of their reactions and attitudes to politics.

The dichotomous cosmology of the conformists and ritualists reflected their marginal position. It was the cosmology of the man at the bottom who felt manipulated by the people at the top, the ones with all the power, and threatened by the influx of foreigners. Particularly with respect to the national authorities in The Hague, the high/low metaphor was common: "They" are the ones with the power, "we" are the ones who have to do what they say.

An Individualistic Culture
of Unemployment

The enterprising and calculating were part of a social environment characterized by a weak group dimension and a weak grid dimension. The enterprising and calculating were mainly found in Het Nieuwe Westen in Rotterdam.

The enterprising and calculating respondents operated in fluctuating social contexts. They generally had a relatively large network of friends. Table IX shows that 79 percent of the enterprising and 75 percent of the calculating respondents had an extensive circle of friends. The geographic range of their social environment extended beyond the borders of the neighborhood. This was also evident from the fact that 70 percent of the enterprising and the calculating often associated with friends who lived in other parts of the city. The social range of their network and their geographical mobility were clearly expressed in interview fragments like the following.

I am in a band in Amsterdam and I have also got a group I play with in France. There are two Frenchmen and two Dutchmen in it, but we rehearse in France. We always rehearse for two weeks at a stretch and then we tour for four weeks. It all started eight years ago here in Holland and there came a time when we realized it was a very tiny country indeed and that you have to tour all around Europe if you want to earn any money. First we book the gigs by phone, and then we do a week in Germany and a week in France, a week in Switzerland, we go all over (28-year-old man, single, 5 years unemployed).

This is a quote from a working saxophone player. Welfare allowed him to be a musician; only the most successful have regulars gigs. This respondent was not representative of all the people in the enterprising and calculating categories. Though it is a rather extreme example, the quote does illustrate that the social borders of their network were far less restricted than those of the conformists and ritualists. They were part of social environments that had no clear group boundaries or group rules.

The groups the enterprising and the calculated operated in often exhibited many of the features of an open network. Open networks are relatively extensive in a social as well as a geographical sense. People who have a network of this kind tend to move relatively frequently, have access to a variety of social circles and live a rather individualistic life.

The grid dimension was similarly weak. The social world the enterprising and the calculating lived in was not dominated by strong social classifications. They had their own internal rules, which served to help them get around the external rules of the authorities. The enterprising and the calculating had managed to create their own individual territory where they could do as they pleased with a certain extent of autonomy.

Job-Seeking Behavior and Work Ethic

The enterprising and the calculating partly coincide with the unemployed people described in Chapter 6 who make hardly any effort, if at all, to find a job and who have found alternatives for formal employment (Tables 6.1 and 6.4). Table VII shows that the enterprising were much less willing to give up their demands regarding the content and the type of work than the conformists and the ritualists. They also had high wage requirements in comparison with the other types of unemployed people: 67 percent of the enterprising and 69 percent of the calculating wanted to earn a monthly wage that was more than 300 Dutch guilders ($150) higher than the welfare benefit.

Most of the calculating and the enterprising had a utilitarian work ethic. Work was not viewed as something of value in itself, but as a way to gain access to a specific consumption level or to a life style that would enable one to develop as freely as possible. It was rather important to the enterprising to reach a certain income level. This also held true for some of the calculating. In addition, the calculating respondents sometimes invested in an education they hoped would eventually get them a job.

The calculating respondents made very little effort to find a job, but the situation was more complicated where the enterprising were concerned. There was a group that had not given up looking for a job through formal channels but at the same time was earning some money on the side by working informally (Table VII). There was a second group that was no longer looking for a job because formal employment would not earn them an income as high as they were now receiving. Most of the calculating and enterprising respondents seemed to prefer the advantages of their situation to those of a formal employment situation. They particularly appreciated the freedom and the leisure time they had living on welfare (Table VIII).

The enterprising and the calculating were much less subject to social pressure to look for a formal job than the conformists and ritualists. They operated within open networks where accepting unemployment had few social repercussions. That did not necessarily mean they were not open to social influences. The contexts they were part of were far looser ones, where a great deal of importance was attributed to freedom and leisure time rather than to having a permanent job. Table IX shows that 40 percent of the enterprising and the calculating had a circle of friends that included many people who were out of work.

Making Ends Meet and Risk Perception

The enterprising and the calculating applied the enterprising strategy described in Chapter 4 to make ends meet. They were able to increase their incomes with informal strategies in order to meet their specific needs. The enterprising and the calculating had a relatively high monthly income per person, without including whatever they managed to earn on the side (Table VII). In addition, they had an extra income based either on the informal work they did or on the advantageous arrangements they were able to make. The enterprising and the calculating managed to get around the external rules imposed by the authorities or to use them to their own advantage. In Rotterdam, they took advantage of the atomized social structure of parts of the neighborhood where their behavior was not likely to be sanctioned. In certain parts of the neighborhood, no one knew anyone else and social control was virtually non-existent. The risk perception of the enterprising and the calculating in Rotterdam was considerably lower than that of the conformists and ritualists in Enschede. There was much less fear of being reported to the Welfare Department by people in the neighborhood.

Yes, if they wanted to they would be able to find out about it. I think things would be very different in a village, but here in the city it is much easier to get away with these things. And anyway they don't have enough manpower, they are so understaffed those Welfare people. It's pathetic (23-year-old woman, partner, no children, years unemployed).

I don't know anybody. Just the people who live next door. I nod and say hello, that's all. I don't want any problems. If you go see the neighbors, then they will come see you, and I don't want that. I mind my own business and everyone else does the same. I don't recognize any of the people who live in the neighborhood (44-year-old man, three-generation household, 8 years unemployed).

In addition to the anonymity of the immediate residential environment, there were also the anonymity and privacy provided by the open networks the respondents lived in. Besides specific skills, anyone who wants to be successful in the informal economy needs personal contacts (Pahl 1984 and Renooy 1990). People who have an extensive and heterogeneous network that not only provides a certain extent of anonymity but also leads to personal contacts have more of a chance to operate successfully in the informal economy than people who are confined to a small close-knit group.

Many of the enterprising and the calculating respondents were in debt (Table VII). The way the enterprising and the calculating dealt with their debts had more of a strategic element than was the case with the other types of respondents. For the conformists and ritualists, going into debt was primarily a sign of financial problems and a method of dealing with these problems. For the enterprising and the calculating, however, going into debt was a consciously utilized strategy for increasing consumption. They ventured to take these risks because the financial repercussions for them were calculable and because there were virtually no social sanctions regarding income strategies of this kind.

Coping with Time and Time Perception

The enterprising and the calculating fell under the category of active unemployed people described in Chapter 5, who are rarely bored and sometimes even feel they don't have enough time for all the things they want to do. The enterprising and the calculating had less difficulty finding satisfying ways to spend their time than the conformists. They had succeeded in developing alternative activities that took the place of a formal job. To differing degrees, these activities had more or less taken over the functions generally attributed to work, providing the respondents with an income and a way to structure time, status, social contacts and self-respect. Most of them had an extra income besides welfare, making it was easier for them to join clubs or other organizations and providing more opportunities to go out (Table VII).

The high extent of social participation was necessary for the enterprising and the calculating if they were to maintain their position within the open networks they were part of. Going out, especially to cafes, was a form of social investment. The social participation of the enterprising and the calculating was also evident from another interesting phenomenon: No fewer than 65 percent of the enterprising and 85 percent of the calculating respondents kept an appointment book (Table VII). Keeping an appointment book was an indication of regular social contacts and social intercourse. The percentages of the other types keeping an appointment book, with the exception of the autonomous, were in no way comparable.

It is striking how often the enterprising and the calculating referred to how little time they had; they had "so much to do" and there were "so many things" they simply didn't have time for. Although comments like these were not made solely by the enterprising and calculating respondents, and they could be viewed as a defense mechanism against the clichés other people were so quick to use about the enormous amounts of time the unemployed were thought to have on their hands, there was still a fundamental difference between the time perception of the enterprising and the calculating and that of the other types. The time perception of the enterprising and the calculating can be comprehended on the basis of the meaning attributed to the activities they engaged in. Whereas many of the unemployed respondents were confronted with a shortage of meaningful activities, so that their social rhythm slowed down and traditional temporal frameworks lost their meaning, this was much less the case with the enterprising and the calculating.

I'm a part-time student. I train twenty hours a week and I go to the club four evenings a week. My traveling expenses and clothing are paid for, otherwise I wouldn't be able to afford it. So that is how I spend almost every evening. I study maybe fifteen hours a week. If you want to live a good life, you have to pace yourself. If you try and do too much all at the same time, it won't work, you know. What you have to do is sit down and think for ten minutes: This is what I want to get done today and this is the time and energy I am prepared to spend on it (30-year-old man, single, 12 years unemployed).

The enterprising invested mainly in short-term strategies. The time horizon of the majority of these respondents was confined to the near future, which was expressed in the numerous debts they incurred. Some of the students among the calculating respondents were an exception in this respect. They had a long-term perspective that was closely linked to the completion of their studies and the possibilities it would present. In this group, there was a certain extent of career planning.

Dependence and Responsibility

The enterprising and the calculating belonged to the unemployed group described in Chapter 7 as having very few problems with their welfare dependency or with manipulating the Welfare Department rules. They had very few compunctions about violating the external rules of the Welfare Department or using them to their own advantage. They made their own rules and were not checked in this respect by coercive group norms. Thus they were not likely to perceive their dependence on the Welfare Department as a problem. By utilizing their own bureaucratic competence, the enterprising and the calculating managed to somehow restructure this dependence on the Welfare Department to their own advantage. An indication of their opportunistic attitude was the fact that the feelings of shame observed in these groups were so negligible (Table VIII).

The system is there to be taken advantage of. You have to make sure you get as much out of it as you can. No one wants to be out of work. If you are in a situation you can't do anything about, you have to look after your own interests. I'm a student who is on welfare and I got my VCR from the Welfare Department. I told them I needed some money to fix up my house (30-year-old man, single, 14 years unemployed).

It has been noted that the internal rule system of the conformists and ritualists was in a harmonious relation with the regulation system of the Welfare Department. The internal rule system of the enterprising and the calculating, however, was in a *discordant relation* with the Welfare Department. They violated the prescribed rules. Their pragmatic and opportunistic attitude, not only toward the Welfare Department but toward people of foreign descent as well, was characteristic of the enterprising and the calculating. The scapegoating observed among the ritualists and conformists was much less common here. Instead, these groups tended to blame themselves for their present situation and to take responsibility for it.

I never felt I had been treated unfairly. I was the one who was responsible for what happened. (. . .) I am pretty right wing in the sense that I feel each individual should take care of himself and see to his own needs. My ideal is to find some way of seeing to it that I don't have to work. That is my ideal, but I don't know if it is feasible (23-year-old man, single, 4 years unemployed).

A Fatalistic Culture of Unemployment

The retreatists can be localized in a social environment with a weak group and a strong grid dimension. In the course of time, the majority of the retreatists had become isolated and totally dependent on welfare. The social and geographical world they lived in had shrunk in size. Only 18 percent of the retreatists associated with friends who lived in other parts of the city and only 29 percent of them had a large network of friends (Table IX). The retreatists' ties with their immediate environment had become closer and closer. Due to their isolated social position, the retreatists were not part of any strong groups.

> Now that they know I am living on Welfare, I don't have any friends any more because there isn't anything left they can get from me, they can't borrow any money from me any more, they can't do anything at all. The fact of the matter is I don't want to have friends any more. I live in my own world and I just keep going round and round in it and I am happy this way (34-year-old man, single, 5 years unemployed).

The grid dimension of the retreatists' social environment was strong. Strong social classifications regulated their behavior, "leaving minimum scope for personal choice, providing instead a set of railway lines with remote control of points for interaction" (Douglas 1978:16). The norms for the retreatists' behavior were prescribed by the authorities they had come to be totally dependent on. The other types made use of their own internal regulations to keep from becoming overly dependent on the Welfare Department, but this was not the case with the retreatists. The control they had over their own behavior had become very limited indeed. The external regulations of the authorities were now dominating many aspects of their social lives.

The only resistance on the part of the retreatists to the government institutions surrounding them was that they failed to meet with certain formal obligations. This withdrawal on their part was expressed in various ways. Often with the permission of the Welfare Department, would ignore the obligation to keep applying for jobs and they would refuse to attend training courses because they no longer had any faith in them. With respect to the other aspects of their lives, however, they remained tied in every conceivable way to the government institutions, particularly since they had no supportive social relations to fall back on.

The size of the retreatist category was virtually the same at the various locations (Table 8.1). At all three locations, the number of retreatists was second only to that of the conformists. In the following section, examples will be given from all three locations.

Job-Seeking Behavior and Work Ethic

The retreatists fell under the category described in Chapter 6 as unemployed people who have given up any chance of ever being able to find a job. The retreatists no longer even made any efforts to find a job. That did not necessarily mean they did not think work was important. Most of them had a traditional work ethic and had done some very heavy work in the course of their employment career. It was characteristic of the retreatists that they were resigned to the fact that they had no prospects of ever finding another job. This was why the retreatists had the largest percentage of unemployed people who were not willing to take training courses and learn new skills. In view of their background and experience, they had no confidence that training of this kind would offer them any new prospects of a job. The retreatists' non-active conduct on the labor market is clear from Table VII. There was very little willingness on their part to accept jobs requiring long commuting times or to make concessions as to the kind of work they wanted to do. They also made high wage demands (see Table 6.4). In Chapter 9, these high demands Will be discussed as a defense mechanism against possible reproaches about their lack of success on the labor market.

The resigned attitude on the part of the retreatists was mainly the result of a realistic assessment of costs and benefits. Time after time, their job applications had been unsuccessful. In the end, this made them not even bother to look for a job because the social costs caused by the loss of self-esteem gradually became too high. Another factor that may have contributed to their resigned attitude was the absence of pressure from other people to go out and look for a job. They had very few friends and were barely active in any social contexts. The social world they lived in had become an small one, and there was so little social pressure to continue looking for a job.

> I don't have any relatives. I am all alone. I live alone. I have very few friends and acquaintances. I am usually home all the time (45-year-old woman, single, 12 years unemployed).

Making Ends Meet and Risk Perception

The retreatists applied the fatalistic strategy described in Chapter 4 in order to make ends meet (Thompson et al. 1990). It can hardly be referred to as a real strategy however. The retreatists had no control over their own finances and it was all they could do to pay their bills with the help of government agencies. They were not able to earn any extra income by way of informal activities. The retreatists were almost incapable of earning any money on the side or engaging in informal activities; only 9 percent of them occasionally earned something by way of informal work (Table VII). They did not have access to the networks that would have made informal work possible, and over time they had lost contact with the other people who could have helped them.

> I would prefer to have some kind of work that I could do off the books. With an extra 150 guilders a week, I would have maybe 1600 guilders a month. That's an amount that you can do something with, but I don't have the contacts to get myself that kind of work. A couple of years back, there was this contractor standing at the Central Station. I would go there and get work for a day. Cleaning out the inside of ships, dirty work. But it was a good way to fill up your day and you had a little extra money. I also worked in gardens, raising the level of the soil, and putting in tiles. But there comes an end to the number of people you know and then that kind of thing stops (32-year old man, single, 6 years unemployed).

The retreatists used individual making-ends-meet strategies that often involved going into debt. Debts were relatively common among the retreatists; 59 percent of them were in debt. Often their payment obligations had been taken over by the Welfare Department. This kind of intervention in the finances of the retreatists implied increased dependence. Their freedom to do as they pleased with their money was very restricted.

The risk perception of the retreatists regarding working off the books was more limited than in the case of the conformists or ritualists (Table VIII). Their social isolation played a role here. However, their isolated social position and their dependence on the Welfare Department led to a "welfare dependence" situation in which taking any risks at all and engaging in informal activities were no longer realistic options.

Coping with Time and Time Perception

The retreatists belonged to the group of passive unemployed people described in Chapter 5 who had trouble killing time. They differed from the conformists in that they exhibited a lower level of social participation and a greater disorientation as regards the most commonplace units of time. The isolated position of the retreatists clearly affected the way they spent and perceived their time. Obviously their poor financial position restricted their chances to participate in leisure activities, which usually cost something. And because of their isolated social position, there were fewer meaningful activities available to them. Tables VII and VIII show that only 5 percent of the retreatists kept an appointment book and that boredom was most widespread in this group. The time strategies the retreatists used consisted mainly of doing nothing and killing time.

The retreatists' time horizon had shrunk. They could barely see any future for themselves. The only part of the future that was clearly visible to them was the next day. Jahoda et al. referred to this attitude as resignation: "It is an attitude of drifting along, indifferently and without expectations, accepting a situation that cannot be changed. . . But the future, even in the shape of plans, has no longer any place in the thought or even dreams of these families. All this seems to us to be best characterized by the word *resignation*" (Jahoda et al. 1972:52-53).

Dependence and Responsibility

The retreatists are somewhere in between the dependence and the independence of the dichotomous schema described in Chapter 7. It was initially difficult for them to accept their welfare dependency, but in the course of time, the retreatists came to view dependence on welfare as something "natural." The retreatists were not in either a harmonious or a discordant relation with the authorities. Their relation with government agencies, particularly the Welfare Department, was simply viewed as a *natural* one. This might explain why the retreatists exhibited less shame or embarrassment than the conformists or ritualists in this connection.

I can't say I have a feeling of dependence. To me, the relation with the Welfare Department has become something I just take for granted (42-year-old man, lives with parents, 5 years unemployed).

Many of the retreatists had been disappointed and unsuccessful so often and had become so dependent on the government that they were convinced there was nothing they could do to improve their situation. A "culture of dependence" could be observed among the retreatists. The idea that they could somehow exert influence was virtually non-existent.

The retreatists had a rather tragic perception of responsibility: "This is fate" and "There is nothing we can do about it." They did not feel there was any way they could alter their situation unless they were very lucky. Merton described this as the "doctrine of luck" and referred in this connection to Bakke's study *The Unemployed Man* (Merton 1957:149). In this study, the unstable position of the unemployed on the labor market served to account for their belief in luck. The unemployed workers never felt there was any kind of influence they could exert: "There is a measure of hopelessness in the situation when a man knows that most of his good or ill fortune is out of his own control and depends on luck" (Bakke 1933:14).

This fatalistic view lacked both the optimism of the enterprising and the calculating and the ability of the conformists to make the best of things. No one knew what the future would bring, it was a matter of blind fate, chance occurrences that would shape the course of individual lives. It was neither the system nor one's own shortcomings that had caused the present situation. What the retreatists did was blame "fate."

An Autonomous Culture of Unemployment

The autonomous were people who liked to do things their own way and who tried to remain as independent as possible. Some of the autonomous lived rather isolated lives, but it was a self-chosen isolation. The autonomous were less active in "network building" than the enterprising and the calculating. They invested less in maintaining social contacts focused on acquiring extra income, and maintained the only the kind of social contacts that were important to their own fields of interest. The autonomous decided for themselves who they wanted to associate with, how they wanted to spend their time and which activities they wanted to engage in. The autonomous could mainly be found in the Rotterdam and Amsterdam neighborhoods. The heterogeneous, often anonymous structure of these suburban neighborhoods created the prerequisites for groups of long-term unemployed people to lead an autonomous life. The social structure of the Enschede neighborhood was much less conducive to a life style of this kind.

Job-Seeking Behavior and Work Ethic

The autonomous belonged to the group of unemployed people described in Chapter 6 as making little if any effort to find a job and as having found alternatives for formal employment. There were two reasons not to look for work. First, there was a sub-group that had an alternative work ethic that rejected the idea of a job as the highest goal in life. Second, there was a sub-group that had accepted the situation of unemployment and had developed alternatives. This sub-group differed from the retreatists in the extent to which they were able to be self-reliant and from the enterprising and the calculating in their rejection of illegal income strategies.

The work ethic of these "alternative" autonomous respondents could differ quite a bit from the traditional work ethic: they only wanted to work in the kind of situation they would be completely happy in. A working situation with strict regulations, particularly a hierarchic one with fixed working hours, was not one they would even consider. The autonomous were not willing to give up the freedom to do as they pleased. The fact that the autonomous were willing to make very few concessions was illustrated by the high demands they made of a prospective job (Table VII). They made the same high demands of whatever training courses were available to them. No less than 89 percent of the autonomous respondents had their own requirements these training courses had to meet with. These requirements often pertained to the nature of the training and the prospects for getting a job afterwards. The autonomous wanted to do "interesting" training courses with prospects for the kind of job they would "enjoy." These demands were such that the autonomous preferred their present situation to a formal working situation and hardly attended any training courses that would strengthen their position on the labor market.

With all the things I am able to do now, I feel much better than I ever did in any of those jobs I had. There is never a dull moment. Lately I have even started to think: would I actually have time for a job? (39-year-old man, single, 3 years unemployed)

As a result of their autonomous position in society, the autonomous respondents did not experience the kind of social pressure that activated the job-seeking behavior on the part of the conformists and ritualists. Like the enterprising and the calculating respondents, the autonomous were not very embarrassed or ashamed of the fact that they were unemployed (Table VIII).

Making Ends Meet and Risk Perception

The autonomous were the most successful of all the respondents at making ends meet. They applied the autonomous strategy described in Chapter 4, harmoniously attuning resources and needs to each other. The autonomous respondents were characterized by a sober life style. The percentage of the autonomous who were in debt was much lower than in the other groups, only 27 percent of them had debts. In part, this was related to their relatively high average spendable monthly income, 696 Dutch guilders or about $350 per person, which in turn had to do with the fact that many of them lived alone and had low living expenses. Almost a quarter of the autonomous respondents living on welfare even managed to save something.

The autonomous also made use of more alternative methods to cut down on their expenses, for example by buying things second hand. The autonomous had hardly any extra income from informal work or from especially advantageous arrangements; only 14 percent of them occasionally earned something extra by working informally. The risk perception of the autonomous regarding informal work of this kind was relatively strong (Table VIII). Their awareness of the risks involved, however, was based much less on their fear of being reported to the authorities by other their neighbors than was the case with the conformists and ritualists. The autonomous led a life of their own and were not corrected by the behavioral norms of other people. When asked about the risks of informal work, the autonomous referred to other factors, for example the activities of Welfare Department investigators. For most of the autonomous respondents, welfare was their only source of income. These benefits constituted the financial guarantee for their autonomous existence. They did not want to endanger that existence by earning an extra income in an illegal way.

Coping with Time and Time Perception

The autonomous were masters over their own time schedules. The autonomous respondents belonged to the group of active unemployed people described in Chapter 5 as not being bored and as attaching a great deal of value to their freedom and leisure time (Table 5.2). For the autonomous, having this kind of control over their own time was one of the most valuable things they had been able to attain in their lives. Whereas the retreatists, conformists and ritualists all had trouble getting through the day and the enterprising and calculating respondents sometimes did not have enough time, the autonomous did as they liked with their time.

> I am very fond of my leisure time and the way I see it my free time would be very threatened by a job, even if it were only for twenty hours a week. For me, life is spending time well, studying a little bit, reading. I view my life as a "permanent education." Now and then studying for a year, then doing nothing for a year. I don't go to the university to get myself a better position on the job market. No matter how much fun work can be, no matter how convinced you are that it is really your hobby, there are always sides to it that are not that attractive, the pressure. And now if there is something you don't feel like doing, you just don't do it. You have more freedom. You can devote more time to the things you really want to do (27-year-old man, 4 years unemployed).

None of the autonomous said they were often bored (Table VIII). The freedom and the leisure time the unemployment situation entailed were something the autonomous felt a great deal of appreciation for. They used their time to develop their talents and personality. For the autonomous, time did not threaten or restrict their social functioning in any way. Their time was spent as they wished and was used to develop themselves in their own way, independently of any social pressure exerted by individuals, groups or institutions. The time perception of the autonomous was diametrically opposed to that of the retreatists.

Dependence and Responsibility

The autonomous respondents were the prototype of the unemployed category described in Chapter 7 who view their welfare dependency as a prerequisite for an independent life. The autonomous did not perceive their dependence on welfare as a problem. Van Stolk and Wouters (1983) referred to the "peace of mind of the welfare state" to indicate that the social security provided by the welfare state has been internalized to a certain extent by its citizens and has become personal security. This peace of mind could not be observed in most of the unemployed, though it was clearly evident among the autonomous, who viewed welfare as a reliable foundation for their autonomous existence. By keeping strict control over their financial situation, the autonomous tried to restrict their dependence on relatives, friends and authorities as much as they could. This also held true for their relation with the Welfare Department. They tried to maintain as impersonal a relation as they could with it. Most of the autonomous respondents had an *administrative relation* with the Welfare Department. In other words, as much of their contact with the Welfare Department as possible was by way of letters and of an anonymous nature, and there was hardly any direct personal contact between the autonomous and the Welfare Department social workers.

In part, the autonomous respondents' perception of their own responsibility corresponded to that of the enterprising and the calculating. The autonomous did not refer to any external factors or segments of society (the Dutch National Parliament in The Hague, fate, foreigners) to justify the situation they were in. The autonomous viewed themselves as being responsible for their own situation and their own behavior. However, there was no evidence of the right wing perspective that characterized the attitude of many of the enterprising respondents. The notion that anyone who was not successful was at fault (blaming the victim) was totally alien to the autonomous line of reasoning.

A CULTURE OF MODERN POVERTY

In the Dutch inner cities where unemployment figures are highest, long-term unemployment is thought to have led to a specific jobless culture characterized by the rejection of the work norm, the acceptance of unemployment and the generation of informal survival strategies that sharply deviate from those of the dominant culture (De Neubourg 1986). This characterization contains elements of what has been described in this chapter as an individualistic culture of unemployment. In addition, three other cultures of employment have been described: conformist, autonomous and fatalistic. In the conformist culture of unemployment, the work norm still prevailed, but in the autonomous one, there was an alternative interpretation of the very concept of work. Both of these cultures were characterized, however, by a rejection of informal strategies. In the fatalistic culture of unemployment, there was no longer any prospect of employment in either the official or the informal labor market. Together, the four cultures reflected the wide range of ways the long-term unemployed dealt with their situation.

Almost half the respondents were part of a conformist culture of unemployment and a quarter belonged to a fatalistic one. The relative size of these two cultures belies the commonly held view that people who are out of work no longer look for a job because they can earn enough on the side. This assumption held true mainly for the enterprising and calculating members in an individualistic culture of unemployment. They constituted one fifth of the research population. Some of them would re-enter the labor market at some point in the future. This was particularly true for the small group that was getting an education on welfare instead of on a scholarship.

The fatalistic culture of unemployment could be viewed as a modern version of what the anthropologist Lewis (1968) described as a "culture of poverty."[8] In the case of some of the respondents, long-term unemployment had led to their exclusion from social institutions and networks and had made them completely dependent on the government. This group reacted to its situation by developing feelings of fatalism and resignation. Hence, our use of the concept of culture implies an integration of the situational and the cultural view on poverty and unemployment (see Gans 1991). The behavior of the unemployed results initially from an adaption to their existential situation. Some of these adaptations change according to changes in their situation. Some adaptations, however, will be "culturally hardened" when their social position and social environment continues to be the same. This process of cultural hardening manifests itself in some behavioral patterns and aspirations toward work, time and money, as demonstrated in this chapter.

It is important to examine the extent to which the various cultures of unemployment precede and succeed each other in time. Can a conformist or an individualistic culture gradually turn into a fatalistic one? It is difficult to make any definitive statements on the development of long-term unemployment based on the data from our study. After all, no longitudinal research was conducted. There are nonetheless several tendencies that were evident from the research material.

If we examine the individual unemployment careers of the respondents, we can cautiously conclude that the longer a person is out of work, the more of a tendency there is toward retreatist behavior. Over time, there would seem to be a conversion from conformist to retreatist behavior. The negligible success on the labor market, the high social costs that continual job-seeking behavior entails and the reduction or disappearance of social frameworks can all serve to account for this shift from conformist to retreatist behavior, and the longer the unemployment lasts, the more this is the case. The fact that the longer the unemployment continued, the fewer conformists there were was also due to the fact that some of them managed to find a job. It is also clear that the older the respondents were, the more common retreatist and ritualistic behavior became. The older, often poorly educated respondents realized that they no longer had any prospect of ever finding a job, and they were resigned to their situation.

The shift from conformist to retreatist or ritualist behavior did not apply to all the of respondents. Quite different processes could be observed among the enterprising and the calculating. The tendency for enterprising behavior to increase with the unemployment duration was largely explained by the fact that many enterprising respondents preferred to remain in a welfare situation. For them, the advantages of living on welfare were more attractive than the income and obligations of a formal job. Some of the calculating respondents did eventually reject the welfare situation, because, for example, they had completed their education.

No one single development line could be discerned. As has been extensively noted, the unemployment careers of the individual respondents were also shaped by their social environment. The social environment of many of the Enschede respondents stimulated the behavior of the long-term unemployed more in the direction of conformism than did the social environments of the Amsterdam or Rotterdam respondents. Nonetheless, for a relatively large number of the respondents, especially the older ones with a low educational level, long-term unemployment eventually led to a shrinking of the social and geographic world they lived in and thus to a more isolated existence in which they became increasingly dependent on the facilities provided by the government. In terms of the cultural theory, this implies that the group dimension became weaker and the grid dimension stronger. In other words, as a result of a lengthy period of time spent on the lowest social and financial level, the nature of the group and grid dimensions altered and individuals could gradually move from a conformist to a fatalist culture of unemployment. Within a fatalistic culture, the prerequisites for collective action and resistance are non-existent; there is no group consciousness and no faith in the idea that people can exert influence over their own lives.

THE MAKING OF A DUTCH UNDERCLASS

Cultural Heterogeneity as an Unintended Consequence of Welfare Policy

The most important conclusion that can be drawn from our study is that in a sociological sense, the long-term unemployed are not one uniform, homogeneous group, even though all the members of this group do have several statistical features in common. On the basis of the research material, six types of unemployed are constructed. Typologies of the unemployed have been constructed before. One well-known typology is that drawn up by Lazarsfeld-Jahoda and Zeisel (1933). The prevalent resignation observed among 70 percent of their respondents was also noted in our own study. If we were to group the ritualists and the retreatists together, we would see that at the time of our study, certain forms of resignation were still in evidence, although to a lesser extent (34 percent). The dangers of continual resignation—that one is caught up in a downward spiral of passivity, waiting for something to happen rather than taking the initiative—also played a role in the lives of some of the conformists (36 percent).

The remaining types in our study (30 percent)—the enterprising, the calculating and the autonomous respondents—could be viewed only against the background of the most important features of the contemporary social security system. The Murray thesis (1984) that, on the basis of rational calculations, citizens decide to remain or to become dependent on welfare, since the net results yield more financial advantages than the income of a regular job, can be applied to the enterprising and the calculating unemployed. The autonomous, on the other hand, go their own way and use the welfare benefit as a basic income. These behavioral reactions are unforeseen and unintended consequences of the Dutch welfare policy. The changes in society, especially the individualization, also contribute to the existence of these new categories. Most of the modern types are single or childless, statuses that increase the varieties of coping with unemployment. As demonstrated in Chapter 4, parents with children take fewer risks and react in a conformist way to unemployment. Nonetheless, the 70 to 30 ratio of the "traditional" to the "modern" reaction patterns makes it clear that in a quantitative sense, the long-term unemployed could not soon be expected to exhibit a completely new mentality. For this, the composition of the new group itself is far too heterogeneous. This ratio does, however, indicate that we should be very careful about making oversimplified generalizations. It is easy to put the long-term unemployed whose reactions are traditional in the same category with those whose reactions are "modern." The less acceptable aspects of the modern reactions are often also attributed to the traditional ones, though our study proved this to be an erroneous assumption.

A Differentiated Social Policy

In the policy figures, our research population is categorized as "long-term unemployed," but in the reality of actual society, policy categories of this kind include a far more complex system of multifarious categories. Some of the long-term unemployed were not really out of work at all, and some of them lived far above the national poverty line. The aim of the cultural analysis of long-term unemployment presented here is to provide greater insight into the heterogeneous reality of the long-term unemployed. The six types of long-term unemployed people and the four cultures of unemployment described here constitute an effort to construct a sturdy foundation for a sociological categorization based on the everyday reality of the long-term unemployed. In their article, "A Poverty of Distinction," Thompson and Wildavsky had a comparable point of departure. Using their cultural theory they made it clear that there were various types of poor people who used various strategies. No matter how greatly these strategies differed from each other, they were "perfectly rational in relation to a distinct social context" (Thompson and Wildavsky 1986:178).

The subtitle of the article by Thompson and Wildavsky would also have been a very appropriate one for this chapter: "From economic homogeneity to cultural heterogeneity in the classification of poor people." That also applies to their most important recommendation that the heterogeneity of poverty (in our case unemployment) should lead to a more differentiated social policy. Policy measures designed to either help certain groups of unemployed people or to keep a stricter check on them cannot be effective if they are applied to all long-term unemployed people with totally different sociological features. For example, if the aim is to reduce the abuse of social security rights on the part of the long-term unemployed, then stricter policies and stricter checks would be justified. However, if stricter checks were applied mainly to the groups described in our study as conformists, ritualists and retreatists, often poorly educated people above the age of 40, they would probably be counterproductive and lead to a great deal of bad feelings and unfairness.

Underclass Formation in the Netherlands

For a large segment of the long-term unemployed population, especially the ritualists and the retreatists, it is probable that their situation will continue unchanged. Even if these groups should become far more active than in the past, on the grounds of our research findings they would be unlikely to do much to alter their situation. Intensive personal counseling combined with the effective implementation of a structural labor market policy would be called for. Dutch policies should concentrate more on the reintegration of the unemployed into the labor market. Compared with other countries in Western Europe, the Netherlands spends far less on an active and activating labor market policy. The Dutch unemployment policy provides an income through the social security system and fails to stimulate employment growth by means of a coherent and effective economic policy (SCP 1990).

The Dutch policy concerning the long-term unemployed is contradictory: if the unemployed become resigned to the situation, it does not get them any farther, but if they take the initiative and actively pursue unofficial alternatives, they run the risk of being punished for it. Thus "doing nothing" does not pay off, but neither does "doing something." Resignation reinforces the downward spiral, going from bad to worse, and operating outside the rules is a risky business. The unemployed consider the two alternatives and often "choose" the one that may contain no prospect of any improvement in the future but gives them the safety and protection welfare can provide. For this group of resigned individuals, there is no longer any actual link between work and income. Particularly for the unemployed above the age of 40, it does not seem as if this situation is likely to change soon. Many of them, especially the retreatists, withdraw from society in reaction to their diminishing life chances. This process of social exclusion escapes regular observation, and this is typical of the marginal position this category occupies in society (Dahrendorf 1988).

In the Netherlands, an underclass is threatening to emerge. This underclass has some of the characteristics Wilson (1987, 1991) describes as essential. Its emergence can be explained by economic changes and the lack of a structural labor market policy. It can be recognized by its geographically limited position (the inner cities), its weak attachment to the labor force and its fatalistic culture of unemployment. There are, however, striking differences: the Dutch long-term unemployed do not live in highly segregated areas, nor do they live far below the poverty line or have great difficulties getting access to decent housing, health care and education. The American and Dutch welfare states show different faces of underclass formation: in the United States, the making of the "ghetto poor", and in the Netherlands the emergence of a category of very long-term unemployed, living in inner cities, permanently dependent on welfare.

NOTES

1. For this chapter, the interview material was coded to a more detailed extent. On the basis of the initial analyses and results of the research material, six types of unemployed people were distinguished. The 221 processed interviews were subsequently scored again. Since the recoding entailed the precise interpretation of the sometimes contradictory information given by the respondents, use was only made of the interviews that had been processed word for word. The recoding was done by various staff members. After that, all the interviews were compared with the recodings of the original interviewers. In cases where the recodings deviated from each other, further analysis and interpretation was required in order to arrive at intersubjective agreement. The tables belonging to this chapter can be found in Appendix V.

2. In order to be eligible for RWW, a person is under the obligation to remain available for employment and to apply for jobs. Some unemployed people are actually part-time students. They study in the evenings, which enables them to continue to receive the RWW benefits. However, the respondents in question studied or did volunteer work related to their study in the daytime. A scholarship amounts to about $300 and an RWW benefit for a single person to about $500. What is more, part of the scholarship has to be paid back later, which is not the case with an RWW benefit. More information about welfare benefits can be found in Appendix IV.

3. In her introduction to *Measuring Culture; A Paradigm for the Analysis of Social Organization* by Gross and Rayner, Douglas wrote: "Grid/group analysis is part of an approach whose data are either actions or statements in defense of actions. It looks at public allegiances, tributes, incorporations, and rejections, seeking positivistically to construct from unquestionable bases a social environment that people say constrains them, or act as if it constrains them." Mary Douglas, "Introduction," in: Jonathan Gross and Steve Rayner, *Measuring Culture: A Paradigm for the Analysis of Social Organization*, New York: Columbia University Press, 1985: XXI.

4. The autonomous culture is an invention by Thompson: (1982). One of the main problems of Douglas' group/grid model was where to put the hermit or autonomous individual. Douglas herself did not provide a decisive solution to this problem. She may have preferred "to leave the hermit off the map of social controls, crediting him with full escape" (Mary Douglas (ed.), *Essays in Sociology of Perception*, London/Boston: Routledge & Kegan Paul/Russell Sage Foundation, 1982:11), but she did seem to situate "the hermit" in the lower left hand corner of Square A (Mary Douglas,

Cultural Bias, (Royal Anthropological Institute of Great Britain and Ireland, Occasional Paper no.35), London: Royal Anthropological Institute of Great Britain and Ireland, 1978:42). Situating him there presents a new problem, i.e. this corner is then occupied by two very different individuals with greatly differing cosmologies, the successful entrepreneur and the hermit who has voluntarily withdrawn from society. Douglas did however cite two fundamental differences between the social environment of the hermit and that of the entrepreneur. Firstly, the hermit or autonomous individual received very little stimulation to enter into transactions with other individuals: "His transactions are sporadic, spontaneous and uncalculated" (Douglas 1978:42). Secondly, the hermit or autonomous individual lived much more in the periphery of the dominant institutions of society. This is one of the reasons why Thompson et al. situated the hermit at the grid/group intersection (Michael Thompson, Richard Ellis and Aaron Wildavsky, *Cultural Theory*, Boulder, Colorado: Westview Press, 1990:17).

5. Douglas also uses the concept of "cultural theory." See Mary Douglas and Marcel Calves, "The Self as Risk Taker: A Cultural Theory of Contagion in Relation to AIDS," in: *The Sociological Review*, 38,3:445-464, 1990.

6. The research locations did not coincide with the squares described here. The neighborhoods where the research was conducted were areas with clear boundaries, and within these boundaries various cultures could be observed which each provided different opportunities and imposed different restrictions on the behavior of individuals. The various cultures could be observed at each of the research locations, though there were clear differences in their sizes.

7. See also Gerald Mars, *Cheats at Work: An Anthropology of Workplace Crime*, Allen and Unwin, London, 1982; Michael Thompson and Aaron Wildavsky, "A Cultural Theory of Information Bias in Organizations", in: *Journal of Management Studies* 23, 3, (1986): 273-86, Louis Boon, *De list der Wetenschap*, Baarn: Ambo 1983.

8. The crux of Oscar Lewis' thesis was that the culture of poverty is transmitted from one generation to another and thus could immobilize generations. Since we did not investigate the effects of long-term unemployment on the life chances of children, our statement of the coming into existence of a 'modern culture of poverty' must be understood within the limitations of our study. This culture has to be viewed as a medium-term adaption of the unemployed to their bad labor market chances and their isolated social position. It is an empirical question whether children growing up in a fatalistic culture have a less future perspective than children growing up in a conformist culture. There are, however, some indications that this is the case in the Netherlands (Hannie Te Grotenhuis, *The Bottom Side of Prosperity: Children of Long-Term Unemployed Parents in the Dutch Welfare State*, Paper prepared for the Workshop on the Effects of Parental Joblessness on the Social Outcomes of Adolescence: Cross-Cultural Perspectives, New York, 21 November 1991).

CHAPTER 9

Homo Calculans and Homo Honoris

In the foreword to the English edition of the Marienthal study, Lazarsfeld cited as one of the most important findings that long-term unemployment "leads to a state of apathy in which the victims do not utilize any longer even the few opportunities left to them" (Lazarsfeld, in Jahoda et al. 1972:vii). Lazarsfeld noted the parallel between the Marienthal study and the poverty studies by Lewis and Harrington published in the United States in the late 1950s and early 1960s (Lewis 1959, 1961 and Harrington 1962). These studies concluded that long-term poverty could lead to a culture of poverty that perpetuated the poverty situation. The authors were referring to a culture characterized by exclusion from societal institutions, the disintegration of direct relations with friends, relatives or neighbors, and a fatalistic mentality. People imprisoned in a culture of poverty had a short-term perspective on life, an inferior self image, feelings of helplessness and very few aspirations. Lewis viewed fatalism and a low aspiration level as the central features of a culture of poverty (Lewis 1968).

In the literature on the social consequences of long-term unemployment, comparable notions are very much in evidence, particularly in studies written from the perspective of social psychology.[1] Within this tradition, attention has been focused mainly on changes in the attitudes of the long-term unemployed and on the different stages distinguished in this connection (Bakke 1960). The Marienthal study was partly an example of this. Four attitudes were distinguished: "unbroken," "resigned," "apathetic," and "in despair." The social psychology approach focused attention on specific mental features of the long-term unemployed that were thought to perpetuate the unemployment situation. These features, in particular their motivation and aspiration, were viewed as problems, and far less attention was focused on the underlying socio-economic process of exclusion from the labor market and societal institutions. This has been most explicit in studies on the motivation of the long-term unemployed and the poor. In research of this kind, the resigned behavior of the long-term unemployed has often been dismissed as irrational (Hayes and Nutman 1981).

A second objection to many of the studies on the social consequences of unemployment is that they stipulated the options open to the unemployed in a highly deterministic fashion. People who had been out of work for a lengthy period of time no longer had any firm ground to stand on; their lives were adrift and they were in danger of floating off on the waves of unemployment. This is one point where they coincided with the "culture of poverty" approach and its deterministic conception of culture. This is clearly illustrated by Lewis' often quoted comment: "By the time slum children are age six or seven, they have usually absorbed the basic values and attitudes of their subculture and are not psychologically geared to take full advantage of changing conditions or increased opportunities which may occur in their lifetime" (Lewis 1968:188). This line of reasoning was also evident in Lazarsfeld's foreword, although formulated in a less outspoken fashion. This could lead researchers to overlook the diversity and creativity of the various strategies of the long-term unemployed (Gans 1991). In Chapter 8, the differences were described between various types of unemployed people, not only in their personal biographies but also in the ways they coped with the triad of unemployment problems.

In this chapter, we rebut the ill-considered use of such terms as "apathy" or "irrational" to describe the behavior of the unemployed. We are convinced instead of the rational orientation of their conduct. This standpoint would seem to coincide with Murray's; in *Losing Ground* (1984) he introduced the concept of the calculating poor. His depiction of the *homo calculans*, who makes strategic use of the welfare system, is, however based on the rational choice theory, exemplified by individuals with fixed, coherent preferences who are able to maximize their own utility. We would like to give the term "rationality" a more sociological interpretation. This corresponds with the premise of cultural theory; namely, that the rational conduct of individuals is dependent on their social position and the social context they are functioning in. In other words, "What is rational depends on the social or institutional setting within which the act is embedded" (Thompson et al. 1990:22-23). The instruments and goals the unemployed utilize and aspire to vary in accordance with their chances on the labor market and in accordance with the specific instruments and aims that are perceived as legitimate within a specific social context.

THE LONG-TERM UNEMPLOYED AS RATIONAL PROBLEM-SOLVERS

In descriptions of the behavior of the long-term unemployed, implicit references are often made to what Weber called emotional or traditional action. The behavior of the long-term unemployed is not thought to involve much concrete planning and is held to be oriented toward the immediate future (emotional action). At the same time, the behavior of the long-term unemployed is thought to be shaped by internalized patterns based on specific values, norms and traditions (traditional action). This one-sided view of the behavior of the long-term unemployed is misleading. We feel that much of the conduct of the long-term unemployed is goal-oriented and many of their choices are rational and directed toward the promotion of their own social and economic interests.[2] The ways the long-term unemployed deal with work, time and money can be viewed as strategies aimed at the attainment of realistic ends (Portes 1972). In the following section, a number of these realistic ends are described. The main ones are

- increasing one's income, for example, by moonlighting without informing the Welfare Department;
- minimizing the chance of social injury in the labor market, for example, by becoming resigned to the unemployment situation;
- killing time, for example, by developing and expanding new meaningful activities;
- and enlarging the pattern of expenditures, for example, by going into debt.

The four aims differ from the primary goal many people think the long-term unemployed should be making every effort to attain—finding a new job. The reality of long-term unemployment, however, makes it clear that the goals of the long-term unemployed are not fixed; they are shifting. With these shifts, the strategies the long-term unemployed use to attain the goals change as well. A simple example can illustrate what we mean. In most cases, a person who is out of work will maximize the chance of getting a new job by applying for as many jobs as possible. In Chapters 6 and 8, however, it was noted that the longer a person has been out of work, the lower the application frequency. Sometimes the goal of finding a new job is gradually replaced by the different goal of minimizing the chance of social injury. These two goals are diametrically opposed. If a person wants to have as much of a chance as possible of finding a new job, he should keep applying for whatever jobs might be available, but then he runs the risk of constantly being confronted with his own shortcomings and lack of success. If a person wants to do all he or she can to keep from being humiliated and rejected, he or she would be wise to avoid confrontations with potential employers. As soon as a person has accepted the unemployment situation, and has to make ends meet on a minimum income, other goals loom on the horizon; for example, earning some extra money on the side or enlarging the spending pattern in order to not lose contact with society.

The rational goal-oriented conduct of the unemployed depends on their social position and their chances in the labor market. Someone who has no chances in either the formal or the informal labor market will have different goals and will use corresponding means to reach these goals. A second factor has to do with the social environment or culture the unemployed are part of (see Chapter 8). Moral considerations that are derived from the values and norms of their culture also influence the cost-benefit analyses made by the unemployed (see also Jordan et al. 1992). Both of these factors will be referred to in the following sections.

RATIONALITY AND THE TRIAD OF UNEMPLOYMENT PROBLEMS

In this section, various strategies of the unemployed are described as rational solutions to the problems they are faced with. In the field of *work*, we examine the position of the long-term unemployed who barely made any effort to find a new job and the position of the "officially unemployed" who were regularly "unofficially employed." In terms of *time*, we focus on the unemployed who had trouble coping with it, and regarding *money*, we devote attention to the long-term unemployed who went into debt and moonlighted without informing the Welfare Department.

Work

In Chapter 8, six types of unemployed people were described. The conformists and ritualists among them were still looking for a job, though this was barely true of the others. The question is: Why did they stop looking for a job? The first reason might be that the advantages of a jobless life were greater than those of a working life. A second reason could be that the disadvantages of looking for a job were so great and the chance of finding one so negligible that they simply stopped trying. There was evidence of both of these reasons in our research results.

Moonlighting

Individuals are often assumed to opt for welfare rather than wages if and when the difference between the two has reached a certain minimum (De Neubourg 1986). An individual who acts rationally opts for a life on welfare if the advantages of the unemployment situation are greater than those of the working situation. This economic rationality would seem to be applicable to the enterprising who were regularly unofficially employed without informing the Welfare Department. The following calculations demonstrate a certain attitude:

> If I moonlight, I get twelve and a half guilders an hour. Say I moonlighted one day a week. Then together with my Welfare check, I would have more than if I had a formal job for thirty-two hours a week (30-year-old man, single, 4 years unemployed).

> That little bit of welfare money I get every week, it doesn't really get me very far. No. But I do what I can to add to it. Maybe five hundred guilders a week. Something like that. And add that to what I get, it's about seven hundred a week. I can live on that, can't I? (32-year-old man, single, 11 years unemployed).

Chapter 4 made clear that some unemployed people had a higher income than they could have earned with a regular job. For these individuals, the informal sector functioned as an alternative for the regular labor market. They were mainly educated Dutch people with an extensive network of friends. According to the Employment Office records, they had been out of work for lengthy periods of time. The average official unemployment duration in this category was seven years. The long unemployment duration seemed to be linked to a deliberate decision to remain dependent on welfare. In their own opinion, they would have a reasonable chance of getting a job. However, they barely made any effort to find one since they preferred the advantages of their present situation. These advantages were not solely financial. Social considerations also played a role. Welfare plus the extra income they earned on the side gave them more freedom and leisure time than they would have with a regular job.

For the enterprising unemployed, the combination of welfare and the extra income they earned on the side was preferable to a regular job. The result of a cost-benefit consideration of this kind was that this group was not active in the formal labor market. In Chapter 8, the size of this group was estimated at 10 percent of the research population. It also held true of the calculating respondents that they profited from the welfare-dependent situation. We discuss the cost-benefit analyses of this group in section "Money".

Sour Grapes

We observed a sizeable group who no longer made any effort to find a job and who were resigned to being dependent on welfare. The interesting thing about this group was that they did not have any income from the informal economy and really would have liked to have a job. The financial advantage of the unemployment situation was non-existent, and the people in this group experienced only the disadvantages. Reasons related to greater freedom or more leisure time barely played a role. This group was convinced of the drawbacks of unemployment and attributed much less value to the leisure time and freedom it gave them than the enterprising respondents did. These were unemployed people with an extremely poor labor market position. In Chapter 8, the size of the retreatist group was estimated at 25 percent of the research population.

Signs of resignation and apathy were observed mainly among the retreatists. How should this resignation be interpreted? As a specific mental or cultural feature, due to which people excluded themselves from the labor market? Or as the consequence of structurally impeded possibilities? This group's resigned attitude should be viewed as a "coping mechanism." The social costs of continuing to apply for jobs in either the formal or the informal labor market were too high to live with on a more or less permanent basis (Willis 1986). If a person was told again and again that there were no jobs available, that he or she was too old, did not have enough work experience or did not have the required diplomas, accepting the situation was the most rational reaction. The following interview fragment describes the process leading to an attitude of this kind:

Applying for jobs, you know, looking at the ads in the papers. Calling, writing letters. They did not even send my letters back, I did not get any kind of reaction at all, so you can keep doing that for a while but there comes a moment when you just don't feel like writing one more letter. Then all you do is call, and as soon as they hear how old you are, they say something like: Don't call us, we'll call you, and of course you don't hear anything or maybe you get a form letter saying the vacancy has been filled. And it just keeps getting worse and worse. In the beginning I did it every day, I would apply for maybe twenty or thirty jobs a month, but that doesn't go on forever because you keep getting the same reaction. You lose your enthusiasm. Now I do it sporadically. . . (40-year-old man, partner and children, 7 years unemployed).

Resignation is an adapting mechanism, a form of strategic behavior. In a study conducted among young working-class people in northeast England, behavior of this kind was viewed as a "long-term strategy" (Coffield et al. 1986:80). This corresponds with the ideas of American authors who have interpreted the behavior and aspirations of the poor in America, including long-term unemployed people, as realistic adaptations to situations of restricted possibilities (Rodman 1963, Liebow 1967, Valentine 1968). The social costs of continuing to aspire to a working career gradually became too high. Time after time, the self-esteem of the unemployed had to endure rejections and humiliating experiences. For this group, rather drastic modifications had to be made in the dominant societal norm of striving for paid employment—not because they rejected the idea of work or because they didn't want a job, but because they had to learn to live with the fact that they no longer had any prospect of a working career. In view of their labor market position, an attitude of this kind is certainly not unrealistic. The awareness of how hopeless one's situation is eventually changes the aim of maximizing the chance of a job into the aim of minimizing the chance of social injury.

This change in goals can be justified and accounted for in a number of ways. Not everyone comes right out and admits that he or she has no prospect of ever finding another job. In an effort to save face, people sometimes say they would only consider a job that met with relatively high requirements. It would have to be a permanent, well-paid job in the same line of work as their former position (see Table VII). They use these relatively high demands to justify to the outside world why they have had so little success in the labor market. This does not necessarily mean the compromises they are willing to make to get a job should not be taken seriously. All it means is that these rationalizations can be observed.

In *Sour Grapes, Studies in the Subversion of Rationality* (1985), Jon Elster discussed the tendency of individuals to adapt their aspirations to their possibilities. He called it "adaptive preference formation." The term "sour grapes" refers to Aesop's fable "The Fox and the Grapes." Some of the reactions on the part of the long-term unemployed can be viewed as "adaptive preference formation." This pertains in particular to their refusal to make any compromises when it comes to their demands: "I could get a job if I wanted, but it would be underpaid or temporary or the work would be too dirty." In the framework of maximizing one's chance of a job, this attitude would be irrational, but in view of the new goal of minimizing the chance of social injury, it is far less irrational. This type of reaction is a way to make the situation more bearable and not to lose one's self-respect. Anyone who expects the long-term unemployed to keep relishing the sour grapes of constant rejection on the labor market has very little insight into their need to maintain their self esteem.

Time

In Chapter 6, we described how different types of unemployed people spent and perceived time. The picture presented there was far more differentiated than in the Marienthal study. The authors noted that "the workers of Marienthal have lost the material and moral incentives to make use of their time. Now that they are no longer under any pressure, they undertake nothing new and drift gradually out of an ordered existence into one that is undisciplined and empty" (Jahoda et al. 1972:66). The quote expresses a normative and deterministic view. The notion, however, that this drift always takes place is one we have our doubts about.

In Western society, the conception of time is closely linked to work. In literature on the functions of work, numerous references are made to three elements related to time structuring and time orientation: work structures the day, work is a binding activity, and work gives people a point of orientation in life. In the literature on unemployment, the other side of the coin is discussed: people who have lost their jobs get lost in time and lose their social orientation. Regarding the way the long-term unemployed spend their time, the same paradox keeps coming up: the unlimited quantity of leisure time keeps them from making good use of it (Jahoda 1987). The results of our study confirmed and refuted the time paradox. There were respondents who made excellent use of their leisure time, but there were also those who did not know what to do with their time, especially the ritualists and the retreatists. Here, we examine how this category of unemployed people spent their time. The reason for this special attention is that the time orientation of this group, which coincides with the classic picture of the long-term unemployed, is often cited as a specific cultural feature, which is then taken to be responsible for the fact that the unemployed are not able to take advantage of the opportunities there are in the labor market (Banfield 1974).

Killing Time

In the first instance, it would seem as if the ways the unemployed who did not know what to do with their time actually spent it were rather irrational. They would sleep late, hang around on the street, go window shopping and watch television, all activities that did not offer much of a prospect for a successful comeback in the job circuit. Nonetheless, the behavior of this group was understandable. Boredom was most prevalent among the weakest groups in the labor market, particularly among the people who had been out of work for extremely long periods of time, the people of foreign descent and the people with the lowest educational levels.

The most vulnerable groups had less access to networks of friends and were not active in the informal sector. Their social position greatly affected the way they spent their time. Their unfavorable financial position restricted their participation in leisure time activities, most of which cost money. Their isolated social position also meant there were fewer meaningful activities open to them. Previously relevant time classifications gradually became meaningless. People structurally excluded from the labor market do not have to get up at seven o'clock in the morning or draw a distinction between weekdays and weekends. Other time classifications become more meaningful, such as "television time," "outdoor time in the summer," "indoor time in the winter," "time for the check to come," and for some of them "time for methadon."[3] The following fragments are illustrative.

> It's okay in the summer. Then you go do some work on the house outside and in the garden. But in the winter when the days get shorter, that's when it gets hard. Then you just sit indoors all the time (44-year-old man, partner and children, 1 year unemployed).

> Watching television takes up a lot of my time. If we get bored then we play games or watch something on television (30-year-old woman, partner, no children, 4 years unemployed).

> I have been in a methadon program for about four years now. At eleven o'clock in the morning, I have to go get my methadon. I have to be on time, otherwise I don't get anything. So I have to get up on time. That makes it easier to keep a certain kind of rhythm (31-year-old man, single, 12 years unemployed).

Sorokin and Merton once defined social time or experienced time as the relation between meaningful activities (Sorokin and Merton 1937). In the cases of many of our respondents, loss of jobs this also meant a sharp fall in the quantity of their meaningful activities and an essential change in their nature. This resulted in an altered time orientation. In its most extreme form, this manifested itself in a much slower rhythm and a time perception in which the usual time units had lost their meaning.

> For me there isn't any time, no real strict time. For me, it is always Sunday, you might say (46-year-old man, single, 6 years unemployed).

> When I had a job, the weekend was the end of the week. Two days at home. But now we just kind of fool around all day long. There isn't really any beginning and end of the week (42-year-old man, partner and children, 6 years unemployed).

These interview fragments indicate a time perspective which has "gone back to a more primitive, less differentiated experience of time. The new circumstances no longer fit an established time schedule. A life that is poorer in demands and activities has gradually begun to develop on a timetable that is correspondingly poor" (Jahoda et al. 1972:77). The periods without meaningful activities tended to go by without a schedule to define when they started or finished. This also applied to the respondents in the category who did not know what to do with their time and were consequently bored. "Too much time" mainly meant too few meaningful activities. Thus time also involved a problem of scarcity. The activities they could engage in were stretched out to last as long as possible, and the intervals between them were filled up with doing nothing or killing time. The time strategies our respondents used were realistic reactions to a scarcity of meaningful activities. A few examples can illustrate this point.

You go to bed as late as you can, two, three o'clock at night, and that way you get up later in the morning so that the day is shorter. Certainly in the winter, you make a real effort to do this (32-year-old man, partner no children, 6 years unemployed).

I go shopping every day. I never buy enough for the whole week. Whatever I need, I go out and get every day (43-year-old woman, single, 5 years unemployed).

You spend enormous amounts of time reading the paper, doing little things around the house. You postpone things, why do it now, you might as well do it later. Sometimes you take longer doing something than you really have to. Consciously or unconsciously. Time isn't the same as what it used to be (29-year-old man, single, 6 years unemployed).

The Time Horizon

Another characteristic element of the time perception of some long-term unemployed groups is the disappearance of a long-term perspective. People in various classes in society tend to differ in the extent to which they focus on the future. There is a difference between the long-term future orientation characteristic of the middle classes and the short-term future orientation characteristic of the lower classes (Rubin 1976, MacLeod 1987). If people can only perceive the future in terms of uncertainty and insecurity, then living from one day to the next is a rational course of action. This short-term rationality was evident in the unstable employment histories of some of the respondents. When they lost their jobs, the short-term perspective became even shorter: the future became tomorrow.

No, I don't look ahead. It's too scary. We'll just wait and see (49-year-old man, multi-family household, 6 years unemployed).

I am the kind of guy who lives from one day to the next. If it isn't here today, then it will be here tomorrow. And that is the kind of attitude I go through life with, you know. There are a lot of people who try and build something up in their life, but what can you build up on welfare? (27-year-old man, partner no children, 12 years unemployed).

The short-term orientation of the poor and the unemployed has often been discussed in connection with the absence of rational planning. Banfield's book *The Unheavenly City Revisited* (1974) is interesting in this respect. In the following passage, he commented on the time perception of people imprisoned in a culture of the lowest class: "The lower-class individual lives from moment to moment.

If he has any awareness of a future, it is of something fixed, fated, beyond his control: things happen to him, he does not make them happen. Impulse governs his behavior, either because he cannot discipline himself to sacrifice a present for a future satisfaction or because he has no sense of the future. He is therefore radically improvident: whatever he cannot consume immediately he considers valueless" (Banfield 1974:61).

If there is no clear picture of the future, then why bother planning for it? The time orientation of the long-term unemployed has nothing to do with mental features; it is related instead to the absence of a future perspective and the dearth of socially meaningful activities. The resigned category of unemployed (especially the retreatists) no longer had the luxury of being able to think ahead. They adapted their behavior to the possibilities they had. These adaptations manifested themselves in an altered time perception and specific time strategies such as doing nothing or killing time. They lived in a social time that was functional for them.

Money

Much as the Marienthal study was among the first to focus on the social consequences of mass unemployment, *The Poor Pay More* (1963) by Caplovitz was among the first to provide insight into the consumer patterns of low-income groups in America. However, it had the same shortcoming as so many publications about poverty and unemployment. The consumer customs of the low-income groups were explained on the basis of their inability to cope with money and consumer problems in a more rational way. Caplovitz distinguished three "coping patterns" in the low-income groups: apathy (nothing was done), ignorance (people did not know their rights) and ineffectiveness (whatever they did do failed to have any effect). It was their cultural traditionalism that was mainly responsible, he felt, for the inability evident in these three coping patterns. This explanation was applied particularly to newcomers such as Puerto Ricans and blacks from the South, who were thought to have a traditional consumer pattern and to thus be unable to cope with the impersonal but cheap department stores that were outside the neighborhood. These newcomers had a marked preference for personal contact with shopkeepers in the immediate vicinity and for local creditors who personalized their services. Thus they fell into the hands of unscrupulous businessmen who gave them low quality and high interest rates: "The Poor Pay More."

In the same study, paths were opened to a different approach to this issue of how people cope with money. It was noted that the consumer behavior of low-income groups might sometimes be rational indeed: "interpretations in terms of adaptive rationality cannot be ignored. Families who buy food at small groceries may do so in part because they feel more at home with the storekeeper; but it is also true that they can get credit there which is not available at the supermarket. And the same pervasive need for credit may explain why some shop for durables only in the neighborhood" (Caplovitz 1963:11). In other words, they did not shop at the store on the corner for traditional reasons but for rational ones. The neighborhood storekeepers were willing to let them buy now and pay later.

Caplovitz also made it clear that for the low-income groups, "the scope of shopping" was very limited and subject to financial obstacles. There were fewer opportunities to go shopping in the large stores outside the neighborhood where prices were cheaper. People who had to make do with a low income had to buy by the day and pay their bills by the month, even if this meant they had to pay more. The income of the poor was too low to allow for bulk buying or immediate payment. Caplovitz also noted that although people who lived on welfare did not stand a chance of getting credit through the regular channels, they could buy durable goods on the informal consumer market. These observations bear witness to far more realistic insight than the explanations in terms of traditionalism. This is illustrated by the following two quotes:

> There is a guy like that across the street here and he is very easy about it. He writes these things down, you know. It happens often enough, if we haven't got the money. Then we just have him write it all down (27-year-old man, partner, no children, 12 years unemployed).

> If I didn't have Wehkamp [a mail order company], I don't know what I would do. Because the Welfare Department won't let you buy a rug. And they certainly won't let you just go out and buy a couch. So this is the only way. How else could I do it? And they can trust me to pay the installments on time, down to the very last penny. Never any problems, I make sure it goes smoothly. Wehkamp is a godsend. Some people think it isn't smart. But to me, it is the best there is. You do pay a lot of interest, but at least it's a way to buy things (30-year-old man, partner and children, 14 years unemployed).

We now focus on two controversial ways that people can expand their income: by going into debt and by manipulating the Welfare system. These are strategies for temporarily enlarging the spending options or increasing the income on a more permanent basis.

Problem Debts

Almost half the respondents had some debts. Going into debt was thus one of the main strategies of people on welfare for making ends meet. Other recent research also illustrated that approximately half the households on the national poverty line borrowed money (Oude Engberink 1984 and 1987). It is estimated that more than a third of these households had what could be called "problem debts." This meant their debt situation was such that they could no longer meet with the financial obligations they had incurred. Problem debt situations occurred mainly in households that were dependent on welfare. This is a conclusion that can not be stressed emphatically enough: the less money people have, the more likely they are to have problem debts. In addition, the following relevant factors have been noted in the literature: (1) young couples with children have relatively numerous debts; (2) debtors often have various debt relations and tend to find their way to the less common and the less critical creditors such as the municipal electricity board, the city credit bank, private landlords, financing companies, mail order companies and the Welfare Department itself; (3) mismanagement and poor financial management can be noted on the part of some of the debtors. The third point touches on notions of irrationality in the behavior of people who are dependent on welfare. Going into debt could be attributed to personal shortcomings. In a Rotterdam report, in 20 percent of the cases mismanagement was cited as the main cause of problem debts (Van Hulst 1987). Based on this definition of the problem, it is obvious that government intervention would be called for. People who are deeply in debt should be given special training courses and budget counseling. Diametrically opposed to this view is the question of the rationality of going into debt. The mismanagement or irresponsible spending pattern of people who are dependent on welfare is often an attempt to keep up with the rest of the consuming world and to meet with certain obligations, for example, to their children. Consumer goods have undeniable social functions, and anyone who does not have a certain something—whether it is a telephone, a television, candy, a bottle of whiskey, a car or a pair of Nikes—is apt to be excluded from a social framework one might want very much to be part of. People who are dependent on welfare are no more and no less the victims of this consumer industry than the high-income groups. Going into debt is a rational choice. It is a choice between social participation and social exclusion. In this light, it is easy to account for the fact that it was mainly young people and families with children who went into debt. Sometimes risky purchases were made in an effort to avoid being ostracized. The following quote illustrates that although unemployed young people want to invest in social contacts and relations, their options are limited (Coffield et al. 1986).

> It is often the same every single day. I sit around the house and if I have got a little bit of money then I go to the café or I go watch something on the VCR at someone's house. A lot of my friends hang out at Café Istanbul. We talk about work, we keep each other informed. If you have got money, you can go out. But if you go out with a Dutch girl, it costs you a good hundred guilders. Then you have to borrow some money from your friends (24-year-old man, multi-family household, 5 years unemployed).

The rationality of going into debt was expressed in the debt relations the respondents maintained. They had devoted quite a bit of thought to the risks involved. By failing to pay the rent and the electricity bill, borrowing money from the Welfare Department and buying goods from mail order companies, they could spend more on other things. The immediate consequences of these strategies and transactions remained rather limited. In Rotterdam, for example, it was quite some time before any action was taken against people who had not paid their rent or electricity bills. The results of the Rotterdam Budget Counseling Project showed that 75 percent of the participating households had unpaid electricity bills and 50 percent were behind on the rent (Van Hulst 1987). The average rent debt was 3,200 guilders ($1,600) and the average electricity debt was 3,700 guilders

($1,750), in other words most of these people had not paid their rent or electricity bills in more than a year. They calculated the risks in advance and knew the risks would be limited. It was only in few cases that even sizeable debts meant they would be evicted or have the electricity shut off. In most cases, arrangements were made to have the debts paid off in installments.

> There are some things you deliberately do not pay for now and then. You start to take advantage of things. Gas and electricity for example. You would know that you hadn't paid the bill for six or seven months. Once we didn't pay the rent for more than a year. It was up to more than a thousand guilders that we owed. If we hadn't paid in the end, we would have been out on the street. We have paid it all off now. But me, I can always fall back on my parents. So you can take that risk because you know that they will always help you make some kind of arrangement (32-year-old man, partner, no children, 6 years unemployed).

Calculating Behavior

It was noted in Chapters 4 and 8 that the calculating unemployed took advantage of the state by manipulating the welfare system. They were willing to take risks in order to enlarge their incomes. This kind of behavior was particularly widespread in Rotterdam. The most common strategic arrangements pertained to relations with partners or other members of the household. Either fictitiously or in reality, these relations could be adapted to meet with the requirements of the government agency involved.

> I have got a bit of a problem in that although I do want to live with my boyfriend, I am on welfare and I don't want to be financially dependent on someone else . . . When I was getting Unemployment Insurance, we were living together, but when that stopped and I started getting my Welfare I said to my boyfriend "You'll have to move out now." Because I can not lie. So just for the Welfare Department, we don't live together any more. Actually it is more fiction than fact. My boyfriend lives here in the neighborhood and he is here a lot of the time (31-year-old woman, no partner, one child, 3 years unemployed).

> If I were registered as living with my girlfriend, it would cost her quite a bit of money. Even though we do have a very intimate relationship, when it comes to the salary she earns, she says, "I don't love you enough to sacrifice that much of my income for you." So when I lost my job, as far as the records are concerned I moved back to live with my parents (30-year-old man, lives with parents, 3 years unemployed).

Other strategies included finishing one's education on welfare rather than on a scholarship and taking advantage of the individualization principle of the Welfare Department.[4] The various strategies could be viewed partially as short-term and partially as long-term investments. The future focus of various categories of unemployed people were evident in the strategic behavior they chose. Middle-class students who completed the university on welfare were simply taking advantage of the fact that their benefits were higher than a scholarship and didn't have to be paid back, and were thus investing in their own future.

The strategies implied different degrees of risk. It was relatively easy to conceal the fact that two people were living together and thus no longer had the right to two separate benefits, or to one income and one complete benefit, just as it was not difficult to go to school while receiving welfare. Welfare Department social workers tended to turn a blind eye to both of these forms of fraud. Getting a divorce in order to receive two benefits (pseudo-divorce) meant much more of a risk. The same held true of having a separate mailing address or working off the books while receiving welfare. A small and specific group of respondents engaged in these two strategies. They were long-term unemployed people with certain qualities and networks that enabled them to operate efficiently in the informal sector. Relatively speaking, they were willing to take larger risks that they hoped would lead to greater profits.

BOUNDED RATIONALITY

In the previous sections, we discussed the rationality of the behavior of the long-term unemployed. Moonlighting, becoming resigned to the unemployment situation, killing time, going into debt, making strategic use of the welfare system —these were all viewed as rational solutions to the problems they had to cope with. Nonetheless, Chapter 8 made it clear that these strategies were not evenly distributed over the research locations. If we focus on moonlighting and going into debt and compare the respondents in Rotterdam with those in Enschede, we see that these two strategies were more prevalent in Rotterdam than in Enschede (Tables 9.1 and 9.2).

In order to explain the differences between the two locations, we need to know more about the influence of the social environments on the choices the individual respondents made. If we draw a *general* comparison between the two locations

TABLE 9.1 Earnings From Informal Labor in Het Nieuwe Westen (Rotterdam) and Stadsveld/Pathmos (Enschede) (in percentages)

	Het Nieuwe Westen	*Stadsveld/Pathmos*
Yes	19	16
occasionally	3	13
regularly	16	3
No	81	84
Total	100	100
N	86	77

TABLE 9.2 Debts in Het Nieuwe Westen (Rotterdam) and Stadsveld/Pathmos (Enschede) (in percentages)

	Het Nieuwe Westen	*Stadsveld/Pathmos*
No Debts	41	56
One Debt	33	41
More than one Debt	26	3
Total	100	100
N	85	88

we see two different social organizational forms that imposed different restrictions on the behavior of individuals. Pathmos in Enschede still exhibited the features of a small, close-knit social network. It was a homogeneous neighborhood rooted in what had once been a textile-industry community. Sixty percent of the respondents were part of a conformist culture of unemployment, and only 9 percent could be said to be part of an individualistic one (Table 8.1). Obeying the rules and refraining from becoming dependent were dominant values in this neighborhood.

Het Nieuwe Westen in Rotterdam was a multicultural neighborhood where many people lived in looser, more anonymous settings. Unlike the case in Enschede, social control had been greatly reduced in large parts of the neighborhood. The Enschede neighborhood had a more homogeneous and egalitarian structure. Anyone who violated the rules was ostracized. The strong social control was expressed in the risk perception regarding working off the books: when they were asked why they did not work unofficially, 65 percent of the respondents in Enschede said it involved too much of a risk. Only 45 percent of the respondents in Rotterdam felt this way. In Rotterdam the percentage of respondents who were part of a conformist culture was the same as the percentage who were part of an individualistic one, namely 34 percent (Table 8.1). The enterprising and calculating reactions described here were observed mainly on the part of the Rotterdam respondents. The different ways of life or cultures were what bounded the rationality. As Thompson et al. wrote, "Rather than counterpoising rationality and irrationality, we refer to competing social definitions of what will count as rational. No act can be classified as in and of itself rational or irrational. What is rational depends on the social or institutional setting within which the act is embedded. Acts that are rational from the perspective of one way of life may be the height of irrationality from the perspective of a competing way of life" (Thompson et al. 1990:22-23).

If we apply this line of reasoning to our study, we see that working informally or making strategic use of the welfare system was "irrational" to most of the unemployed in Enschede but "rational" to many of them in Rotterdam. Unlike the case in Enschede, giving a neighbor a helping hand was "irrational" in Rotterdam because this kind of social investment was not likely to pay off in an individualistic culture of unemployment. As to the question of debts, despite the fact that many of the unemployed people in Enschede lived under a strict financial regime because they were responsible for a family with children, we see that debt accumulation occurred much less frequently in Enschede than in Rotterdam (Table 9.2). The low debt accumulation level can be explained by the relatively close-knit social structure. People could more easily fall back on others for help. In addition, there was wider social correction regarding excessive conspicuous consumption. These examples make it clear that the strategic behavior of the unemployed was influenced by moral considerations that can differ from one culture to the next.

HOMO CALCULANS AND HOMO HONORIS

The world of the long-term unemployed is often judged by the moral standards of the working middle classes. The unemployed are expected to behave in accordance with the norms and values of the middle classes, to work hard, to apply for jobs in the formal economy, not to be lazy, to take initiative and to improve their skills. Viewed from these standards, the behavior described in our study might sometimes be "irrational." In this chapter we described and interpreted the behavior patterns by way of a conceptual apparatus that was not founded on the models often tacitly accepted by the active middle classes or the authorities. Viewed from this cultural theory perspective, the unemployed did indeed turn out to be rational problem-solvers who were quite sensitive where matters of self-esteem and maintaining their social relations were involved.

Caution is called for in using such terms as apathy, ignorance and irresponsibility to describe the behavior of the unemployed. These terms are indicative of the assumed irrationality of their behavior. Unemployed people are assumed to belong to a culture in which rational calculations fail to play any role whatsoever and in which people act impulsively. In opposition to this view, this chapter has focused on the strategic behavior of the long-term unemployed. Becoming resigned to a jobless life, killing time, moonlighting, calculating behavior and going into debt have all been described as strategies that one might find morally reprehensible but are certainly not irrational.

Overlapping and interrelated economic and cultural factors shape and influence the tactics the long-term unemployed use to attain certain goals. In day-to-day reality, it is not only the economic costs and profits that count, but the social ones as well. Keeping one's self-respect, participating in social and cultural activities and having a certain status within the community are all things that count. A long-term unemployed individual is also a *homo honoris* who wants to keep his self-esteem and protect himself from the humiliation and shame that can result from long-term unemployment and from ostracism and isolation. There are nonetheless unemployed individuals who coincide with the prototype of the "homo calculans," such as the enterprising and the calculating categories. In addition, there are other types of unemployed individuals who make rational calculations that are not informed by any economic usefulness.

We hope this interpretation model will help policy-makers see the normal aspects in the behavioral reactions of the long-term unemployed, thus making it easier to take these aspects into consideration. People in situations of dependence have a normal sense of pride and honor that are often overlooked in policy studies, and these feelings should be taken into consideration. From the perspective of the unemployed people themselves, action programs could then be better adapted to their social conditions and attitudes.

NOTES

1. See Donald W. Tiffany, James R. Cowan, and Phyllis M. Tiffany, *The Unemployed: A Socio-psychological Portrait*, Englewood Cliffs N.J., 1970.; John Hayes and Peter Nutman, *Understanding the Unemployed: Psychological Effects of Unemployment*, London/New York: Tavistock 1981.; N. T. Feather, *The Psychological Impact of Unemployment*, New York: Springer Verlag, 1990.

2. This line of reasoning is based in part on the book by Samuel L. Popkin: *The Rational Peasant: The Political Economy of Rural Society in Vietnam*, Berkeley: The University of California Press, 1979., and the article by Alejandro Portes, "Rationality in the Slum: An Essay on Interpretive Sociology", in: *Comparative Studies in Society and History*, Vol. 14 (3) 1972, 268-286.

3. Chemical drug provided by municipal health agencies to heroin addicts in an effort to decriminalize them and to keep them under surveillance.

4. The Welfare Department has an "individualization principle". On the basis of this key National Assistance Act principle, households can receive extra funds if and when their specific situation calls for it.

CHAPTER 10

A Profile of
Urban Poverty

In Chapter 8, cultural theory was used to distinguish various types of unemployed people and cultures of unemployment in Dutch inner cities. It was thus demonstrated that behind a seemingly unambiguous policy classification such as "the long-term unemployed," in fact a heterogeneous reality is concealed. The long-term unemployed can be sub-classified not only by ethnic background, age, the length of time they have been out of a job and so forth, but also by the ways they cope with the triad of unemployment problems (work, time and money) and the ways they perceive their position in society and justify their strategies. The various differences were described on the basis of four cultures of unemployment.

In this chapter, the usefulness of cultural theory will be demonstrated for the analysis of the heterogeneity of urban unemployment and poverty in the United States. Since the majority of the American poor do work, we do not confine ourselves to the situation of the unemployed, but also include that of the working poor in the analysis (see Ellwood 1988). We focus on the social worlds of unemployed and poor Americans who live in areas where the poverty rate is high. In America, using the concept of culture in relation to poverty and unemployment is often interpreted as a form of "blaming the victim," which is why we examine the "culture of poverty" thesis here. After all, the culture of poverty theme does bear a conceptual resemblance to the cultures of unemployment discussed here. We shall then apply cultural theory to various ethnographic studies. Based on these applications, we try to illustrate the importance of cultural theory in contemporary debates on the urban underclass and the unintended consequences of social policy.

In the next section we give a brief sketch of the American welfare system. Our study has shown that some of the behavioral reactions of the long-term unemployed can be properly understood only against the background of a highly developed social security system in combination with a weakly developed activating labor market policy. Comparable conclusions have been drawn in America, where social policies are sometimes felt to have a suction effect and to contribute to the perpetuation of poverty and welfare dependency (Murray 1984). Other authors feel that exactly the opposite is true and hold the lack of effective social policies responsible for the continuation of poverty and welfare dependency (Wilson 1987). At the end of this chapter, we refer to the Murray Paradox as we elaborate on our own position. This paradox assumes that Murray's hypothesis on the perverse effects of welfare policy has some relevance for highly developed welfare states but has very little, if any, significance for the American semi-welfare state for which it was initially designed.[1]

SOME NOTES ON THE AMERICAN WELFARE SYSTEM

In Chapter 1, the development of the Dutch welfare state was briefly described. Ellwood formulated a comparable analysis of the development of the American welfare system. He distinguished three periods: the foundation (1930-1960), the take-off (1960-1976) and the retrenchment (1976-1987). In the foundation period, the basic structure of the social welfare system was formed. "The mission was clear: help only those who cannot work through no fault of their own. Protection was offered at three levels: Social Security, employment-related benefits and means-tested benefits" (Ellwood 1988:27). Social Security is by far the major program and mainly covers people with a working past, especially the elderly and the disabled. It is a relatively universal program. Welfare has not been developed to any sizable extent. It mainly pertains to selective means-tested programs for the benefit of specific groups, most specifically single mothers. During the take-off period, there was a rise in expenditures for Social Security and employment-related benefits. In addition, more was invested in means-tested programs (e.g. aid to Families with Dependent Children, or AFDC) to benefit the growing numbers of single mothers. In the framework of the War on Poverty and the Great Society, more job training, educational and neighborhood service programs were developed to improve the position of vulnerable groups. During the retrenchment period, it was mainly these programs and the means-tested programs that were affected by budget cuts. Eligibility criteria were made stricter and benefits were no longer adjusted to the inflation rate. This had widespread repercussions for the still growing group of single mothers living on AFDC benefits, "so, in the next decade in most states, their real value per family fell by 30-50 percent" (Ellwood 1988:40). In the period from 1976 to 1984, the number of poor people rose from 25 million to 34 million. In the following years, poverty mushroomed mainly in the central cities (Peterson 1991).

Anyone who examines the development of the American welfare system cannot help but conclude that its dimensions have always been restricted. Specific groups benefit from the system, but there are also large groups who remain, at least in part, outside the system, such as working two-parent families, single people and couples without children. People who have been in a position to safeguard themselves with stable and decent jobs do have a certain extent of security, but people who have hardly been able to do so, if at all, have little choice but to rely on the support of their relatives and on means-tested programs.

Welfare is largely in-kind rather than in-cash. The range of welfare programs is restricted, and only certain categories of "deserving" candidates are eligible for them. In addition, the administration and implementation of welfare are organized by state and local governments, and there is no national minimum benefit level. This means enormous state-to-state differences in the benefit levels. This is why Piven and Cloward preferred to refer to the United States as a "semi-welfare state" (Piven and Cloward 1982). Esping-Andersen classified it as a "liberal welfare state," in which the benefit level is relatively low. Facilities are often income-dependent and quite modest. In order not to infringe on the functioning of the free market, social rights to housing, education, income and work are restricted (Esping-Andersen 1990). The liberal system is characterized not only by the lack of facilities and the low benefit level, but also by the production of specific symbols and systems of regulation. These symbols pertain to the primacy of the work ethic and the emphasis on individual responsibility. The system of regulation pertains to the classification of deserving and undeserving poor and the moral degrading and disciplining of people who are dependent on welfare. Handler and Hasenfeld wrote: "While the programs themselves are myth and ceremony, the consequences for the undeserving poor are concrete and serious. Especially today, with the increase in eligibility requirements, verifications, quality control, and work requirements, those who are admitted to welfare are subject to suspicion, humiliation, stigmatization, and various forms of harassment" (Handler and Hasenfeld 1991:42).

The development of the American welfare state differs significantly from the Dutch (see Chapter 1). The transformation from a hierarchical-authoritarian social environment to an individualized social environment has not taken place. According to the group/grid model, the American welfare state has always been characterized by relatively weak group and weak grid. This is evident in the characteristics of the American welfare state: limited social security programs, economic opportunity and the associated concern for individual and local responsibility (Marmor et al. 1990). The matching culture has been called "competitive individualism" (Wildavsky 1982:47).[2] This market-oriented individualism, however, is different from the cultural individualism in the Netherlands, which stems from a highly developed welfare state in which individuals are taken care of "from the cradle to the grave." Unlike the Dutch individualist, the American individualist is not protected by a comprehensive welfare state. Poor people who cannot survive in such a competitive and hard environment are in danger of ending up in a position of "minimum choice and maximum isolation" (Douglas and Isherwood 1979: 43). What that means will come up in our discussion of several of ethnographic studies.

These studies were conducted during the take-off and retrenchment periods. In the following section, we shall examine the debate on the culture of poverty, a debate that played a central role during the take-off period. This was when poverty was rediscovered and specific programs were designed to combat it during the War on Poverty. Theories on a culture of poverty constituted a major legitimation for job training and educational programs designed to improve and alter the individual characteristics of the poor. Analyzing the debate on the culture of poverty enables us to more acutely address the relevance of a cultural analysis. Discussions on the emergence of an urban underclass and the perverse effects of official social policies took place mainly in the retrenchment period, a period Katz referred to as the War on Welfare (Katz 1986 and 1989).

THE CULTURE OF POVERTY AND
THE RELEVANCE OF CULTURE

Based on various studies among the urban poor of Mexico and Puerto Rico, Oscar Lewis introduced the notion of a "culture of poverty" (Lewis 1959, 1961, 1966). A culture of poverty emerges in the event of long-term exposure to economic deprivation. What Lewis meant by "long-term" bears very little similarity to present-day policy classifications, where it usually refers to one, two or three-year periods of unemployment or welfare dependence. Lewis uses "long-term" to refer to poverty that goes from one generation to the next. In an effort to ward off the perils of a life without security, the poor adjust their values, aspirations and local institutions accordingly. Over time, these institutionalized ways of thinking, acting and interacting develop a relative autonomy vis-à-vis the social circumstances that produced them. The elimination of these circumstances does not necessarily mean that the cultural patterns will immediately disappear as well. The most important features of a culture of poverty are inadequate participation in the dominant institutions of a society; the disintegration of the residential environment;, the crumbling of family units; and feelings of dependence, inferiority and fatalism. The culture of poverty makes escape from poverty impossible, even if the circumstances would allow it. What we are talking about here is in essence the perpetual motion of poverty. The ideas first conceived by Lewis, and even more so the imprudent application of these ideas, have been heatedly refuted (see Valentine 1968 and Ryan 1971). Katz (1989) cited the following points of criticism:

- No systematic thought has been focused on the various dimensions in a culture of poverty. No clear distinction is drawn between behavior and personality features.
- Assumptions about the mechanisms perpetuating a culture of poverty are inadequate because they assume the primacy of socialization. Various competing

explanations are equally feasible, such as the situational approach based on adaptations of individuals to societal restrictions.

* The culture of poverty thesis has a tautological structure. Pathological behavior leads to poverty, which causes pathological behavior. No clear distinctions are drawn between the causes and the symptoms of poverty.
* The relations between subcultures, social institutions and social structures remain unspecified.
* The culture of poverty is an ethno-centric idea. Middle-class standards are applied to low-income groups.
* The culture of poverty thesis has a weak empirical basis. It is difficult to generalize specific case studies and apply the conclusions to other groups and situations. Much of the culture of poverty research is focused on families and too easily applies the conclusions to other social situations.
* Culture of poverty research largely lacks a developmental perspective. This is why it is not possible to observe changes in the way the poor think and act.

The criticism also pertained to the presumed uniqueness of the culture of poverty. The poor differ far less from the rest of society than Lewis presumed. Their behavior should be viewed as a reaction to situational constraints, such as a position in the labor market with no prospects whatsoever, a low income and an isolated position in society. This is what is referred to as the situational approach. The poor have values and norms comparable to those of the middle class, but they do not have the channels or instruments to achieve them (see Valentine 1968 and Liebow 1967). Once a number of situational restrictions have been eliminated, however, there is no culture of poverty to keep the poor from benefiting from it (Gans 1977).

Finally, there is the criticism pertaining to the political exploitation of the very concept of a culture of poverty. Leeds reproached Lewis for providing the ideological legitimation at the time of the War on Poverty for situating the cause of poverty among the poor themselves rather than in the socio-economic structure (Leeds 1971). Lewis ignored reproaches of this kind. He acknowledged that the most important cause of poverty lies in the socio-economic structure of a society, but added: "However, this is not the only reason. The subculture develops mechanisms that tend to perpetuate it, especially as to the world view, aspirations, and the character of the children who grow up in it" (Lewis 1968:20). Lewis thus clearly continued to hold that a culture of poverty can become so deeply embedded in people themselves that it plays a role in the continuation of poverty.

The Relevance of the Cultural Factor

Whatever criticism there might be of the culture of poverty thesis, there are still authors who advocate focusing on the cultural dimensions of poverty. The anthropological argument for devoting attention to the cultural factor was formulated by Hannerz. In his study entitled *Soulside* (1969), he advanced a "soft culture concept." Cultural transference takes place by way of contextual learning processes and the reproduction of specific behavior patterns. This is how youngsters in a ghetto learn a specific idiom and acquire the behavior pattern of the relevant peer groups outside as well as inside the ghetto. A cultural concept based solely on the generational transference of fixed norms overlooks the more subtle transference of ghetto-specific behavior and ignores the changes that take place within the ghetto in relation to society as a whole.

The relevance of the cultural factor is also evident in studies on job training programs for the long-term unemployed, particularly where attention is focused on the problematic interaction between the unemployed and instructors or employment officers.[3] Anderson (1990b) made specific mention of the clash between the content and design of training programs and the street culture of the hard-core unemployed. There is a clear discrepancy between street-oriented values and school-oriented values. Anderson was of the opinion that instructors ought to be more sensitive to the background and cultural problems of the hard-core unemployed.

The significance of the cultural factor was also evident in Wilson's influential study, *The Truly Disadvantaged* (1987). He made an effort to link the culture of poverty thesis to a structural analysis of poverty by way of the concept of social isolation: ". . . the concept of social isolation does not mean that cultural traits are irrelevant in understanding behavior in highly concentrated poverty areas: rather, it highlights the fact that culture is a response to social structural constraints and opportunities" (Wilson 1987:61). Wilson noted the growing concentration of vulnerable groups in high poverty areas. They have a weak labor-market attachment and no access to the dominant institutions and social networks of people with a stable job. The result is a perpetuation of unemployment, a rise in the number of female-headed households and an increase of informal survival strategies. In his presidential address to the American Sociological Association, Wilson presented a more detailed framework linking structural and cultural arguments. He explicated the micro-social effects of life in an environment where formal work no longer plays a prominent role. He noted the slow development of children who are unable to develop "disciplined habits associated with stable or steady employment" because they have no contact with people with stable jobs (Wilson 1991a:10). Referring to the Algerian study by Bourdieu (1965), he stressed the absence of a temporal framework for the organization of daily life due to the lack of steady employment. Stable work structures life and implies concrete aims and prospects for the future. Finally, Wilson noted the meaning of a crucial cultural mechanism, the development of feelings of "low perceived self-efficacy" as a result of long-term unemployment. People lose confidence and feel marginal and futile. These feelings are reinforced by the social environment and have a detrimental influence on the ghetto poor's life chances.

The concept of culture adhered to by Hannerz, Anderson and Wilson is less deterministic than the one held by Lewis. Hannerz wrote: "We have seen culture above all as providing adaptations and reactions to a given situation rather than as a completely autonomous determinant of behavior" (1969:193). Wilson's analysis differed on two major points from Lewis'. Wilson devoted more attention to macro-structural processes and made an effort to link structural and cultural arguments with his social isolation thesis and the self-efficacy theory. In his terms: "The psychological self-efficacy theory is used here not in isolation but in relation to the *structural problem of weak labor-force attachment* and the *cultural problem of the transmission of self and collective beliefs in the neighborhood*" (Wilson 1991a:11).

The Relevance of Cultural Theory

The group/grid model developed by Douglas and the further elaborations on it by Thompson et al. provide a useful tool for the reformulation of the culture of poverty debate in less emotional terms. The group/grid model combines the situational and the cultural approaches. It leaves room for the social context or social structure people are either part of or excluded from (the situational approach). It also focuses on the shared values, norms and beliefs and on the acts of individuals and how they legitimate them (the cultural approach). In *Cultural Theory* (1990), Thompson, Ellis and Wildavsky made the following observation: "In recent decades, the social sciences have witnessed a dissociation between studies of values, symbols, and ideologies and studies of social relations, modes of organizing, and institutions. Cultural studies proceed as if mental products were manufactured in an institutional vacuum, while studies of social relations ignore how people justify to themselves and others the way in which they live. One of the most important contributions to our sociocultural theory, we believe, is bringing these two aspects of human life together" (1990:21).

An ambitious feature of cultural theory is that it makes an effort to surmount the well-known dualisms between "action" and "structure" and between "order" and "change" as well as between "culture" and "structure." Cultural theory does not work from the assumption that there is a one-sided causal relation between social relations or institutions and cultural values. They are interdependent and intertwined. Douglas works from the notion of a "negotiating individual": an intentionally acting individual who is not completely dominated by the constraints of the social environment. Individuals are the product and the producers of the social environment or the institutions they are part of. This implies that social change is feasible. This change can be the result of the individual striving of citizens, but it can also be reinforced if the nature of the features of the social environment alters.

The ideas of Douglas, Ellis, Thompson and Wildavsky have been received with a certain amount of skepticism regarding their model of the "cultural composition of the world," more so than for their general points of departure. Like every classification model that reduces complex reality, it evokes questions and a certain amount of irritation (see Geertz 1987). Are there really only five viable ways of life (individualism, egalitarianism, hierarchy, fatalism and autonomy)? Thompson et al. have responded by arguing that in many cases, this limited number still doubles the existing theories on social organization. This is a reference to the great dichotomies described in classic works by Weber or Durkheim. Other questions largely pertain to the level of analysis (macro or micro), the fact that individuals can be part of various cultures, the exact status of the autonomous culture and the influence of macro-social and historical processes on the group and grid dimensions.

In this chapter, we work mainly with cultural theory and try to demonstrate that it can be used to illustrate the heterogeneity of poverty and unemployment. In the words of Thompson et al.: "How much behavior in a given domain can be explained by recourse to cultural theory is an empirical question that cannot be settled by fiat" (1990:273). In the second to last section, several limitations of the cultural theory are addressed.

CULTURAL THEORY AND
ETHNOGRAPHIC RESEARCH

In this section, cultural theory is applied to the world of the poor and the unemployed in the United States. Since this requires detailed knowledge of the social worlds of Americans, we shall analyze various ethnographic ghetto studies, the number of which is limited by practical considerations and by the space we have here. It is striking how few ethnographic or community studies have been conducted recently on the subject of poverty compared to the more quantitatively oriented ones. Many contemporary studies on the underclass still fall back on the works of Liebow, Hannerz, Stack and Anderson. Of course this is much to the credit of these authors, whose pioneering research broke new ground. It is lamentable, however, that the meticulous studies of such authors as Ellwood (1988) and Jencks (1992) have barely been complemented by new ethnographic material. Often in a rather perfunctory manner, the old ethnographic studies are still referred to. They constitute the ritual footnotes in the more quantitative analyses. The dearth of more recent ethnographic studies is all the more lamentable because of the drastic changes that have affected the situation in the ghettoes and the inner cities in the past two decades.

Ethnographic Studies: From
Tally's Corner to *Street Wise*

We refer to the following studies here: Elliot Liebow, *Tally's Corner* (1967); Ulf Hannerz, *Soulside* (1969); Elijah Anderson, *A Place on the Corner* (1978);

Jay MacLeod, *Ain't No Making It* (1987); and Elijah Anderson, *Street Wise* (1990a). We have selected these studies because they are widely known and because they present detailed pictures of the way the poor and the unemployed think and act and the social environment they are part of. All of these studies challenge the conventional notions on poverty.[4]

Elliot Liebow, Tally's Corner (1967)

In *Tally's Corner*, Liebow described the world of approximately twenty street corner men in a black neighborhood in Washington, D.C. The central action point was the street corner where the New Deal Carry-Out Shop was located. The field work was conducted in 1962 and 1963. Liebow formulated a comprehensive explanation for the attitudes and behavior of the street corner men, who constituted a small minority in the neighborhood. He referred in particular to the effect of the men's labor and income position on their self-images, and the consequences regarding the development and design of their social relations. Liebow made it clear that the street corner men were not able to earn enough money to support themselves and their wives and children if they had them. The only jobs they could get were the poorly paid ones at the very bottom of the employment ladder. The street corner men all had a history of poorly paid temporary jobs that did not enable them to support themselves or their families. Their experiences had led to feelings of marginality and low self-esteem and affected their aspiration level accordingly. Liebow suggested that the low aspiration level was an intergenerational phenomenon—not because a low aspiration level was passed on from generation to generation, but because the various generations were all exposed to the same experiences.

Due to their poor position in the labor market and their lack of prospects for the future, the street corner men came to view work from a particular perspective. Liebow noted in this connection that the street corner men did not attribute any less value to their jobs than the society around them; they were "dead end jobs" with no prospects for advancement. The reality of this evaluation had social and psychological repercussions, lowering the men's aspiration level and shortening their time perspective: "Living on the edge of both economic and psychological subsistence, the street corner man is obliged to expend all his resources on maintaining himself from moment to moment. . . He does so precisely because he is aware of the future and the hopelessness of it all" (pp. 65-66). The poor prospects for the future also affected their commitments to their families, friends and other people. Excessively strong ties led to responsibilities they could not fulfill. One example was marriage. Marriages were either not entered into or broke up because of the insecurity of their economic position. Liebow observed that the freedom of the street corner was one of the certainties the men would not abandon. The looser their ties with other people were, the better able they were to survive.

The temporary and vulnerable nature of their personal relations were typical of the position of men barely able to make any regular investments in them. As Liebow observed, "fully aware of his friends' limited resources and the demands of their self-interest, each person is ultimately prepared to look to himself alone. . . . Lacking depth in both past and present, friendship is easily uprooted by the tug of economic or psychological self-interest or by external forces acting against it" (pp. 180, 206-207).

The world the street corner men lived in bore a number of similarities to the culture of poverty described by Lewis. Liebow noted, however, that the social world of the street corner was not a self-generating or self-sustaining system with clear borders separating it from the rest of society. The world of the street corner men should be viewed instead as an integral component of society. This was manifest in the construction of a shadow system of values: "There, on the street corner, public fictions support a system of values which, together with the value system of society at large, make for a world of ambivalence. contradiction and paradox, where failures are rationalized into phantom successes and weaknesses magically transformed into strengths" (p. 214).

Ulf Hannerz, Soulside (1969)

In this study Hannerz tried to give a complete picture of the residents of the Winston Street neighborhood in Washington, D.C. Hannerz, who conducted his study from 1966 to 1968, started from the following assumption: "If there is a 'ghetto way of life' it consists of a web of intertwining but different individual and group life styles" (p. 12). Hannerz depicted the heterogeneity of the ghetto population by focusing on four life style types: mainstreamers, swingers, street families and street corner men.

The *mainstreamers* were "those who conform most closely to mainstream American assumptions about the 'normal life'" (p. 38). They belonged to the relatively stable working class. Most of them were married and lived in a nuclear family with a rather stable composition. Often the husband and wife both worked, so that these families were financially relatively well off. The mainstreamers had a strong work ethic and a feeling of superiority toward the other neighborhood residents. They viewed themselves as the "respectable" people of the neighborhood. They spent much of their leisure time with the members of their immediate family. The social networks they moved in were nonetheless relatively extensive: "Most of their friends are scattered over the town—particularly in the ghetto of course, but some friends have also moved to somewhat more affluent areas. Many households maintain contacts with friends, and in particular with kin, in the South or in other Northeastern cities, and on occasional weekends and holidays the family may drive for example to New York or Philadelphia for a visit, or receive visitors from such cities" (p. 40). Some mainstreamers went through a process of social advancement, which could result in their moving to a better neighborhood outside the ghetto.

The *swingers* were younger than the mainstreamers. Many of them were not yet responsible for a family. There was very little long-term unemployment among the swingers, though they might be temporarily out of a job. Unemployed swingers lived on the income earned by their girlfriends or wives or engaged in informal activities such as stealing or gambling. The life style of the swingers entailed a lot of going out, which was done mainly outside the neighborhood and outside the family circle. Many-branched and shifting networks and a large extent of residential mobility were typical of the swingers. As Hannerz noted: "All factors taken together, with their investment of time and effort in sociability and entertainment, their mobility, and their living in a large metropolis where people's paths need not often cross accidentally, the swingers are in a position to make a great number of acquaintances, but they also easily come to an end if not pursued actively" (p. 45). Hannerz used the term "loose-knit" to characterize the networks of the swingers.

The *street families* fit the prototype of the ghetto family. The father was absent in half of these child-rearing families, where several generations often lived together. These families were dominated by women, some of whom had jobs and some of whom were dependent on welfare benefits (AFDC). Their poor income position put the majority of the street families below the poverty line. The household composition was frequently altered by the birth of children, the start of new relationships and the termination of old ones. Street families were characterized by looser living together relationships than the mainstreamer families. This was evident in the segregated relations that men and women were likely to have. Women mainly associated with a circle of close kin—mother, sisters, daughters—and other women who lived in the neighborhood. Men had their own peer group life on the street corner. The social network of the street families was clearly confined within certain borders. Their social life was concentrated within a rather small area around the neighborhood. Participation in street life contributed toward the growth of informal channels of information and informal sources of care.

In part, the *street corner men* belonged to the category of street families described above. In addition, there were men who had little or no family context to fall back on. They were "unattached men" who lived an isolated life and did not maintain any ties with mainstream institutions. The men who were members of street families mainly did unskilled work or were temporarily out of work. The unattached men were more or less permanently unemployed. The everyday social life of these men took place within the same group. As Hannerz wrote, "Most days in the life of a street corner man, then, are filled with the same faces, the same hangout, the same struggle for food and drink, the same kind of talk—in short, the same routine" (p. 57).

Hannerz presented the four types of life styles as ideal types. The borders between the various life styles were permeable, and ghetto dwellers could change their life style if and when their social circumstances allowed. Individuals could also adopt several life styles.

Elijah Anderson, A Place on the Corner (1978)

Anderson's study *A Place on the Corner* (1978) was based on participant observation at Jelly's Bar and Liquor Store on the South Side of Chicago. The field work was conducted from 1970 to 1973. In this study, Anderson demonstrated that the people who patronized this bar constituted a coherent group composed in turn of a number of subgroups. Anderson distinguished the following three groups, referring to them by the terms they used themselves:

The *regulars* adhered to "the more general social, moral and legal codes" of mainstream society (p. 38). It was important to them to have a steady job that enabled them to support themselves. "Central to their values is the notion of 'decency', which includes a willingness to work and to be law-abiding" (p. 38). The regulars were generally older married men who supported each other by exchanging various kinds of help. Their relatively strong financial position provided them with a basis for this type of exchange. "For the regulars, the ability to be trustworthy and dependable in reciprocating social favors comes first and foremost from a strong financial base. Being a good and decent person is often equated with having a job and the ready money that is expected to go along with it" (p. 65). The regulars looked down on the other two groups, the hoodlums and the wineheads. There was a strong us-and-them perspective. The regulars took it for granted that their values were superior to those of the other categories. They felt more connected to mainstream society than the other categories.

The *hoodlums* had a strongly ambivalent attitude toward the morals and values of conventional society. "Hoodlums, unlike the regulars, tend to exhibit a high degree of alienation. Many feel wronged by the system, and thus its rules do not seem to them to be legitimate" (p. 130). They mainly operated in the informal economy or in the criminal circuit. Their activities included robbing, gambling, fencing and selling dope. Some of them had a steady job, others lived on unemployment or welfare benefits. The hoodlums were younger than the regulars and were the product of the street gang they grew up in. Many of them had a criminal record. The hoodlums felt it was important to be tough and to earn money, but they were not particularly interested in having a job. Anderson noted: "If regulars mainly value a 'visible means of support' and 'decency', and wineheads care about 'getting some wine' and 'having some fun,' then hoodlums appear to care mainly about presenting themselves as 'tough' and able to 'get big money'" (p. 130). The hoodlums could be viewed as the entrepreneurs of the ghetto. They operated within loose networks that were instrumental for their informal activities.

The *wineheads*, a residual category, were the lowest in the informal hierarchy at Jelly's Bar. Most of them were out of work and had no fixed address. They spent most of their time at Jelly's Bar. They were alcoholics who lived from hand to mouth, begging to get money for a drink. Most of the wineheads had not always been this way, but had gradually slid down the social ladder. They were not even remotely interested in a formal job and were not active in any way in the informal economy. They lacked the required skills, channels and incentive: "Most wineheads lack the ability and motivation to hustle the streets as many hoodlums do. They do not possess the personal organization necessary to steal and then fence the goods, and most also lack the will, the nerve, and the cunning to be a good stickup man" (p. 96). The wineheads were viewed as "social nobodies" who were not able to take control over their own lives.

Like Hannerz, Anderson noted the interaction between the various groups and the upward and downward social mobility, which was closely linked to getting or losing a job. The various groups could also exert influence on potential transitions from one group to another. The regulars for example tried to keep each other from "degenerating" into wineheads or hoodlums when times were hard.

Jay MacLeod, Ain't No Making It (1987)

MacLeod focused on youngsters in Clarendon Heights, a low-income housing development in a northeastern city. Unlike the neighborhoods in the studies described, Clarendon Heights was not a ghetto. It was a relatively small development situated in a traditional working-class community. The majority of the households in Clarendon Heights consisted of single-parent families, and approximately 70 percent of the families received some form of welfare. MacLeod described two different peer groups in the teenage world of Clarendon Heights, the Brothers and the Hallway Hangers. MacLeod observed these youngsters during and after high school in the 1981-1983 period, mainly focusing on their occupational aspirations. What has made MacLeod's study so important is its complex analysis of the reproduction of inequality through the cultural mechanism of leveled aspirations. Two comparable groups of youngsters behaved in opposite fashions and developed very different aspiration levels.

The *Hallway Hangers* were "tough, street wise individuals who form a distinctive subculture" (p. 23). They rejected such dominant values as doing your best at school and trying to hold down a job. In their sub-culture, the central value was "being bad." This value was closely linked to masculinity, physical toughness and street wisdom. They used drugs and drank alcohol, which youngsters of their age were not legally allowed to do. Many of them earned some extra money in the drug economy. Solidarity was powerful among the Hallway Hangers. MacLeod noted "their adoption of communitarian values" (p. 33). Their relations with each other were more important to them than their relations with the members of their families. Most of the Hallway Hangers grew up in white families with an absentee father and with older brothers who had been in trouble with the Police in the past. Neither of their parents were apt to have played much of a role in the lives of the Hallway Hangers. The Hallway Hangers had a limited aspiration level regarding paid employment. MacLeod used such terms as pessimism, insecurity, short-term focus and modesty to refer to their limited aspiration level.

The *Brothers* similarly came from families that were low on the occupational ladder. The Brothers behaved in a conformist fashion and did not have a clearly separate sub-culture of their own. They did their best at school, spent their leisure time doing things they felt were useful, had steady girlfriends, and did not engage in any informal activities. As MacLeod wrote, "the Brothers accept the dominant culture's definition of success and judge themselves by these criteria . . . their behavior generally conforms to societal expectations" (p. 44).

Unlike the Hallway Hangers, the Brothers were part of "loose and shifting cliques." Like the Hallway Hangers, most of the Brothers grew up in female-headed households, although there was often a male authority figure around. Almost all the fathers of the Brothers were employed, and their older brothers and sisters, who did well at school and in the labor market, served as role models. The Brothers were stimulated by their parents to work hard and accept what they felt were important social values. The Brothers had a relatively positive picture of the future in mind. This positive picture entailed middle-class aspirations such as having a good job, raising a family and owning durable consumer goods. The American achievement ideology was reflected in the expectations regarding their own future. In this respect, they differed markedly from the Hallway Hangers: "The Hallway Hangers reject this ideology, the Brothers accept it" (p. 129).

MacLeod explained the differences in the behavior and aspirations of the two groups on the basis of three interacting societal fields: (1) the upbringing in the family, (2) the experiences in the labor market and (3) the functioning of the school system. He also noted the achievement ideology that permeates American society and exerts a considerable amount of influence on the design of such social institutions as schools. MacLeod was convinced that the disappointing experiences of the Hallway Hangers in the societal fields of the family and the labor market had made them lower their aspiration level and that the effect of the school system had been to reproduce and perpetuate these low aspirations. In response to the obstacles the Hallway Hangers were confronted with, they had developed their own sub-culture to preserve their self-respect. The Brothers, however, had positive role models and were stimulated by their parents. Since they had internalized the dominant achievement ideology, they were more vulnerable if and when they did not succeed in realizing their aspirations. They could not fall back on alternative values to defend themselves against potential damage to their self-respect.

Elijah Anderson, Street Wise (1990a)

This study was based on field work conducted from 1975 to 1989 in Village Northon. This big city area consisted of two districts, an impoverished black community and a primarily white, middle-class neighborhood. Anderson's study described the social life in both of the neighborhoods, the various ways use was made of the public space and the street etiquette that regulated the interaction between groups. We confine ourselves here to Anderson's analysis of two contrasting neighborhood institutions in Northon: the *old heads* versus the *new old heads* and the stable *family culture* versus the *street culture*.

Anderson described a central local institution in Northon, the relation between the old heads and the young men. An old head was someone who was impartial and felt responsible for the functioning of the community. He frequently served as an intermediary between the youngsters and the privileged groups. The old head fulfilled a normative and integrating function. He drew the youngsters' attention to their obligations and responsibilities and helped them find a place for themselves in the community. "The old head's acknowledged role was to teach, support, encourage, and in effect socialize young men to meet their responsibilities with regard to work ethic, family life, the law, and decency" (p. 69).

In the 1980s, due to the altered social structure and changes in the use of public space, the old heads lost much of their significance as role models. The middle-class groups had moved to the suburbs and the public space had become less and less safe, making it increasingly difficult for the old head to fulfill his public role. Another factor was the reduced access to the kind of stable jobs that offered some extent of security. As Anderson wrote, "When gainful employment and its rewards are not forthcoming, boys easily conclude that the moral lessons of the old head concerning the work ethic, punctuality, and honesty do not fit their own circumstances" (p. 72). The new old head was the antithesis of the traditional old head. He was younger and did not attribute much significance to traditional values with respect to work, the family and the community. The new old head was mainly active in the informal economy. In Anderson's words, "He makes ends meet through the underground economy, dabbling in the drug trade or participating full time. As far as family life goes, he shuns the traditional father's role. His is a 'get over' mentality, and as the traditional old heads comment, he is out to beat the next fellow" (p. 103).

The changes in the role models were reflected in the altered balance among various types of families. The ghetto family was becoming less widespread and the female-headed household more common. Anderson noted the importance of the "strong ghetto family" (p. 91). He was referring to two-parent families who had strong ties with their relatives and were well integrated in the neighborhood. These inner city families adhered to traditional values regarding work, the family and law-abiding behavior. As Anderson wrote, "The father usually works at a regular job and has a sense that his values have paid off. Both parents, or close kin, strive to instill in the children the work ethic, common decency, and social and moral responsibility" (p. 91). Families like these constituted an important buffer against the dangers of the neighborhood. "Two parents, together with the extended network of cousins, aunts, uncles, grandparents, nieces and nephews can form a durable team, a viable supportive unit engaged to fight in a most committed manner the various problems confronting inner city teenagers, including drugs, crime, pregnancy and the lack of social mobility. This unit, when it does endure, tends to be equipped with a survivor's mentality. It has weathered a good many storms, which have given it wisdom and strength" (p. 123).

The conventional two-parent family had lost much of its significance. Due to the lack of gainful employment, many men and women were not in a position to build up stable relationships. What is more, the drug economy had emerged as a destructive functional alternative. Children from single-parent families grew up with very little supervision at home and barely any stimulation to try for upward social mobility by way of school or work. They saw that the opportunity structure was relatively closed to them and that the drug economy offered them an alternative way to acquire status and money. It was far more difficult for single mothers than for traditional families to protect their children from the dangers of the neighborhood.

The ghetto street culture the young children grew up in was a competitive culture where toughness, opportunism and individualism were highly valued. This was illustrated by the tough and calculating etiquette within the drug economy and in the relations between men and women. Many young men had a hit-and-run mentality toward women and a preoccupation with keeping their freedom. Making women pregnant so they would be insured of a regular welfare benefit was one strategy for strengthening their own financial basis. However, the power relations between men and women were not one-sided. Young women also used sexual relations to improve their options. Having a baby and acquiring the status of welfare mother was one of their options. It would guarantee a regular welfare check, thus giving women a source of power vis-à-vis men. "In fact, in cold economic terms, a baby can be an asset, which is without a doubt an important factor behind exploitative sex and out-of-wedlock babies. Public assistance is one of the few reliable sources of money and, for many, drugs are another. Babies and sex may be used for income; women receive money from welfare for having babies, and men sometimes act as prostitutes to pry money from them" (Anderson 1990a:136).

Anderson's study illustrated the extent to which the communal ghetto of the fifties had been affected by the fall in employment, the migration process and the advent of the drug economy. Traditional role models and institutions lost ground to the new role models and the socializing institutions that served only to widen the gap between the ghetto dwellers and the rest of society.

A Cultural Analysis

The reaction patterns described above coincide with those of the long-term unemployed in the Netherlands, particularly the ones exhibiting retreatist, conformist or enterprising behavior. As is the case with the long-term unemployed in the Netherlands as well, these reactions can be comprehended better in their specific social context. In the ghettoes, various ways of life are in evidence, including a fatalistic street culture, a conformist working-class culture and an individualistic entrepreneurial culture. We have not come across any mention of an autonomous culture, and we feel this is related to the fact that the benefits are so much lower in America. In ethnographic literature, there was also no mention of a hierarchic culture.[5] The following observations can be made.

1. The street corner men described by Liebow, Hannerz and Anderson can be viewed as retreatists. As Hylan Lewis noted in the foreword to *Tally's Corner*, they were losers who were not able to achieve such dominant values as having a stable job and raising a family (Liebow 1967: xi-i). "In self-defence," he wrote, "the husband retreats to the street corner" (Liebow 1967:136).

These retreatists were part of a fatalistic culture. This was particularly true of the unattached men and wineheads described by Hannerz and Anderson, who were permanently unemployed and had given up any hope of a working career. In Ferman's terms, they were "economic retreatists who did not participate in either the formal or the informal sector of the economy" (Ferman 1990:131). They were socially isolated and barely in a position to take control of their own lives. A culture of this kind is characterized by weak group ties and a strong grid. The weak group ties were evident in the restricted and superficial social relations of the street corner men and their inability to enter into long-term commitments to other people. The strong grid dimension was evident in the realization that their power to design their own lives as they saw fit was very limited indeed. Liebow cited this tragic realization in describing the reactions of the street corner men when one of them (Sea Cat) had a relationship with a girl (Gloria) who had a lot to offer him: "The men on the corner, like the chorus in a Greek tragedy, watched its development, analyzed it, and commented on it. They saw—or talked as if they saw—Sea Cat and Gloria as the user and the used, with Sea Cat a kind of Streetcorner Everyman who hunts for A Good Thing, finds it and inevitably loses it" (Liebow 1967:157).

2. The mainstreamers, the regulars, the Brothers, the old heads and the heads of the strong ghetto families all bore a striking resemblance to the conformists. They attached a great deal of value to work and self-reliance and they all obeyed the rules. They also had clear ties to the labor market. As the heads of families, all of them except the Brothers tried to inculcate their children with traditional values regarding work, the family and the community. They stimulated their children to get ahead and tried to shelter them from the temptations and hazards of the street.

In the Dutch study, we observed that the conformists were part of an egalitarian working-class culture with strong group ties and considerable social control, particularly within the family circle. The same held true to an even greater degree for the strong ghetto families. The contours of a comparable culture were evident in the case of the mainstreamers and the regulars, who were often involved "in a few close relationships, many of which are with relatives, and enjoy the stable day-to-day life with home and family" (Hannerz 1969:45). The grid dimension was weak, social contact was egalitarian and there was a general distrust of outsiders. The us-them perspective was evident in the distinction drawn between "respectable" or "decent" people and "the undesirables" or "the street" (Hannerz 1969:35, Anderson 1991:379). It was also clear however that the mainstreamers Hannerz described functioned in part within a more individualistically oriented middle-class culture. The same held true for the Brothers MacLeod described. Although they had to obey the strict rules of a rather close-knit family, they were also active in relatively open networks. In other words, conformism regarding paid employment did not necessarily coincide with an egalitarian culture.

3. The hoodlums, the new old heads and some of the swingers could be categorized as enterprising. They were active within the informal circuit of the drug economy. This circuit gave them an alternative that enabled them to acquire status and money. As to black youngsters active in the drug circuit, Anderson observed that "many adjust to the situation of desire for material things coupled with severe economic dislocation by becoming entrepreneurs of drugs and vice" (Anderson 1990a:243). The enterprising among them put the value of work into a perspective all their own, and it was not a work ethic but a "consumption ethic" that occupied a central position. In addition, there were sizable differences between the groups. The new old heads could be classified as successful entrepreneurs, but this was far less the case for some of the hoodlums.

The enterprising individuals were part of an individualistic culture. The group and grid dimensions were relatively weak. The enterprising individuals operated within relatively open networks and were not obstructed in any of their activities by strong classifications; in part they made their rules themselves. The drug culture Anderson described was a typical example of a competitive individualistic culture where individuals took considerable risks and where Darwin's survival of the fittest prevailed.

Other groups are more difficult to classify. Some of the Hallway Hangers, for example, could be classified as enterprising and some as retreatists.[6] To a modest degree, they were active in the informal economy. MacLeod interpreted their conduct as "resistance" (see Willis 1977). On the other hand, their attitude and behavior exhibited forms of retreatism. The longer they went on that way and the more serious their alcohol or drug addiction became, the more likely they were to join the category of the street corner men. Their social network could disintegrate and their attitude of resistance could then easily turn into fatalism. Elements for the development of a fatalistic culture were already in evidence.

The street families were also difficult to classify. These female-dominated family configurations were relatively close-knit. There was an extensive network of reciprocal relations, whereby use was made of whatever means were at hand, formal, informal, to reinforce the family income (see Stack 1974). Informal strategies were illustrated by their calculating behavior when it came to forming a family and insuring social security. There were also women who worked in the formal circuit. In the street families, there was thus evidence of both conformist and calculating behavior. A crucial factor was that their scarce income there was divided among the members of the street family. The functioning of the street family was a good example of how an egalitarian culture worked. Thompson and Wildavsky put it as follows: "No one in this elaborate network of kin is necessarily better off financially in the long run. But the exchange strengthens the group collectively, reinforcing social norms, making a whole that is greater than the sum of its parts" (Thompson and Wildavsky 1986:190).

THE PERIMETERS OF A CULTURAL ANALYSIS

Cultural theory fails to devote much attention to macro-structural processes that influence group and grid dimensions. In a certain sense, though quite the opposite might seem to be the case, cultural theory is characterized by a cautious form of voluntarism. It seems to suggest that the individual can freely choose from the five ways of life. Take a sentence like "Plural ways of life, we respond, give individuals a chance for extensive, if finite, choice" (Thompson et al. 1990:13). The choices people make are affected, however, by the scarcity or abundance of means and opportunities available to them. This is why the relation between structural possibilities and limitations on the one hand and forms of cultural expression on the other deserves more attention. This is evident from the ghetto studies discussed here. A stable position on the labor market has a sizable effect on the development of social relations and ways of life and on the cultural bias of parents and their children. The Dutch study made it clear that a relatively highly developed social security system could also influence the way people act and the choices they make.

The second point of criticism pertains to what Thompson et al. called their "impossibility theorem," namely that there are only five possible ways of life: hierarchy, egalitarianism, fatalism, individualism and autonomy. MacLeod's portrait of the Hallway Hangers illustrated that mixtures were also feasible. Thompson et al. partially solved this problem with two concepts, the "multiple self" and the "compartmentalization of biases" (Thompson et al. 1990: 265-266). People participate in various social contexts where different biases are dominant. A good example are the mainstreamers described by Hannerz, whose members functioned simultaneously in an egalitarian (communal) context and a more individualized context. Daniel Bell's comment on the American middle groups, "one is to be 'straight' by day and a 'swinger' by night" (Bell 1978:72) holds partially true for the mainstreamers, who doubled as swingers in their free time. It would be worthwhile to think in terms of viable mixtures. Research on minority entrepreneurs illustrates this, such as the studies by Portes on the informal economy in Miami (Portes 1987, 1991), in which he introduced such concepts as "bounded loyalty" and "enforceable trust." Being a successful entrepreneur depends on receiving adequate support (money and manpower) from one's own close-knit circle, and on being able to move outside one's ethnic circle and gain access to open networks. The boundedness of one's ethnic group and the loyalty to one's community should not serve as obstacles. In essence, what Portes was describing was a combination of an egalitarian and an individualistic culture. It was precisely this intermediate form that made successful entrepreneurship feasible (see Waldinger et al. 1990).

CULTURAL THEORY AND
THE POVERTY DEBATES

With the aid of cultural theory, the analysis of American studies on the world of the poor yields information and ideas that are relevant to the three central debates on poverty, unemployment and social policies. We shall first evaluate what the cultural analysis has contributed to the debate on the culture of poverty and then examine present-day controversies on the existence of an urban underclass and the unintended consequences of social policies.

Cultural Theory and
the Culture of Poverty

It is particularly the fatalistic culture of unemployment that we view as a variant of the culture of poverty. Cultural theory views it as only logical that a fatalistic culture should exhibit an institutional "solidity" that does not automatically disappear under altered external circumstances. The crucial element of cultural theory is that in addition to experiences that may push people in a fatalistic direction, fatalists constitute a fatalistic culture in and of itself. That means that they share values and beliefs that legitimate their passivity. In other words, they contribute to their own situation and are not only acted upon (Wildavsky 1987). The same holds true of the other cultures. Thus disintegration of the communal or institutional ghetto does not lead to the disappearance of this solidity or of a local institute like the "old head." It is clear, however, that the emergence and perpetuation of a fatalistic culture can be comprehended only in relation to the rest of a society. Street corner men and wineheads were not born as fatalists. Fatalism emerges as a reaction to frustrated potentials and is reinforced by the social environment one is part of. As Gans wrote, "Many poor people in our society are . . . fatalists, not because they are unable to conceive of alternative conditions, but because they have been frustrated in the realization of alternatives" (Gans 1991:305).[7]

Wilson's social isolation thesis has been confirmed by various ghetto studies, particularly if they are viewed from a *developmental perspective*. When Liebow observed the social world of the street corner men in the early 1960s, they constituted a small minority and most ghetto residents had a job; they were the people Hannerz and Anderson later called mainstreamers or regulars, the people who maintained a link with the world outside the ghetto. The drug economy was less dominant at the time. It was a crucial factor for these people that they had regular ties with the labor market and were in a position to maintain relatively stable personal relationships. Over time, most of these mainstreamers and regulars moved to the suburbs. They gradually served less and less of a normative and integrating function. The reduced significance of the old heads and the strong ghetto family was a good illustration of this change. Anderson's *Street Wise* (1990) showed how much had changed since *Tally's Corner* and *Soulside*, especially the diminishing number of industrial jobs and the growing influence of the drug economy on public life. While the street gained ground, the family and the formal labor market as socializing agencies lost ground. Youngsters were consequently more likely to grow up to be Hallway Hangers than Brothers. Even in the "hyperghetto" (Wacquant 1989:509), however, some Brothers still did grow up who, stimulated by their parents or other relatives, tried to escape from the poverty around them (see Williams and Kornblum 1985).

It is important remember that side by side with the fatalistic street culture, there are the conformist working-class culture and the individualistic entrepreneurial culture, both of which emanate a resilient fighting spirit, gumption and vitality. The conformist culture does not question the dominant values, norms and objectives of mainstream society. In the individualistic culture, attempts are made to acquire such mainstreams symbols as material prosperity, but through informal channels (see Jankowski 1991). In the studies discussed here, entrepreneurship is closely linked to crime. Recent studies on ethnic entrepreneurs in industrialized societies demonstrate that other informal routes of a less destructive nature can also be taken (see Portes 1987 and Waldinger et al. 1990). In order to properly understand these forms of entrepreneurship, specific information is required on the social context in which minority entrepreneurs operate successfully.

Cultural Theory and the Underclass

For a number of reasons, cultural theory is relevant to the present-day discussion on the underclass and the formulation of social policies. First, a cultural analysis undermines the notion of the poor as a homogeneous category. At the moment, there is a tendency to view all the people who live in a black ghetto as members of an underclass. Herbert Gans has voiced various objections to the imprudent use of the term underclass. He took exception to the generalizing nature of the term, noting that underclass is a "synthesizing notion" that overlooks the enormous differences between various categories of poor people (Gans 1991:334). Quantitative analyses also stress the diversity within these categories. The significance of cultural theory lies in the fact that it assesses differences in group and class-linked features and in ways of thinking and acting as well. We would like to reserve the term underclass for the people who are part of a fatalistic street culture. We thus use the term underclass in the same sense as Wilson (1991a); to refer to a category of people who are shut off from the labor market and have become socially isolated in an impoverished neighborhood. In response, they develop feelings of fatalism and low perceived self-efficacy. The people who operate within a destructive entrepreneurial culture can also be classified as belonging to the underclass. Although they often live far above the poverty line, they nonetheless remain shut off from mainstream society (Hochschild 1989: 151).

Studies by Dahrendorf (1985, 1988) gave a comparable account of the European underclass, which consists of the long-term unemployed, the poor and the discriminated against ethnic minorities. They do not have access to the labor market, the political community or networks of social relations. Dahrendorf localized the underclass in the inner cities of the leading European metropolises and analyzed their problems in terms of anomie. Anomie describes a state of extreme uncertainty in which no one knows what behavior to expect from others in given situations. As Dahrendorf wrote, "Anomie then is a condition in which both the social effectiveness and the cultural morality of norms tends toward zero" (Dahrendorf 1985:26). On certain points, Dahrendorf's analysis made a moralistic impression. In addition, one might doubt the usefulness of the notion of anomie. The American ghetto studies have demonstrated first, that even in extreme situations, behavior is still shaped by certain norms and rules and second, that various cultures can be observed side by side. When Dahrendorf referred to "The Road to Anomia," what he implicitly meant was an individualistic culture with a weak grid and weak group ties.[8] In *Law and Order* (1985) and *The Modern Social Conflict* (1988), he referred to "no-go areas" in the social as well as the physical sense, where anything could happen and anomie reigned.

The acknowledgement of cultural diversity can be one of the building blocks for realistic and differentiated social policies to improve the life chances of the ghetto poor. This is the second reason why cultural theory is relevant. There can be no doubt that it the conformist majority of the working poor would benefit by having a better chance of getting a decent job or an adequate education. Other groups should be approached and helped in a more intensive manner. That holds particularly true of the homeless and youngsters who are part of a fatalistic street culture or an individualistic drug culture. These groups, however, constitute only a small minority of the poor. They are the "estranged poor" (Hochschild 1989: 143). In their case, reintegration policies imply eradicating the thinking and behavior patterns that can stand in the way of returning to the formal labor market. This in turn requires programs that are expensive and intensive. As Hochschild wrote, "Successful efforts to aid the estranged poor cost a lot, last a long time and involve a wide array of activities aimed at changing skills, views, and life circumstances" (Hochschild 1989:151.[9]

The cultural analysis also makes clear the importance of reinforcing the societal position of what few regulars, mainstreamers or strong ghetto families might still reside in high poverty areas. All of the studies demonstrate the significant normative and integrating function of traditional families. In this connection, a definite moralizing factor is clear. What remains important, however, is the empirical observation that in an environment where insecurity is rampant, care facilities are inadequate and labor market attachments are threatened, a relatively stable family constitutes a crucial factor in the protection and socialization of its members. The members of the family form a social buffer, a "last line of defense" or a "fighting unit" against the perils of the ghetto (Wilson 1987:56, Anderson 1990a:107).

In other words, as far as social policies are concerned the cultural analysis leads to a "three-stage rocket" to combat the formation of an underclass. What we would recommend would be a strong universal educational, labor market and training policy (see Wilson 1987 and 1991b). In addition, targeted social policies are needed for specific groups, and the cultural dimensions of poverty and unemployment have to be taken into consideration in this connection (see Skocpol 1991). Finally, neighborhood programs and welfare programs should be developed to reinforce the positions and functions of working people and families with children in ghettoes and high poverty areas (see Ellwood 1988).

Cultural Theory and the Unintended Consequences of Welfare Policies

In the controversial study *Losing Ground* (1984), Murray expounded the theory that in the United States, the welfare system has reinforced rather than alleviated problems related to poverty. He did not seek the causes of the perpetuation of poverty in the culture of the poor or the socio-economic structure, but in the unintended consequences of the welfare policies developed with good intentions in the 1960s. The system of social benefits led, he felt, to a state-dependent leisure class of the poor. The main point Murray made was that the poor made rational cost-profit analyses and then decided to opt for a life on welfare. The AFDC benefits in combination with food stamps would, he claimed, give a person more of an income than the minimum wage, thus not leaving a very difficult choice. From Murray's point of view, the decision on the part of young ghetto women to live on welfare as unmarried mothers instead of getting married or finishing school and getting a job was rational and sensible, at any rate within the welfare system of the United States. The interesting thing about Murray's analysis is that he started from the assumption that a poor person is a rationally calculating individual who tries to optimize his or her own interest. Murray focused mainly on the AFDC mothers. His analysis has been criticized on several grounds, particularly for its selective and shaky empirical foundation. We will not go into this in detail here and refer the reader to the critical analyses by Danzinger and Gottschalk (1985) and Wilson (1987). We do, however, question the assumption about the calculating poor. It is evident from the cultural analysis that in many cases, the behavior of individuals is not solely steered by economic incentives. In some contexts, traditional values regarding work and the family (the conformist working-class culture), preserving self-respect and minimizing the chance of being offended socially (the fatalistic street culture) are of greater significance than calculating conduct regarding social benefits.

The calculating individual Murray described can be located within the confines of the individualistic entrepreneurial culture. The youngsters who operated there did not have a choice between a welfare check or a job. In most cases, they were not eligible for welfare and the only choice they had was between unemployment (or a very poorly paid job) and participation in the drug economy. We did see, however, that living on welfare was a realistic option for black women in the impoverished ghettoes. Since there were so few eligible employed black males who were able to support a family, these women opted for AFDC, which guaranteed them a fixed income. They did not have much of a choice. The tough, competitive world these boys and girls grew up in made it a logical choice. As Anderson wrote, "The economic noose restricting ghetto life encourages both men and women to try to extract maximum personal benefit from sexual relationships" (Anderson 1990a:135).

In the past few decades, there have been drastic changes in the social structure of the ghetto. In terms of the group/grid model, this transformation, which Wacquant (1989, 1992c) referred to as the shift from the "communal ghetto" to the "hyperghetto," affected the thinking and the (strategic) behavior of everyone involved. The erosion of the social frameworks that had characterized the communal ghetto contributed to the emergence of a tough competitive environment and a fragmented social environment where relatively isolated individuals shut themselves off from the rest of society.

The following passage sums up the repercussions of the British crusade for privatization—less government, more market—led by Prime Minister Thatcher group/grid terms. It clearly pertains as well to what happened in the 1970s and the 1980s in the American ghettoes: "Creating a more individualized social context, in which group relationships are absent or little developed, forces individuals to rely on their own resources. Some—the energetic, the skillful, the adventurous, the lucky—will be able to set themselves up at the center of personal networks and prosper. Others—those less energetic, less skillful, less adventurous, less lucky—will find themselves always out at the peripheries of other people's networks. The push toward 'privatization', we predict, will have not only the intended effect of strengthening individualism, but also the unintended consequence of increasing fatalism" (Thompson et al. 1990:79). In this quote, the strengthening of individualism is viewed as an intended effect and increasing fatalism as an unintended consequence. Whoever examines the destructive situation in the American ghettoes can hardly fail to see the unintended effects of rough individualism, particularly the crime rise in the inner cities.

Cultural theory puts into perspective the portrayal of the calculating individual and the notion that the calculating individual is a function of social policies. A cultural analysis makes it clear that it is precisely the cutbacks on welfare arrangements in a period of economic restructuring that have stimulated the rise of a tough and strategic environment where opportunism and rash behavior dominate. In the Netherlands, a different process can be observed: unemployed people with bureaucratic skills are able to profit from the relatively highly developed welfare system. The autonomous and calculating and to a lesser degree the enterprising behavioral reactions of the Dutch unemployed can be comprehended only against the background of an advanced system of social security. It should be noted that these reactions are feasible because, as in America, there is so little evidence of activating labor market policies in the Netherlands.

THE MURRAY PARADOX: AMERICA VERSUS THE NETHERLANDS

At first glance, reading about the poverty and social policies in the United States might make one quite content with the Dutch welfare state. The relatively high level of social security, with all the undesirable and unexpected side effects, still unmistakably implies a more humane society (Engbersen en Van der Veen 1992). There are no destructive ghettoes in the Netherlands, and even the people who live on the minimum social benefits are relatively more comfortable materially. Impoverishment and the most clearly visible signs of poverty are far less evident on the streets of Dutch cities. And yet there are developments taking place in the Netherlands at the moment that give very little reason for contentment. The Dutch welfare system seems to keep unemployed people in their place: passive, not really trying to move out. Perhaps this welfare system functions in more or less the same way as the social environment in American cities, which keeps people detached from mainstream society and in their place. The working of the Dutch welfare system is a cultural condition for the emergence of a Dutch underclass. Besides this cultural condition, there are the structural ones as well, such as the economic restructuring.

In the Netherlands, a counterpart to the American underclass is in danger of coming into existence: a group of people who are structurally excluded from the formal and informal labor markets and have become completely dependent on the care of the state. This group consists mainly of older unskilled workers and people of foreign descent who have very little chance of succeeding in the labor market (the retreatists and the ritualists in this study). As in the United States, the Dutch underclass is too far away from the labor market to benefit from the demand for labor. This can be concluded from the fact that despite the success of the Dutch "job machine," long-term unemployment still remains as sizable as ever. The educational level of long-term unemployed people is generally too low to make them eligible for the highly qualified jobs in the service sector, and the less highly qualified jobs are often part-time, which would earn them less than their welfare benefit (Kloosterman and Elfring 1991). In addition to this category, a group of enterprising and calculating unemployed people emerged in the 1980s, who fit well into the picture Murray presented of the strategically operating welfare client. And this brings us to the Murray Paradox: In the Netherlands, a mixture of a corporatist, social democratic and liberal welfare state, this group would seem to be of more significance than in the liberal American welfare state. Murray's neo-conservative criticism of the welfare state would thus seem to be more applicable in the Old World than in the New.

NOTES

1. This paradox was formulated by Loïc J. D. Wacquant at the Leiden Workshop on Modern Poverty, Unemployment and the Emergence of a Dutch Underclass in August 1990. See also Godfried Engbersen and Robert Kloosterman, "William Julius Wilson en het debat over de onderklasse," *Intermediair*, Vol. 26, No. 34 (August 1990): 43-49.

2. Wildavsky describes two other cultures of the American welfare state "hierarchical collectivism" and "egalitarian sectarianism." In our opinion these two cultures are less dominant in the American welfare state. See Aaron Wildavsky, "The Three Cultures: Explaining Anomalies in the American Welfare State," in: *The Public Interest*, Number 69, Fall 1982: 45-58.

3. See Yeheskel Hasenfeld, "The Role of Employment Placement Services in Maintaining Poverty" in: *Social Service Review*, December 1975, 569-587.; Michael Lipsky, *Street-Level Bureaucracy: Dilemmas of the Individual in Public Services*, New York: Russell Sage Foundation, 1980; Ken Auletta, *The Underclass*, New York: Random House, 1982; and Anderson, Elijah, "Racial Tension, Cultural Conflicts, and Problems of Employment Training Programs," in: Kai Erikson and Steven Peter Valas, *The Nature of Work: Sociological Perspectives*, New Haven and London: American Sociological Association Series and Yale University Press, 1990b, 214-234.

4. There are, of course, other important ethnographic studies (in the making). See for example the work of Wacquant on Woodlawn, a section of Chicago's South Side: Loïc J. D. Wacquant, "The Comparative Social Structure and Experience of Urban Exclusion: Race, Class, and Space in Chicago and Paris," in R. Lawson, C. McFate, and W. J. Wilson (eds.), *Urban Marginality and Social Policy in America and Western Europe*, Newbury Park: Sage Publications, 1992a. Loïc J. D. Wacquant, "'The Zone': Le métier de *hustler* dans le ghetto noir americain," in: *Actes de la recherche en sciences sociales*, 92, juin 1992b.

Besides, there are important ethnographic studies on the crack economy, youth crime and gangs. See for example: Mercer L. Sullivan, *Getting paid: Youth Crime and Work in the Inner City*, Ithaca: Cornell University Press, 1990; Martin Sanches Jankowski, *Islands in the Street: Gangs and American Urban Society*, Berkeley: University of California Press, 1991. Philippe Bourgois, "In Search of Horatio Alger: Culture and Ideology in the Crack Economy," in: *Contemporary Drug Problems* (Winter): 619-649.

5. Examples of hierarchical cultures are described by Martin Sanches Jankowski in his study on the organization of gangs *Islands in the Street: Gangs and American Urban Society*, Berkeley: University of California Press, 1991.

6. It is striking that the Hallway Hangers belonged to a close-knit group with a strong feeling of group solidarity. One might wonder however whether MacLeod did not overestimate the communitarian attitude of this group. Liebow and Hannerz rightly noted the relative fragility of group relations among men who are not in a position to make any investments in these relations.

7. Merton writes in this respect: ". . . fatalism tends to develop among those living under conditions of extreme stress or rigorous arbitrary rule. Philosophy and conditions of live interact and reinforce one another: men are apt to think fatalistically under depressed conditions and they are apt to remain under these conditions because they think fatalistically. This fatalistic acceptance of things as they are develops among the extremely deprived social stratum described by Karl Marx as the *Lumpenproletariat* (the aggregate of demoralized workers), by Lloyd Warner as the lower-lower class and

by many others, in the recent past, as the underclass" (Robert K. Merton, and Robert Nisbett, *Contemporary Social Problems*, New York: Harcourt, Brace, Jovanovich, 1971: 814-815).

8. Dahrendorf's four-fold classification model regarding patterns of life chances bears certain similarities to Douglas' group/grid model. Dahrendorf used two dimensions: options and ligatures. Options are structural opportunities for choice, ligatures are allegiances or bonds and linkages (Ralf Dahrendorf, *Life Chances*, London: Weidenfeld & Nicolson, 1979:30 and 80-81).

9. Intensive programs often imply intervention in the way people live. A certain moralizing factor unmistakably plays a role. It is important, however, that something is indeed offered to the individuals involved. If that is not the case, the contours loom of what Polsky called the "therapeutic state," which intervenes in the lives of marginal groups in an authoritarian manner but in the end does more harm than good (Andrew J. Polsky, *The Rise of the Therapeutic State*, Princeton, New Jersey: Princeton University Press, 1991).

APPENDIXES

UNEMPLOYMENT AND
THE LABOR MARKET

In this Appendix, we present the unemployment figures of the Netherlands compared to the United States and to the international figures. For the sake of comparability over time and countries, we use the OECD figures. Table I shows that until recently, the Dutch unemployment rate was comparatively high. These are the same unemployment rates as shown in Figure 2.1 in Chapter 2.

TABLE I Unemployment in the Netherlands, the EC, the OECD and the United States (1960-1990, percentages of work force)

	1960	1974	1980	1984	1986	1987	1988	1989	1990	1991	1992[a]
Netherlands	0.7	2.7	6.0	11.9	10.3	9.6	9.2	8.3	7.5	7.0	6.5
EC	2.4	2.9	6.2	10.9	11.1	10.8	10.2	9.0	8.4	8.7	9.3
OECD	3.4	3.9	5.9	8.1	7.9	7.5	6.9	6.2	6.1	6.8	7.4
United States	5.4	5.5	7.0	7.4	6.9	6.1	5.4	5.2	5.4	6.5	7.4

[a] Figures for May 1992.
Source: OECD 1991 and 1992.

Unemployment figures are not undisputable. Since the OECD figures on unemployment do not give full account of the welfare state and labor market problems, we briefly discuss both the measuring of unemployment and the low level of labor force participation in the Netherlands.

Until 1989, the total number of people registered as unemployed at the District Employment Offices was the official Dutch figure. This figure, however, had several biases. It included people who were no longer "available" for a job for various reasons: they had already found a job but had not reported it to the Employment Office or were not willing to accept a job within two weeks or for more than 20 hours a week. To avoid the bias of the old definition, the Dutch government decided to calculate the official unemployment figures from a quarterly survey together with the Employment Office registration figures (CBS 1988).

But these figures are not fully accurate either. The field work for this study made it clear that certain long-term unemployed categories are virtually inaccessible to researchers. Especially at the Amsterdam and Rotterdam locations, we could only reach many of the extremely long-term unemployed people only after coming to their door again and again at various times of the day. Certain categories were also inaccessible because they had no telephone or, surprisingly enough, because they had an unlisted telephone number. Thus many of these long-term unemployed people cannot be expected to be included in the official CBS unemployment survey and the official figures drawn from it. This is also reflected in the total number of people who draw unemployment insurance or an unemployment related welfare benefit. In Table II we present the unemployment figures according to the old Dutch definition of unemployment.

TABLE II Unemployment and Duration of Unemployment (1975-1990, thousands)

	1975[a]	1980[a]	1982	1983	1984	1985	1986	1987	1988	1989	1990[a]
< 1 year	–	–	450	449	387	354	334	321	328	318	288
1-2 years	–	–	137	210	185	153	128	122	120	123	
2-3 years	–	–	40	91	121	104	78	72	68	66	
3-4 years	–	–	14	29	73	71	64	50	45	42	
> 4 years	–	–	14	22	57	79	106	121	124	121	
Total			655	801	823	761	710	686	685	670	612
Percentage of Total Working Population	5.0	5.9	12.5	17.0	17.3	15.9	14.7	13.9	13.7	13.2	12.3

[a] More specific duration figures not available.
Source: Ministry of Social Affairs and Employment 1991.

As indicated in Chapter 1 and 2, the problems of the Dutch welfare state are expressed not only in the unemployment rate, but more and more in the labor force participation rate in stead. In the same period that the unemployment rate has gone down, the number of people with a disability benefit has gone up, from 406,000 in 1975, 696,000 in 1980, 772,000 in 1985, to 862,000 in 1990. The numbers of unemployment benefits (insurance plus welfare) were successively 182,000 in 1975, 233,000 in 1980, 646,000 in 1985, and 575,000 in 1990 (CBS 1992).

In addition to the data presented in Chapter 1, Table 1.4, Table III shows the development in gross labor force participation rates for men and women from 1973 to 1990. The reality behind the rising participation rate of women in the Netherlands is that 60 percent of the women work part time.

TABLE III Gross Labor Force Participation in International Comparison (Persons 1973-1990)

	Men					Women				
	1973	1983	1988	1989	1990	1973	1983	1988	1989	1990
Netherlands	86	77	81	81	81	29	33	52	52	54
Belgium	83	77	73	72	–	41	49	51	52	–
France	85	78	75	75	75	50	54	56	56	56
United Kingdom	93	88	87	87	87	53	57	64	67	65
West Germany	89	84	83	82	–	50	52	55	55	–
Sweden	88	86	84	85	86	63	77	80	81	82
United States	86	85	86	86	86	51	62	67	68	68
OECD Europe	89	83	81	81	–	45	50	54	54	–

Source: OECD 1990, 1991 and Ministry of Social Affairs and Employment 1991.

FIELDWORK AND DATA PROCESSING

The research populations consisted of people registered as unemployed for two years or longer at the beginning of 1987, who were between the ages of 23 and 50 and lived in one of the three neighborhoods: Amsterdam (Banne Buiksloot and Overtoomse Veld), Rotterdam (Het Nieuwe Westen) and Enschede (Stadsveld/Pathmos). We were interested in a group that had been excluded from the labor process for quite some time and had thus become dependent on welfare or some other benefit of the same amount. The minimum and maximum ages meant that two groups were excluded, the youngest unemployed people and the ones above 50. For the interviews, samples were drawn from the files of the District Employment Offices and from the Municipal Welfare Departments in Amsterdam, Rotterdam and Enschede. The original samples consisted of 989 people who had been without a job for two years or longer; 237 in Amsterdam, 352 in Rotterdam and 400 in Enschede. We stopped interviewing when we reached a total of 90 interviews in each city.

In view of the comprehensive nature of the questions posed in the study, open interviews were preferred. The subjects were fixed beforehand, but the course of the interviews could differ from one case to the next. The sensitive nature of some of the subjects called for an approach of this kind. The interviews took place in mid-1987, usually in the homes of the respondents. The interviews took from an hour and a half to two hours and with very few exceptions were recorded on tape. In the interviews, the following subjects were discussed:

- personal particulars
- household (type, size, composition)
- housing (past and present situation, satisfaction, environment)
- neighborhood (description, contact, developments, satisfaction)
- educational level, work and loss of it (employment record, occupation, experience, last job, reason for leaving it, duration of unemployment)
- spending time (time elements in the week, planning, perception)
- looking for a job (frequency, channels, experiences, willingness to compromise, expectations, relation with the District Employment Office)
- intermediary facilities (familiarity and experience with training courses, willingness to take them, special projects for the unemployed, measures to stimulate employment, etc.)
- consequences for the family and their reactions to unemployment

- consequences for informal networks (relatives, friends, acquaintances) and their reactions (size and meaning of social relations, changes)
- unemployment and the neighborhood (percentage of people out of work, changes because of it, neighborhood reactions to unemployment, participation in neighborhood activities)
- unemployment and society (participation in social activities, relations with government agencies, ideas about politics, social comparisons, stigmatization)
- financial situation (income and expenditures, strategies for making ends meet, debts, informal earnings)
- health

Listening and transcribing the interviews turned out to be even more labor intensive than we had anticipated. In order to prevent this stage from becoming too time-consuming, 50 of the interviews were not processed in this manner. The other 221 interviews provided more than enough material. The data were processed in WordPerfect, which enabled us to sort, select and arrange data in various ways.

DESCRIPTIONS OF THE THREE RESEARCH LOCATIONS

Here, short descriptions are given of the three locations. It should be kept in mind that they pertain to the situation in late 1986 and early 1987. Changes may have taken place since then. The descriptions refer to figures given in Table IV at the end of this Appendix.

HET NIEUWE WESTEN IN ROTTERDAM

Het Nieuwe Westen, built between 1900 and 1930 on the north shore of the Maas River, was the largest urban renewal area in Rotterdam in the mid-1980s. Het Nieuwe Westen was one of the most densely built up neighborhoods in Rotterdam. Many of the buildings consisted of a basement, two or three stories and an attic. Particularly in the southern part of the neighborhood, the quality was poor. Urban renewal had been slow there, causing a deterioration in the living climate.

Almost 20,000 people of more than twenty nationalities lived in Het Nieuwe Westen. The largest ethnic groups were from Surinam (formerly Dutch Guiana), Turkey and Morocco. By 1994, about half the neighborhood population will consist of people of foreign descent. At the time of the study, they accounted for almost a quarter of the population there. Until the end of the 1960s, Het Nieuwe Westen was a relatively homogeneous neighborhood where blue collar workers and members of the lower middle class lived. The social structure was close knit and kinship relations played an important role. After the 1960s many Dutch families, people above the age of 35 and people with relatively high incomes left the neighborhood. They were replaced by people of foreign descent, single people, women and children who came to join the migrant workers from Turkey and Morocco, people below the age of 35 and people in the low income groups.

As a result of these demographic developments, a wide range of small social networks emerged. Though social cohesion could be strong within these networks, the gaps between people from different networks could be unbridgeable. Social fragmentation had led to a reduction in the social control in the neighborhood. Attracted by the low rents, certain groups that thrive in an anonymous situation such as drug addicts and dealers had settled in the neighborhood.

At the time of the field work, the working-age population in Het Nieuwe Westen consisted of 9,200 people, about 2,800 of whom were unemployed. The unemployment percentage was 31 percent, compared with 21 percent in Rotterdam as a whole. A third of the men and a quarter of the women were unemployed. Figures on Rotterdam as a whole showed that 34 percent of the Turks and 28 percent of the Surinamese and Antilleans were unemployed. No exact figures were available for Het Nieuwe Westen, but there were no indications that they differed greatly from those of Rotterdam as a whole. In view of the above-mentioned development of the population composition, it is probable that the unemployment rate in this neighborhood will rise in the years to come. This is also likely to be the case with the duration of the unemployment. In 1986, 45 percent of the unemployed had already been out of work for more than two years.

BANNE BUIKSLOOT AND OVERTOOMSE VELD IN AMSTERDAM

Research was conducted in two Amsterdam neighborhoods, Banne Buiksloot in Amsterdam North and Overtoomse Veld in Amsterdam New West.

Approximately 12,700 people lived in Banne Buiksloot, many of whom originally came from urban renewal areas elsewhere in the city. In comparison with Amsterdam as a whole, the neighborhood had a high percentage of families with children and a low percentage of people of foreign descent. Banne Buiksloot was built in the 1960s and 1970 as a suburb for commuters. There were high-rise as well as smaller buildings and the quality was generally good. The high-rise section in "Banne I" made an uninteresting, monotonous impression. The lower buildings in "Banne II" had been designed with far more originality and created a pleasant feeling of intimacy. Partly because the residents of entire streets had moved to this neighborhood, there was extensive interpersonal contact.

In the spring of 1987, 660 people in Banne Buiksloot were out of work. The unemployment percentage in the neighborhood was estimated at 12 percent as compared with 24 percent in Amsterdam as a whole, and 14 percent of them had been unemployed for more than two years. A relatively large number of these unemployed people were young. Their educational level was lower than in Amsterdam as a whole, so that a relatively sharp rise in long-term unemployment could be expected in the future.

Overtoomse Veld is part of the "Gordel '20-'40", which includes the parts of the city built in the 1920s and 1930s. In comparison with the buildings in the urban renewal areas, the quality was still good, though an active policy was required to prevent the Gordel from becoming the urban renewal area of tomorrow.

In Overtoomse Veld, consisting of the "Postjes section" and the "Hoofddorp-plein" section, there were more than 19,000 residents. Until long after World War Two, the Postjes section had been known as a very respectable, rather "fancy" area. Post-war rent control had made the area accessible to lower occupational and income groups. In the 1970s, many young couples moved to the section. Since then, the number of residents of foreign descent doubled and at the time of the study accounted for more than 20 percent of the population. The population of the Postjes section did not differ markedly from that of Amsterdam as a whole with respect to gender, type of household or ethnic background. However, the age of the residents was somewhat higher. The Hoofddorpplein section could also be viewed as representative of Amsterdam as a whole, though there were relatively more elderly people and fewer people of foreign descent. The demographic developments remained somewhat behind those in the Postjes section.

In the spring of 1987, almost 2,000 people were out of work in Overtoomse Veld. The unemployment percentage was estimated at the Amsterdam average of 24 percent. The average duration of the unemployment was somewhat below the Amsterdam average. The educational level of the 430 people who had been unemployed for more than two years was quite a bit lower than that of the Amsterdam population, and their average age was higher. The active working population was largely employed outside the neighborhood.

STADSVELD/PATHMOS IN ENSCHEDE

In Enschede, research was conducted in the Pathmos section and the four adjacent areas known collectively as Stadsveld. Pathmos was built from 1914 to 1927 by textile manufacturers to house the families of the workers recruited from the northern provinces of the Netherlands. It was an example of early twentieth-century suburban architecture. With a great deal of variety and a number of squares, the neighborhood constituted one architectural entity. Stadsveld consisted of middle-income and duplex homes constructed in the 1930s and 1940s and low apartment buildings built in the 1950s and 1960s with one-family homes situated among them. Since most of the homes and buildings had a garden, the neighborhood as a whole made a pleasantly "green" impression

More than 15,000 people lived in Stadsveld/Pathmos. Their average age was lower than in Enschede as a whole. The percentage of people of foreign descent, most of whom were of Turkish descent, was 9 percent compared with 6 percent in Enschede as a whole.

Pathmos would qualify as a "homogeneous working-class neighborhood," though in part this had ceased to be the case as a result of urban renewal completed in 1985. In connection with the urban renewal, the original residents were temporarily housed elsewhere in the city. A number of them, particularly elderly people, did not return. This greatly reduced the average age in the neighborhood. Skilled workers and low or medium level employees lived in the older section of Stadsveld, where 60 percent of them owned their own homes, a much higher percentage than in the rest of the neighborhood.

In Stadsveld/Pathmos, the dominant residential unit was the family. More than 80 percent of the residents lived in a family arrangement. Social control was strong, particularly in Pathmos and in the older areas of Stadsveld. In Stadsveld-

Noord, the population was more heterogeneous and there were more people moving in and out.

In 1987, more than 1,100 neighborhood residents were out of work. The exact unemployment percentage was not available, but it certainly exceeded the 21 percent registered for Enschede as a whole. In the neighborhood, 48 percent of the unemployed people had been out of work for more than two years, whereas in Enschede as a whole this was true only of 42 percent. Compared with the city as a whole, this group included relatively large numbers of men, older people, people with a low educational level and people of foreign descent.

COMPARISON OF THE LOCATIONS

A comparison of the three locations described above illustrates that similarities in one aspect could be accompanied by great differences in another. Table IV shows that the populations of the Rotterdam and the Enschede locations were very similar in gender and age, but differed considerably in type of household and nationality. For an accurate interpretation of the differences and similarities, insight into the development of the various locations is necessary.

TABLE IV Several Features of the Populations of the Research Locations (in percentages for 1987)

City	Rotterdam	Amsterdam		Enschede
Neighborhood	Nieuwe Westen	Overtoomse Veld	Banne Buiksloot	Stadsveld/Pathmos
Number of Inhabitants	20,000	19,000	12,700	15,000
Sex				
Male	52	46	47	50
Female	48	54	53	50
Total	100	100	100	100
Age				
0–14	19	13	17	19
15–64	71	67	67	69
65 and older	10	20	16	12
Total	100	100	100	100
Type of Household				
Couple with/without children	36	31	47	52
One-parent Family	14	9	10	7
Single	50	60	43	41
Total	100	100	100	100
Descent				
Dutch	77	80	92	91
Foreign	23	20	8	9
Total	100	100	100	100
*Unemployment Figure**	31	24	12	27
*Unemployed for two years and more Figure***	50	31	14	48

* Percentage of the Total Working Population
** Percentage of the Total Number of Unemployed People

The figures presented in Table VIII indicate a severe unemployment problem in Het Nieuwe Westen in Rotterdam and Stadsveld/Pathmos in Enschede. The macro-economic causes of the problem at the two locations might have been similar, but the local labor market developments behind them were quite different (see Chapter 3). It is important in this connection to note the demographic factor. In Het Nieuwe Westen, the problem had been partially "imported" the influx of young people and migrants with a poor position in the labor market. In Stadsveld/Pathmos, it was mainly the original population, which had formerly been employed at the textile factories and in other unskilled jobs, that was affected. In this sense, the Amsterdam location occupied an intermediate position.

DUTCH AND AMERICAN
INCOMES COMPARED

The Dutch and American welfare states differ greatly, as do the wages, prices and benefits and the relations between them. In general, one can state that the Dutch welfare state is much more generous than the American. For a study like this it is useful have a somewhat more precise comparison. In order to describe socio-economic context of the financial position of long-term unemployed people in the Netherlands compared to that of long-term unemployed people in the United States, we present in this appendix some general data and tendencies, concentrated on the second half of the 1980s.

Important socio-economic aspects, not in the least as a frame of reference for the unemployed themselves, are the income levels and purchasing power. The average income per employed person in the United States in 1987 amounted to $39,090, the average Dutch employed person earned 78 percent of this income, and his German counterpart 76.5 percent (WRR 1990). The average 1987 income per capita amounted to $18,297 in the United States. Given the relatively low participation in the labor force in the Netherlands (see Appendix I), the Dutch average income was 66.6 percent of the American average income.

Countries differ importantly in the mechanisms on their of their markets and consequently in wages and prices and the outcome of the two: purchasing power. For the purpose of adapting salaries of personnel working abroad, statistical bureaus publish so-called purchasing power parities. Here we present the purchasing power parities given by the Netherlands Central Bureau of Statistics (CBS), which are based on the German figures. The purchasing power parity is a complex measure, based on mainly the price index development and the international exchange rates. It expresses the costs one would have to fill one's basket with a similar set of products in different countries. For 1987 the differences between the three countries earlier mentioned were small. With Germany at 100, the purchasing power needed in the United States was 96 and in the Netherlands 98. For 1991 these figures were 96 for the United States and 96 for the Netherlands. It has to be noted here that the purchasing power parities can change drastically over time, most often because of changes in the exchange rates. In the years before 1987, the parity for the U.S. developed from 143 in 1984 to 149 in 1985 and 112 in 1986. The U.S. figures are the figures for Washington, D.C. (CBS 1987, 1989, 1991 and 1992).

When it comes to saving and spending, the Netherlands and the United States differ significantly. In 1987 the total private savings of the Dutch amounted to 38 percent of the GNP, while the Americans saved 3 percent of their GNP (data provided by De Nederlandsche Bank, the Netherlands Central Bank). The largest difference between the two countries is shown in the extent to which people live and buy with of consumer credit. In the Netherlands the total sum of consumer credits amounted to 0.3 percent of the 1987 GNP, whereas in the United States the total sum of consumer credit was 13 percent of the GNP. From these figures one could conclude that being in debt in the Netherlands or in the United States has different connotations. On the other hand, for unemployed people in the United States it is much more difficult to get a loan than it is for the unemployed in the Netherlands.

Comparing the financial position of long-term unemployed people in the United States and the Netherlands is difficult (Table V), not only because of the different levels of benefits, but predominantly because of the differences in entitlements and the structure of the regulations (see also Gordon 1988, Smeeding et al. 1990 and Adler et al. 1991). In the section "Financial Position" in Chapter 4, we describe the social security route a Dutch worker travels after having lost his or her job, from unemployment benefit to welfare. In the Netherlands, someone who has been employed for at least six months and loses his or her job is entitled to a benefit of 70 percent of the last paid wage according to the national Unemployment Insurance Act. The duration of this entitlement depends on the work history and age of the beneficiary and can vary from several months to several years. In the United States unemployment benefits last 26 weeks (Unemployment Insurance Benefit, UIB) or 39 weeks (Supplemental Unemployment Benefits, SUB), depending on the industry in which one has worked (Bluestone and Harrison 1982, OECD 1991). The UIB applies to most economic industries, the SUB to a small number of industries such as automobile manufacturing. The more generous Trade Readjustment Assistance applies to only a few categories of workers. Accordingly, the loss of earnings after losing one's job differs from industry to industry. Jacobson found the biggest loss of income in steel manufacturing, 46.6 percent after the first two years (Bluestone and Harrison 1982). The smallest loss was found in the manufacturing of TV receivers, 0.7 percent. Even after six years, income of former workers who remained unemployed continued to fall (for instance 18.1 percent for meat packers in the subsequent four years).

The financial positions of Americans in welfare programs (Unemployment Insurance, UI; Aid to Families with Dependent Children, AFDC, General Assistance, GA and Supplemental Security Income, SSI) differ from state to state. This is mainly because of the differences in the accepted minimum standards of living. In 1979, the maximum unemployment insurance benefit in Massachusetts was twice as high as it was in Georgia and Alabama (Bluestone and Harrison 1982). AFDC and GA were highest in states such as Connecticut, Michigan and California and lowest in the southern states; for example, AFDC amounted to $363 a month in New York but to $80 in Mississippi. In 1987, an unemployed AFDC mother with two children living in Pennsylvania had a net income of $7080, while an employed mother with a comparable family earning $4.90 an hour had a net income of $7632, after having paid for childcare (Edin and Jencks 1992). In 1989, for instance, the monthly need standard for a family of three persons was $539 in New York, $421 in Colorado, and $368 in Mississippi (Social Security Bulletin, July 1989/Vol. 52, No. 7, 66). To be eligible for AFDC households must have a gross income that is at or below 185 percent of the State standard of need.

Singles, elderly and other people who are not eligible for AFDC may apply for food stamps if the income is at or below 130 percent of the poverty income guidelines for that particular size of household. In 1988, a four-person household, for example, received $300 per month in food stamps. AFDC receivers may also be eligible for food stamps, if their benefit is not sufficient. Between 1973 and 1989, the mean income deficit (the dollar gap between actual income and the poverty line) grew from $1,162 per family member to $1,416 per family member and for singles from $2,608 to $2,836 (Mishel and Frankel 1991).

In 1989, 44,000 inhabitants of Washington D.C. received an AFDC benefit of an average of $359 per month (U.S. Department of Commerce 1992). In Washington D.C. in 1990, 16,000 people received a Supplemental Security Income (SSI) benefit of $281 per month. Table V shows that these benefits differ significantly form the European standard, especially comparing the percentages of the national average income that are covered.

TABLE V Minimum Welfare Benefits in the Netherlands, the United States and Germany: Several Western Countries (1988)

	Singles		One parents[a]		Couples[b]		Couples-kids[c]	
	A	B	A	B	A	B	A	B
Netherlands[d]	616	66	944	64	878	53	1026	50
United States[e]	281	9	—		—		367	12
West Germany[f]	430	41	886	54	669	33	1033	40

A = In U.S. dollars, net monthly on basis of purchasing power parities.
B = Percentage of average income per category.

[a] One-parent family with two children aged 6 to 11.
[b] Couple with no children.
[c] Couple with two children aged 6 to 11.
[d] National Assistance Act (ABW) and State Group Regulations for Unemployed Persons (RWW), including child benefit, excluding rent subsidy.
[e] Singles; SSI benefit in Washington D.C., 1990. Couples with children: national average AFDC benefit, 1989. Average income not available per category.
[f] "Sozialhilfe," including allowances for children and an average benefit for actual living costs.

Sources: SCP 1990 for the Netherlands and Germany, Social Security Bulletin, July 1989/Vol. 52, No. 7 and U.S. Department of Commerce 1992 for the U.S.

TABLES FROM CHAPTER 8
(except for Table 8.1)

TABLE VI Personal Features of the Types of Long-Term Unemployed People (in percentages, N=221)

	Conform- ists	Ritual- ists	Retreat- ists	Enter- prising	Calcu- lating	Auto- nomous	Total
Sex							
Male	83	100	86	91	50	64	81
Female	17	–	14	9	50	36	19
Total	100	100	100	100	100	100	100
N	80	20	56	23	20	22	221
Age							
< 30	35	10	11	44	65	32	30
30-40	39	35	37	43	35	18	36
40-50	26	55	52	13	–	50	34
Total	100	100	100	100	100	100	100
N	80	20	56	23	20	22	221
Education*							
Primary	29	30	45	5	–	5	26
< L.V./L.G.S.	11	30	22	18	5	32	18
L.V./L.G.S.	44	35	29	41	25	45	37
> L.V./L.G.S.	16	5	4	36	70	18	19
Total	100	100	100	100	100	100	100
N	80	20	55	22	20	22	219
Descent							
Dutch	63	50	48	87	90	90	66
Surinam/ Antilles	14	25	20	4	10	5	14
Mediterranean	16	15	28	–	–	–	14
Rest	7	10	4	9	–	5	6
Total	100	100	100	100	100	100	100
N	80	20	56	23	20	22	221
Household							
Married/ Living Together	48	50	48	39	15	32	43
Single/Rest	52	50	52	61	85	68	57
Total	100	100	100	100	100	100	100
N	80	20	56	23	20	22	221

(to be continued on the next page)

(TABLE VI cont.)

Labor Market Position

Fully Unemployed	71	90	84	78	60	86	77
(Partly) Disabled	–	10	16	–	–	9	6
(Partly) Employed	28	–	–	18	5	–	12
(Partly) Studying	1	–	–	4	35	5	5
Total	100	100	100	100	100	100	100
N	80	20	56	23	20	22	221

Unemployment Duration

<2 Years	16	–	4	–	10	–	7
2-4 Years	21	5	14	18	30	27	19
4-6 Years	39	20	30	27	30	55	35
>6 Years	24	75	52	55	30	18	39
Total	100	100	100	100	100	100	100
N	76	20	56	22	20	22	216

* L.V.: lower vocational school. L.G.S.: lower general school.

Table VII Types of Long-Term Unemployed People and the Triad of Unemployment Problems (in percentages, N=216)

	Conform- ists	Ritual- ists	Retreat- ists	Enter- prising	Calcu- lating	Auto- nomous	Total
WORK							
Willing to Make Concessions as to Type of Work							
Yes, no conditions	26	35	21	6	–	9	21
Yes, under conditions	42	35	47	44	18	27	40
No	32	30	32	50	82	64	39
Total	100	100	100	100	100	100	100
N	69	17	38	18	11	11	164
Willing to Commute Longer Distances							
Yes, no conditions	32	17	14	18	–	25	22
Yes, under conditions	59	75	45	46	70	38	56
No	9	8	41	36	30	37	22
Total	100	100	100	100	100	100	100
N	46	12	22	11	10	8	109
Willing to Undergo Training							
Yes, no conditions	24	20	13	13	18	11	19
Yes, under conditions	47	60	29	40	55	89	46
No	29	20	58	47	27	–	35
Total	100	100	100	100	100	100	100
N	68	15	38	15	11	9	156
Salary Demands							
No demands	12	10	3	6	–	13	8
Dfl. 100 to 200 raise	29	45	25	22	12	14	26
>= Dfl. 300 raise	54	25	65	67	69	40	55
No opinion	5	20	7	5	19	33	11
Total	100	100	100	100	100	100	100
N	58	20	40	18	16	15	167
TIME							
Went Out							
Frequently	18	10	13	36	42	15	20
Irregularly	16	–	19	32	32	35	20
Seldom	66	90	68	32	26	50	60
Total	100	100	100	100	100	100	100
N	73	19	54	22	19	20	207
Kept Appointment Book							
Yes	21	6	5	65	85	54	28
No	79	94	95	35	15	46	72
Total	100	100	100	100	100	100	100
N	56	17	41	17	13	13	157
Joined Clubs etc.							
Yes	45	32	24	52	55	47	40
No	55	68	76	48	45	53	60
Total	100	100	100	100	100	100	100
N	74	19	54	21	20	19	207
MONEY							
Average Spendable Monthly Income (per person in Dfl.)							
Total	559	479	505	634	771	696	590
N	49	11	36	17	16	12	141

(to be continued on the next page)

(TABLE VII cont.)

Debts

Yes	42	42	59	74	55	27	49
No	58	58	41	26	45	73	51
Total	100	100	100	100	100	100	100
N	79	19	53	23	20	22	216

Informal Income

Regularly	–	–	–	95	–	–	9
Incidentally	10	5	9	–	30	14	10
No	81	90	87	–	65	86	75
No Answer	9	5	4	5	5	–	6
Total	100	100	100	100	100	100	100
N	77	20	55	22	20	22	216

TABLE VIII Types of Long-Term Unemployed People and Several Perceptual Aspects of Unemployment (in percentages)

	Conform-ists	Ritual-ists	Retreat-ists	Enter-prising	Calcu-lating	Auto-nomous	Total
Shame							
Yes	21	40	21	9	15	14	20
No	79	60	79	91	85	86	80
Total	100	100	100	100	100	100	100
N	76	20	52	23	20	22	213
ADVANTAGES AND DISADVANTAGES OF UNEMPLOYMENT							
Leisure							
Yes	38	37	38	58	74	84	48
No	62	63	62	42	26	16	52
Total	100	100	100	100	100	100	100
N	71	19	37	19	19	19	184
Freedom							
Yes	32	35	35	73	79	94	49
No	68	65	65	27	21	6	51
Total	100	100	100	100	100	100	100
N	69	17	37	22	19	18	182
Boredom							
Often	38	47	42	9	–	–	29
Sometimes	22	21	33	22	30	32	26
Seldom/Never	40	32	25	69	70	68	45
Total	100	100	100	100	100	100	100
N	56	19	48	23	20	22	208
Is risk a reason not to work in informal economy?							
Yes	74	60	41	17	15	39	52
No	26	40	59	83	85	61	48
Total	100	100	100	100	100	100	100
N	49	15	29	6	13	13	125

TABLE IX Types of Long-Term Unemployed People and Several Aspects of their Social Environment (in percentages)

	Conform-ists	Ritual-ists	Retreat-ists	Enter-prising	Calcu-lating	Auto-nomous	Total
Location							
Rotterdam	19	45	29	52	60	36	32
Amsterdam	38	20	39	31	30	46	36
Enschede	43	35	32	17	10	18	32
Total	100	100	100	100	100	100	100
N	80	20	56	23	20	22	221
Support from Friends							
None	28	45	49	16	–	14	30
Little	25	15	22	5	25	29	22
Much	47	40	29	79	75	57	48
Total	100	100	100	100	100	100	100
N	79	20	55	19	20	21	214
Seeing Friends outside Neighborhood							
Often	44	44	18	70	70	57	45
Sometimes	42	19	52	26	30	33	38
Never	14	37	30	4	–	10	17
Total	100	100	100	100	100	100	100
N	70	16	44	23	20	21	194
Unemployment among Friends							
Few/None	74	69	48	59	60	80	65
Many/All	26	31	52	41	40	20	35
Total	100	100	100	100	100	100	100
N	61	13	40	17	20	20	171

ACKNOWLEDGEMENTS

In the 1980s, long-term unemployment in the Netherlands proved to be very persistent. More than half of the unemployed had been out of work for more than one year. Despite the interest on the part of social scientists, very little data had been gathered on the daily life of the long-term unemployed. This stimulated us to investigate the social consequences of long-term unemployment. A team of eleven researchers from the Department of Sociology at the University of Leiden, inspired by the classical study *Die Arbeitlosen von Marienthal* by Marie Lazarsfeld-Jahoda and Hans Zeisel (1933), designed and conducted an intensive study in three Dutch cities with high unemployment rates.[1] The study, supervised by Kees Schuyt and coordinated by Hein Kroft, resulted in the publication in Dutch of *Een tijd zonder werk* (Kroft et al. 1989).

Cultures of Unemployment is a revised edition of this book. Some of the original chapters have been left out; others have been abridged or revised. Three new chapters have been added. Chapter 1 puts the developments of the Dutch welfare state into comparative perspective and shows the relevance of a cultural analysis of social problems in the Netherlands for international research. Chapter 2 summarizes the central issues of our study, and Chapter 10, in which the analytic apparatus is applied to the problems of urban poverty in the United States. Godfried Engbersen and Jaap Timmer, with the help of Frans van Waarden, revised and adapted the original material for this American edition. They are grateful to the authors of the original chapters for allowing them to use their material. Frans Van Waarden wrote the new Chapter 1, with contributions from Kees Schuyt and Godfried Engbersen. Kees Schuyt wrote Chapter 2. Jaap Timmer wrote Chapter 3 on urban labor markets and unemployment careers. Stefan Hoegen described the financial problems in Chapter 4. Hein Kroft analyzed the job-seeking behavior of the long-term unemployed in Chapter 6, and Frans van Waarden wrote about how the unemployed spend their time and perceive their rights and obligations in Chapters 5 and 7. Godfried Engbersen summarized the most important findings in Chapters 8 and 9 and wrote Chapter 10.

---

1 Christien Brinkgreve, Godfried Engbersen, Stefan Hoegen, Hein Kroft, Hans Lenters, Hennie Müller, Kees Schuyt, Jan van der Sluis, Anki Tan, Jaap Timmer and Frans van Waarden.

In the Dutch edition, we expressed our gratitude to numerous individuals and agencies. Here we would like to once again thank the Ministry of Social Affairs and Employment in The Hague for commissioning the study and Ed van de Beek, Christien Brinkgreve, Robert Kloosterman, Aafke Komter, Hans Lenters, Henny Müller, Gerard Oude Engberink, Jan van der Sluis, Anki Tan and Romke van der Veen for their contributions at various stages of the study. In addition, we would like to thank the members of "The City and the State" project group at the University of Utrecht Department of General Social Sciences for their useful suggestions on improving the manuscript, the Department of Sociology at the University of Leiden for the support past and present, and Jan van der Sluis for helping us with the finishing touch of the manuscript.

The opportunities we had to meet foreign scholars were important. Aaron Wildavsky's visit to the Leyden Institute for Law and Public Policy in spring 1988 was a crucial stimulus for us to go further in applying Mary Douglas' cultural theory. Meeting William Julius Wilson and Loïc J. D. Waquant at "The Leiden Workshop on Modern Poverty" in the summer of 1990 was also important for our further conceptualization. They convinced us of the necessity of linking a structural with a cultural analysis of unemployment. They also brought us into contact with members of the International Network in Comparative Sociology and History, which addresses "Poverty, Immigration and Urban Marginality in Advanced Societies." We are thankful to the people from the Network, especially to Loïc J. D. Waquant and Pierre Bourdieu, for the fruitful formulation of ideas during the Paris conference in May 1991. We were particularly interested in their comments on the rationality of the conduct of the unemployed. We would also like to thank Herbert J. Gans for his constructive criticism and stimulating remarks on some of our draft texts. All of these people gave us the idea that our Dutch study could make a contribution to the debate on unemployment, poverty and social policy and stimulated us to go on with this American edition. In this book, with its own Dutch history behind it, we were able to incorporate only a very small fraction of the overwhelming wealth of ideas they presented us with. One consolation is that science is an ongoing process, and in our future work we hope to make up for the shortcomings of this study.

Finally, we thank Sheila Gogol for her translation and Thea de Beer for turning the manuscript into a book.

Godfried Engbersen
Kees Schuyt
Jaap Timmer
Frans van Waarden

Adler, Michael, Colin Beel, Jochen Clasen, and Adrian Sinfield (eds.). *The Sociology of Social Security*. Edinburgh Education & Society Series, Edinburgh: Edinburgh University Press, 1991.

Alber, Jens. "Government Responses to the Challenge of Unemployment: The Development of Unemployment Insurance in Western Europe." In Peter Flora and Arnold J. Heidenheimer (eds.), *The Development of Welfare States in Europe and America*. New Brunswick and London: Transaction, 1982.

Anderson, Elijah. *A Place on the Corner*. Chicago: University of Chicago Press, 1978.

——. "Sex Codes and Family Life among Poor Inner-City Youths." In W. J. Wilson (ed.), *The Annals of the American Academy of Political and Social Science*, Vol. 501, (January 1989): 59-78.

——. *Street Wise: Class and Change in an Urban Community*. Chicago: The University of Chicago Press, 1990a.

——. "Racial Tension, Cultural Conflicts, and Problems of Employment Training Programs." In Kai Erikson, and Steven Peter Valas, *The Nature of Work: Sociological Perspectives*. New Haven and London: American Sociological Association Series and Yale University Press, 1990b, 214-234.

——. "Neighborhood Effects on Teenage Prenancy." In Christopher Jencks, and Paul E. Peterson (eds.), *The Urban Underclass*. Washington D.C.: The Brookings Institute, 1991, 375-398.

Auletta, Ken. *The Underclass*. New York: Random House, 1982.

Bakke, Edward Wigth. *The Unemployed Man: A Social Study*. London: Nisbet, 1933.

——. "The Cycle of Adjustment to Unemployment." In Norman W. Bell, and Erza F. Vogel (eds.), *A Modern Introduction to the Family*. New York: Free Press, 1960, 112-125.

Banfield, Edward C. *The Unheavenly City Revisited*. Boston: Little, Brown, 1974.

Becker, J. W., R. Vink, and J. J. Godschalk. *Enige aspecten van arbeid in de toekomst: een verkenning tot het begin van de jaren negentig* (Some Future Aspects of Labor: An Exploration until the Beginning of the 1990s). Rijswijk: SDU, 1986.

Bell, Daniel. *The Cultural Contradictions of Capitalism*. New York: Basic Books, 1978.

Berg, Ivar (ed.). *Sociological Perspectives on Labor Markets*. New York: Academic Press, 1981.

Beveridge, William H. *Full Employment in a Free Society: A Report*. London: Allen and Unwin, 1944.

——. *Social Insurance and Allied Services*. London: Report, 2 Volumes, 1945.

Bluestone, Barry, and Bennett Harrison. *The Deindustrialization of America: Plant Closings, Community Abandonment, and the Dismantling of Basic Industry.* New York: Basic Books, 1982.

——. *The Great American Job Machine: The Proliferation of Low Wage Employment in the U.S. Economy.* Paper. Washington: 1986.

Boon, Louis J. *De list der wetenschap: variatie en selectie: vooruitgang zonder rationaliteit* (The Cunning of Science. Variation and Selection: Progress without Rationality). Baarn: Ambo 1983.

Bourdieu, Pierre. *Travail et Travailleurs en Algeria.* Paris: Additions Mouton, 1965.

——. "The Forms of Capital." In John G. Richardson (ed.), *Handbook of Theory and Research for the Society of Education.* New York: Greenwood Press, 1986.

Bourgois, Philippe. "In Search of Horatio Alger: Culture and Ideology in the Crack Economy." *Contemporary Drug Problems* (Winter 1990): 619-649.

Bovenkerk, Frank, Kees Bruin, Lodewijk Brunt, and Huib Wouters. *Vreemd volk, gemengde gevoelens* (Strange People, Mixed Emotions). Amsterdam/Meppel: Boom, 1985.

Buckland, Sarah, and Susanne MacGregor. "Discouraged Workers? The Long-term Unemployed and the Search for Work." In Stephen Fineman (ed.), *Unemployment, Personal and Social Consequences.* London/New York: Tavistock Publications, 1987, 178-194.

Cameron, David R. "Public Expenditure and Economic Performance in International Perspective." In Rudolf Klein, and Michael O'Higgins (eds.), *The Future of Welfare.* Oxford/New York: Basil Blackwell, 1985.

Caplovitz, David. *The Poor Pay More.* New York: Free Press Glencoe, 1963.

——. *Making Ends Meet: How Families Cope with Inflation and Recession.* Beverly Hills/London: Sage Publications, 1979.

CBS (Netherlands Central Bureau of Statistics). *Geregistreerde werkloosheid november 1987-augustus 1988* (Registered Unemployed November 1987-August 1988). The Hague: SDU/CBS, 1988.

——. *Statistiek van de consumptieve kredieten* (Statistics of Consumer Credits). The Hague: SDU/CBS, 1989a.

——. *Maandstatistiek van de prijzen* (Monthly Price Statistics). The Hague: SDU/CBS, 1989b.

——. *1899-1989: Negentig jaar statistiek in tijdreeksen* (1899-1989: Ninety Years Statistics in Time Series). The Hague: SDU/CBS, 1990.

——. *Statistisch Jaarboek 1991* (Statistical Yearbook 1991). The Hague: SDU/CBS, 1991.

——. *Statistisch Jaarboek 1992* (Statistical Yearbook 1992). The Hague: SDU/CBS, 1992.

——. *Statistisch Jaarboek 1993* (Statistical Yearbook 1993). The Hague: SDU/CBS, 1993.

Coffield, Frank, Carol Borril, and Sarah Marshall. *Growing Up at the Margins.* Milton Keynes, Philadelphia: Open University Press, 1986.

Committee on Ways and Means, U.S. House of Representatives, Overview of Entitlement Programs. *1991 Green Book: Background Material and Data on Programs Within the Jurisdiction of the Committee on Ways and Means.* Washington D.C.: U.S. Government Printing Offfice, 1991.

Cox, Robert H. Alternative Patterns of Welfare State Development: The Case of Public Assistance in the Netherlands. *West European Politics* 13 (1990): 85-102.

——. Can Welfare States Grow in Leaps and Bounds? Non-Incremental Policymaking in the Netherlands. *Governance. An International Journal of Policy and Administration*, Vol. 5, No. 1 (January 1992): 68-87.

Daalder, Hans. "The Netherlands: Opposition in a Segmented Society." In Robert A. Dahl (ed.), *Political Opposition in Western Democracies*. New Haven and London, 1966: 188-236.

——. "Consociationalism, Center and Periphery in the Netherlands." In Per Torsvik (ed.), *Mobilization Center-Periphery Structures and Nation-Building. A Volume in Commemoration of Stein Rokkan*. Bergen/Oslo/Tromso, 1981.

——. Countries in Comparative European Politics. *European Journal of Political Research* 15 (1987): 3-21.

Dahrendorf, Ralf. *Life Chances*. London: Weidenfeld & Nicolson, 1979.

——. *Law and Order*. London: Stevens & Sons, 1985

——. *The Modern Social Conflict: An Essay on the Politics of Liberty*. London: Weidenfeld and Nicolson, 1988.

Danzinger, Sheldon, and Peter Gottschalk. The Poverty of Losing Ground. *Challenge*, (May-June 1985): 32-38.

De Grip, Andries, Winnaars en verliezers op de arbeidsmarkt in de jaren '70 (Winners and Losers in the Labor Market in the 1970s). *Tijdschrift voor Arbeidsvraagstukken* No. 1 (1986): 41-51.

——. Winnaars en verliezers op de arbeidsmarkt 1981-1985, Verschuivingen in de beroepen- en opleidingsstructuur (Winners and Losers in the Labor Market 1981-1985). *Tijdschrift voor Arbeidsvraagstukken* No. 4 (1987): 61-69.

Deleeck, Herman, and Karel van den Bosch. Poverty and Adequacy of social security in Europe: A Comparative Analysis. *Journal of European Social Policy* Vol. 2, No. 2 (1992): 107-120.

De Neubourg, Chris. Jantje van Leiden of de cultuur van de werkloosheid (The Culture of Unemployment). *Tijdschrift voor Arbeidsvraagstukken* No. 1 (1986): 26-40.

——. *Unemployment and Labour Market Flexibility: The Netherlands*. Geneva: International Labour Office, 1990.

Dercksen, Willem, and Hans Adriaansens. *Labour Force Participation, Industrial Relations and Policies*. The Hague: Paper WRR (Netherlands Scientific Counsel for Government Policy) 1992.

De Swaan, Abram. *In Care of the State: Health Care, Education and Welfare in Europe and the USA in the Modern Era*. New York: Oxford U.P., 1988.

De Vries, Johan. *De economische achteruitgang der Republiek in de achttiende eeuw* (The Economic Decline of the Dutch Republic in the 18th Century), Leiden, 1968.

Dirven, Henk Jan, and Jos Berghman. *Poverty, Insecurity of Subsistence and Relative Deprivation in the Netherlands*. Report 1991. Tilburg: Department of Social Security Studies and IVA, Institute for Social Research 1991.

Doeringer, Peter B., and Michael Piore. *Internal Labor Markets and Manpower Analysis*. Lexington, Massachusetts: Heath, 1971.

Douglas, Mary. *Natural Symbols: Explorations in Cosmology*. London: Barrie & Rockliff/Cresset Press, 1970.

———. *Cultural Bias* (Royal Anthropological Institute of Great Britain and Ireland, Occasional Paper No. 35). London: Royal Anthropological Institute of Great Britain and Ireland, 1978.

———(ed.), *Essays in Sociology of Perception*. London/Boston: Routledge & Kegan Paul/Russell Sage Foundation, 1982.

———. "Introduction." In Jonathan Gross, and Steve Rayner, *Measuring Culture: A Paradigm for the Analysis of Social Organization*. New York: Columbia University Press, 1985.

———. *Risk Acceptability According to the Social Sciences*. London: Routledge and Kegan Paul, 1986.

———. *How Institutions Think*. Syracuse, N.J.: Syracuse University Press, 1987.

———. "The Self as a Risk Taker: A Cultural Theory of Contagion in Relation to Aids." In Mary Douglas, *Risk and Blame: Essays in Cultural Theory*. London and New York: Routledge, 1992, 102-121.

———, and Baron Isherwood. *The World of Goods: Towards An Anthropology of Consumption*. New York: Basic Books, 1979.

———, and Aaron Wildavsky. *Risk and Culture: An Essay on the Selection of Technical and Environmental Dangers*. Berkeley: University of California Press, 1982.

Edin, Kathryn. "Surviving the Welfare System: How AFDC Recipients Make Ends Meet in Chicago." *Social Problems* Vol. 38, No. 4 (November 1991): 462-473.

———, and Christopher Jencks. "Reforming Welfare." In Christopher Jencks, *Rethinking Social Policy: Race, Poverty and the Underclass*. Cambridge, Massachusetts: Harvard University Press, 1992, 204-235.

Edwards, Richard C. *Contested Terrain: The Transformation of the Workplace in the Twentieth Century*. New York: Basic Books, 1979.

———, Michael Reich, and David M Gordon (eds.). *Labor Market Segmentation*. Lexington, Massachusetts/London: D.C. Heath, 1975.

Elchardus, Mark, and Ignace Glorieux. *De ontwrichting van het levensritme: de effecten van werk en werkloosheid* (The Disruption of the Rhythm of Life: The Effect of Work and Unemployment). Paper gepresenteerd op de Vlaams-Nederlandse studiedagen voor sociologen en antropologen, 7 en 8 april 1988, UFSIA, Antwerpen.

Ellwood, David T. *Poor Support: Poverty in the American Family*. New York: Basic Books, 1988.

Elster, Jon. *Sour Grapes, Studies in the Subversion of Rationality*. Cambridge: Cambridge University Press, 1985.

Engbersen, Godfried. "Cultures of Unemployment in the New West." *The Netherlands Journal of Social Sciences* Vol. 25, No. 2 (October 1989): 73-96.

——— B.M. *Publieke bijstand geheimen: Het ontstaan van een onderklasse in Nederland* (Public Welfare Secrets: The Making of an Underclass in the Netherlands). Leiden/Antwerpen: Stenfert Kroese BV, 1990.

Engbersen, Godfried, and Robert Kloosterman. William Julius Wilson en het debat over de onderklasse (William Julius Wilson and the Underclass Debate). *Intermediair* Vol. 26, No. 34 (August 1990): 43-49.

Engbersen, Godfried, and Romke Van der Veen. *Moderne armoede: overleven op het sociaal minimum* (Modern Poverty: Surviving on Society's Minimum). Leiden/ Antwerpen: Stenfert Kroese BV, 1987.

———. *The Three Faces of Deprivation: The American and the Dutch Welfare State Compared*. Paper prepared for the CES Workshop on "Emergent Supranational Social Policy: The EC's Social Dimension in a Comparative Perspective." Minda de Ginzburg Center for European Studies, Harvard University, November 15th, 16th and 17th 1991.

——— (eds.). Fatale remedies: De onbedoelde effecten van sociaal beleid (Fatal Remedies: The Unintended Effects of Social Policy). Special Issue of *Beleid & Maatschappij*, jaargang XIX (1992): 213-288.

Esping-Andersen, Gösta. *Three Worlds of Welfare Capitalism*. Cambridge: Polity Press, 1990.

Eurostat. *La Pauvreté en Chiffres au début des années 80*. Luxembourg: Office for Official Publications of the European Communities, 1990.

Feather, N. T. *The Psychological Impact of Unemployment*, New York: Springer Verlag, 1990.

Ferman, Louis A. "Participation in the Irregular Economy." In Kai Erikson, and Steven Peter Valas, *The Nature of Work: Sociological Perspectives*. New Haven and London: American Sociological Association Series and Yale University Press, 1990, 119-140.

Fineman, Stephan (ed.). *Unemployment, Personal and Social Consequences*. London: Tavistock Publications, 1987.

Flap, Henk D., and Nanda D. de Graaf. Sociaal kapitaal en bereikte beroepshoogte (Social Capital and Obtained Professional Level). *Mens en Maatschappij* 60 (1985): 325-344.

———, and Frits Tazelaar. "De rol van informele sociale netwerken op de arbeidsmarkt: flexibilisering en uitsluiting" (The Role of Informal Social Networks on the Labor Market). In Henk D. Flap, and Frits Tazelaar, *De flexibele arbeidsmarkt*. Deventer: Van Loghum Slaterus BV, 1988, 48-64.

———. "On the History and Current Problems of the Welfare State." In S. N. Eisenstadt, and Ora Ahimeir (eds.), *The Welfare State and its Aftermath*. London: Croom Helm, 1985.

———. "Introduction." In Peter Flora (ed.), *Growth to Limits: The Western European Welfare States since World War II*. Berlin: De Gruyter, 1986.

———, and Jens Alber. "Modernization, Democratization, and the Development of Welfare States in Western Europe." In Peter Flora, and Arnold J. Heidenheimer (eds.), *The Development of Welfare States in Europe and America*. New Brunswick and London: Transaction, 1982.

Frölich, Dieter. *The Use of Time During Unemployment: A Case Study Carried Out in West Germany*. Assen: Van Gorcum, 1983.

Fryer, David, and Philip Ullah (eds.). *Unemployed People, Social and Psychological Perspectives*. Milton Keynes, Philadelphia: Open University Press, 1987.

Fryer, David, and Stephan McKenna, "The Laying Off of Hands - Unemployment and the Experience of Time." In Stephan Fineman (ed.), *Unemployment, Personal and Social Consequences*. London: Tavistock Publications, 1987, 47-73.

Galtung, Johan, Structure, Culture and Intellectual Style: An Essay comparing Saxonic, Teutonic, Gallic, and Nipponic Approaches. *Social Science Information* 20:6, (1981).

Gans, Herbert J. "Poverty and Culture: Some Basic Questions about Methods of Studying Life-Styles of the Poor." In Peter Townsend (ed.), *The Concept of Poverty*. London: Heinemann Educational Books, 1977, 146-164.

———. *People, Plans, and Policies: Essays on Poverty, Racism, and Other National Urban Problems*. New York: Columbia University Press, 1991.

Geertz, Clifford. The Anthropology at Large. *New Republic* May 25 (1987) 34: 36-37.

Glazer, Nathan. *The Limits of Social Policy*. Cambrigde, Mass.: Harvard University Press, 1988.

Gordon, Alan. *The Crisis of Unemployment*. London: Helm, 1988.

Granovetter, Mark S. The Strength of Weak Ties. *American Journal of Sociology* 78 (1973) 6: 1360-80.

———. *Getting a Job: A Study of Contacts and Careers*. Cambridge Mass.: Harvard University Press, 1974.

Griffiths, Richard T. *Achterlijk, achter of anders?* (Backward, Behind or Different?) Amsterdam: VU Boekhandel, 1980.

Gross, Jonathan L., and Steve Rayner. *Measuring Culture: A Paradigm for the Analysis of Social Organization*. New York: Columbia University Press, 1985.

Gurvitch, Georges. La multiplicité des temps sociaux. *La vocation actuelle de la sociologie* Vol. 2, Chapitre XIII. Paris: Presses Universitaires de France, 1963.

Handler, Joel F., and Yeheskel Hasenfeld. *The Moral Construction of Poverty: Welfare Reform in America*. Newbury Park: Sage Publications, 1991.

Hannerz, Ulf. *Soulside*. New York: Columbia University Press, 1969.

Harrington, Michael. *The Other America: Poverty in the United States*. Harmondsworth, 1962.

Hasenfeld, Yeheskel. The Role of Employment Placement Services in Maintaining Poverty. *Social Service Review* (December 1975): 569-587.

Hasenfeld, Michael, Jane A. Rafferty, and Mayer N. Zald. The Welfare State, Citizenship, and Bureaucratic Encounters. *Annual Review of Sociology* 13 (1987): 387-415.

Hasluck, Chris. *Urban Unemployment: Local Labour Markets and Employment Initiatives*. London and New York: Longman, 1987.

Haveman, Jan. *De ongeschoolde arbeider* (The Unskilled Worker). Assen: Van Gorcum 1952.

Hayes, John, and Peter Nutman. *Understanding the Unemployed: Psychological Effects of Unemployment*. London/New York: Tavistock 1981.

Hochschild, Jennifer L. Equal Opportunity and the Estranged Poor. *Annals of the American Academy of Political and Social Science*: Special Issue "The Ghetto Underclass: Social Science Perspectives," edited by W. J. Wilson, Vol. 501 (January 1989): 143-155.

Hoggart, Richard. *The Uses of Literacy*. London: Penguin Books, 1990 (or. 1957).

Jahoda, Marie. *Employment and Unemployment: A Social-Psychological Analysis*. Cambridge: Cambridge University Press, 1982.

———. "Unemployed Men at Work." In David Fryer, and Philip Ullah (eds.), *Unemployed People, Social and Psychological Perspectives*. Milton Keynes, Philadelphia: Open University Press, 1987, 1-73.

Jahoda, Marie, Paul F. Lazarsfeld, and Hans Zeisel. *Marienthal: The Sociography of an Unemployed Community*. London: Tavistock Publications, 1972.

Jankowski, Martin Sanches. *Islands in the Street: Gangs and American Urban Society*. Berkeley: University of California Press, 1991.

Jencks, Christopher. "Is the American Underclass Growing?" In Christopher Jencks, and Paul E. Peterson (eds.), *The Urban Underclass*. Washington D.C.: The Brookings Institute, 1991, 28-100.

———. *Rethinking Social Policy: Race, Poverty and the Underclass*. Cambridge: Harvard University Press, 1992.

———, and Paul E. Peterson (eds.). *The Urban Underclass*. Washington D.C.: The Brookings Institute, 1991.

Jordan, Bill, Simon James, Helen Kay, and Marcus Redley. *Trapped in Poverty?: Labour-Market Decisions in Low-Income Households*. London/New York: Routledge, 1992.

Katz, Michael B. *In the Shadow of the Poorhouse: A Social History of Welfare in America*. Basic Books: New York, 1986.

———. *The Undeserving Poor: From the War on Poverty to the War on Welfare*. Basic Books: New York, 1989.

Kirschenman, Joleen, and Kathryn M. Neckerman, "'We'd Love to Hire Them, But . . .': The Meaning of Race for Employers." In Christopher Jencks, and Paul E. Peterson (eds.), *The Urban Underclass*. Washington D.C.: The Brookings Institute, 1991, 203-232.

Kloosterman, Robert C. *Achter in de rij: een onderzoek naar de factoren die (her)-intreding van langdurig werklozen belemmeren* (Last in Line: A Study of Factors Hindering the Re-entrance of Unemployed onto the Labor Market). Den Haag: OSA, 1987.

———. *A Capital City's Problem: The Rise of Unemployment in the 1980's in Amsterdam*. Paper prepared for the Conference on Poverty, Immigration and Urban Marginality in Advanced Societies. Paris, May 10-11, 1991.

———, and Tom Elfring. *Werken in Nederland* (Working in the Netherlands). Schoonhoven: Academic Service, 1991.

Knulst, Wim P., and Leo P. II. Schoonderwoerd. *Waar blijft de tijd. Een onderzoek naar de dagelijkse bezigheden van Nederlanders* (Where Does Time Go?: A study of Daily Activities of Dutch People). Den Haag: Staatsuitgeverij, 1983.

Köbben, André J. F., and Jan J. Godschalk. *Een tweedeling van de samenleving?* (Society Divided in Two?). The Hague: Organisatie voor Strategisch Arbeidsmarktonderzoek, 1985.

Kohl, Jürgen. "Trends and Problems in Postwar Public Expenditure Development in Western Europe and North America." In Peter Flora, and Arnold J. Heidenheimer (eds.), *The Development of Welfare States in Europe and America*. New Brunswick and London: Transaction, 1982.

Komarovsky, M. *The Unemployed Man and His Family*. New York: Dreyden Press 1940.

Korpi, Walter. *The Working Class and Welfare Capitalism*. London: Routledge and Kegan Paul, 1980.

Kotlowitz, Alex. *There Are No Children Here: The Study of Two Boys Growing Up in the Other America*. New York: Anchor Books Doubleday, 1991.

Kramer, Ralph. *Voluntary Agencies in the Welfare State*. Berkeley: University of California Press, 1981.

———Kramer, Ralph. "The Welfare State and the Voluntary Sector: The Case of the Personal Social Services." In S. N. Eisenstadt, and Ora Ahimeir (eds.), *The Welfare State and its Aftermath*. London: Croom Helm, 1985.

Kroft, Hein, Godfried Engbersen, Kees Schuyt, and Frans Van Waarden. *Een tijd zonder werk: Een onderzoek naar de levenswereld van langdurig werklozen* (A Period Without Work: A Study of the Social Worlds of Long-Term Unemployed). Leiden/Antwerpen: Stenfert Kroese BV, 1989.

Lauer, Robert H. *Temporal Man: The Meaning and Uses of Social Time.* New York: Praeger Publishers, 1981.

Lawson, Robert, C. McFate, and William J. Wilson (eds.). *Urban Marginality and Social Policy in America and Western Europe.* Newbury Park: Sage Publications, 1992.

Lazarsfeld-Jahoda, Marie, and Hans Zeisel. *Die Arbeitslosen von Marienthal: Ein soziographischer Versuch über die Wirkungen langdauernder Arbeitslosigkeit.* Leipzig: Verlag von S. Hirzel, 1933 (Quotations from Marie Jahoda, Paul F. Lazarsfeld, and Hans Zeisel, *Marienthal: The Sociography of an Unemployed Community,* London: Tavistock Publications 1972).

Leeds, Anthony. "The Concept of the 'Culture of Poverty': Conceptual, Logical, and Empirical Problems, with Perspectives from Brazil and Peru." In Eleanor Burke Leacock (ed.), *The Culture of Poverty: A Critique.* New York: Simon and Schuster 1971, 226-284.

Lewis, Oscar. *Five Families: Mexican Case Studies in the Culture of Poverty.* New York: Basic Books, 1959.

———. *The Children of Sanchez.* New York: Random House, 1961.

———. *La Vida: A Puerto Rican Family in the Culture of Poverty.* San Juan and New York: Random House, 1966.

———. *A Study of Slum Culture: Backgrounds for La Vida.* New York: Random House, 1968.

Liebow, Eliott. *Tally's Corner.* Boston: Little, Brown, 1967.

Lijphart, Arend. *The Politics of Accommodation: Pluralism and Democracy in the Netherlands.* Berkeley: University of California Press, 1975.

Lipsky, Michael. *Street-Level Bureaucracy: Dilemmas of the Individual in Public Services.* New York: Russell Sage Foundation, 1980.

———. "Bureaucratic Disentitlement in Social Welfare Programs." *Social Service Review* 58 (March 1984): 3-27.

Lowi, Theodore J. "Four Systems of Policy, Politics, and Choice." *Public Administration Review* (July/August 1972): 298-310.

Lucassen, Jan. *Naar de kusten van de Noordzee. Trekarbeid in Europees perspectief, 1600-1900* (To the Northsea Coast. Migrant Labor in European Perspective, 1600-1900). Gouda: (s.n.), 1984.

MacLeod, Jay. *Ain't No Making It, Leveled Aspirations in a Low-Income Neighborhood.* London: Tavistock Publications, 1987, and Boulder: Westview Press, 1987.

Marmor, Theodore, Jerry L. Mashaw, and Philip L. Harvey. *America's Misunderstood Welfare State: Persistent Myths, Enduring Realities.* New York: Basic Books, 1990.

Mars, Gerald. *Cheats at Work, An Anthropology of Workplace Crime.* London: Allen and Unwin, 1982.

Marsden, Dennis, and Euan Duff. *Workless: Some Unemployed Men and their Families: An Exploration of the Social Contract Between Society and the Worker.* Harmondsworth: Penguin, 1975.

Mead, Lawrence M. *Beyond Entitlement: The Social Obligations of Citizenship*. New York: The Free Press 1986.

——. "The Logic of Workfare: The Underclass and Work Policy." In William Julius Wilson (ed.), *The Ghetto Underclass: Social Science Perspectives*, Vol. 501 of *Annals of The American Academy of Political and Social Science*, January 1989: 156-169.

——. *The New Politics of Poverty: The Nonworking Poor in America*. New York: Basic Books 1992.

Merton, Robert K. *Social Theory and Social Structure*. New York: The Free Press, 1957.

Merton, Robert K., and Robert Nisbet. *Contemporary Social Problems*. New York: Harcourt, Brace, Jovanovich, 1971.

Ministry of Social Affairs and Employment. "Meerjarenramingen Sociale Zekerheidsregelingen 1981" (Long-Term Calculations of Social Security Regulations). The Hague: Ministry of Social Affairs and Employment.

——. *Rapportage Arbeidsmarkt* (Labor Market Report). The Hague: Ministry of Social Affairs and Employment, 1987.

——. *Rapportage Arbeidsmarkt*. The Hague: Ministry of Social Affairs and Employment, 1991.

Mishel, Lawrence, and David M. Frankel. *The State of Working in America, 1990-91 Edition*. New York: Economic Policy Institute, 1991.

Moore, Sally F. *Law as Process: An Anthropological Approach*. London: Routledge and Keagan Paul, 1978.

Muffels, Ruud, Jos Berghman, and Henk-Jan Dirven. "A Multi-Method Approach to Monitor the Evolution of Poverty." *Journal of European Social Policy* Vol. 2 (1992) No. 3: 193-213.

Murray, Charles. *Losing Ground: American Policy 1950-1980*. New York: Basic Books, 1984.

Nowotny, Helga. *Eigenzeit: Enstehung und Strukturierung eines Zeitgefühls*. Frankfurt am Main: Suhrkamp Verlag, 1990.

OECD. *Measures to Assist the Unemployed*. Paris: OECD, 1988.

——. *National Accounts 1968-1988*. Paris: OECD, 1990.

——. *Employment Outlook 1991*. Paris: OECD, 1991.

——. *Employment Outlook 1992*. Paris: OECD, 1992.

O'Higgins, M., and S. Jenkins. "Poverty in the EC: Estimates for 1975, 1980 and 1985." In R. Teekens, and B. Van Praag (eds.), *Analysing Poverty in the European Community*. Eurostat News Special Edition, Luxembourg: Office of the Official Publications of the European Communities, 1990.

OSA. *Arbeidsmarktperspectieven* (Labor Market Perspectives). The Hague: OSA, 1988.

Oude Engberink, Gerard. *Minima zonder marge* (Poor Without Margins). Rotterdam: GSD, 1984.

——. *Minima zonder marge: de balans 3 jaar later* (Poor Without Margins: The Balance After Three Years). Rotterdam: GSD, 1987.

Pahl, Raymond E. *Divisions of Labour*. Oxford: Basil Blackwell, 1984.

——. "Does Jobless Mean Workless? Unemployment and Informal Work." In Louis A. Ferman et al. (eds.), *The Informal Economy, Annals of the American Academy of Political and Social Science*. September 1987: 36-46.

Peterson, Paul E. "The Urban Underclass and the Poverty Paradox." In Christopher Jencks, and Paul E. Peterson (eds.), *The Urban Underclass*. Washington D.C.: The Brookings Institute, 1991, 3-27.

Pierson, Christopher. *Beyond the Welfare State: The New Political Economy of Welfare*. Cambridge: Polity Press, 1991.

Piven, Frances Fox, and Richard A. Cloward. *The New Class War*. New York: Pantheon Books, 1982.

Polsky, Andrew J. *The Rise of the Therapeutic State*. Princeton, New Jersey: Princeton University Press, 1991.

Popkin, Samuel L. *The Rational Peasant: The Political Economy of Rural Society in Vietnam*. Berkeley: The University of California Press, 1979.

Popkin, Susan J. "Welfare: Views from the Bottom." *Social Problems* Vol. 37, No. 1 (February 1990): 64-79.

Portes, Alejandro. "Rationality in the Slum: An Essay on Interpretive Sociology." *Comparative Studies in Society and History* Vol. 14 (3) (1972): 268-286.

———. "The Social Origins of the Cuban Enclave Economy of Miami." *Sociological Perspectives* Vol. 30, No. 4 (October 1987): 340-372.

———. *Gaining the Upper hand: Old and New Perspectives in the Study of Foreign-Born Minorities*. Paper presented at the Working Conference on Poverty, Immigration and Urban Marginality in Advanced Scieties. Paris, May 10-11, 1991.

Renooy, Piet H. *The Informal Economy: Meaning, Measurement and Social Significance*. Amsterdam: Koninklijk Aardrijkskundig Genootschap, 1990.

Rodman, Hyman. "The Lower-Class Value Stretch." *Social Forces* Vol. 42 (October 1963-May 1964): 205-215.

Rokkan, Stein. "Territories, Nations, Parties: Toward a Geoeconomic-Geopolitical Model for the Explanation of Variations within Western Europe." In Richard L. Merritt, and Bruce Russett (eds.), *From National Development to Global Community*. London: Allen and Unwin, 1981.

Romein, Jan. "De dialectiek van de vooruitgang. Bijdragen tot het ontwikkelingsbegrip in de geschiedenis" (The Dialectic of Progress. Contributions to the Notion of Development in History). In Jan Romein, *Historische lijnen en patronen. Een keuze uit de essays*. Amsterdam: Querido, 1971 (paper orig. 1935).

Rossi, Peter H. *Down and Out in America, The Origins of Homelessness*. Chicago: The University of Chicago Press, 1989.

Rubin, Lilian Breslow. *Worlds of Pain*. New York: Basic Books, 1976.

Ryan, William. *Blaming the Victim*. New York: Vintage Books, 1971.

Schuyt, C. J. M. "Het rechtskarakter van de verzorgingsstaat" (The Legal Character of the Welfare State). In J. A. A. van Doorn, and C. J. M. Schuyt, *De stagnerende verzorgingsstaat* (The Stagnating Welfare State). Meppel: Boom, 1978, 73-97.

———. *Op zoek naar het hart van de verzoringsstaat* (In Search of the Heart of the Welfare State). Leiden/Antwerpen: Stenfert Kroese BV, 1991.

Schuyt, Kees, Kees Groenendijk, and Ben Sloot. *De weg naar het recht* (The Road to Justice). Deventer: Kluwer, 1976.

Schuyt, Kees, and Romke van der Veen (eds.). *De verdeelde samenleving: Een inleiding in de sociologie van de verzorgingsstaat* (Divided Society: An Introduction to the Sociology of the Welfare State). Leiden/Antwerpen: Stenfert Kroese BV, 1990.

Schwartz, Barry. *Queing and Waiting*. Chicago: The University of Chicago Press, 1975.

SCP (Social and Cultural Planning Office). *Social and Cultural Report 1990: The Netherlands*. Rijswijk: SCP, 1991.

Sidel, Ruth. *Women and Children Last*. New York: Viking-Penguin, 1986.

Simonse, Joop. *Belemmerde kansen: sociologische schets van de volksbuurt* (Impeded Chances: A Sociological Sketch of a Working Class Neigborhood). Alphen aan den Rijn: Samson, 1971.

Sinfield, Adrian. *What Unemployment Means*. Oxford: Robertson, 1981.

Skocpol, Theda. "Targeting within Universalism: Politically Viable Policies to Combat Poverty in the United States." In Christopher Jencks, and Paul E. Peterson (eds.), *The Urban Underclass*. Washington D.C.: The Brookings Institute, 1991, 411-436.

Smeeding, Timothy M., Michael O'Higgins, and Lee Rainwater (eds.). *Poverty, Inequality and Income Distribution in Comparative Perspective: The Luxembourg Income Study (LIS)*. New York: Harvester Wheatsheaf, 1990.

Smith, Michael P. *City, State & Market: The Political Economy of Urban Society*. Oxford: Basil Blackwell, 1988.

Sorokin, Pitrim A., and Robert K. Merton. "Social Time: A Methodological and Functional Analysis." *The American Journal of Sociology* Vol. 42 (5 March 1937) 615-629.

Sossin, Michael R. "Legal Rights and Welfare Change, 1960-1980." In Sheldon H. Danziger, and Daniel H. Weinberg (eds.), *Fighting Poverty: What Works and What Doesn't*. Cambridge: Harvard University Press, 1986, 260-283.

Stack, Carol. *All Our Kin, Strategies for Survival in a Black Community*. New York: Harperz Row, 1974.

Stephens, John D. *The Transition from Capitalism to Socialism*. London: Macmillan, 1979.

Tebbutt, Melanie. *Making Ends Meet: Pawnbroking and Working-Class Credit*. Leicester: Leicester University Press, 1983.

Te Grotenhuis, Hannic. *The Bottom Side of Prosperity: Children of Long-Term Unemployed Parents in the Dutch Welfare State*. Paper prepared for the Workshop on the Effects of Parental Joblessness on the Social Outcomes of Adolescence: Cross-Cultural Perspectives. New York, November 21, 1991.

Therborn, Göran. *Why Some Peoples Are More Unemployed than Others: The Strange Paradox of Growth and Unemployment*. London: Verso, 1986.

Thompson, Michael. "The Problem of the Centre: 'An Autonomous Cosmology.'" In Mary Douglas (ed.), *Essays in the Sociology of Perception*. London: Routledge and Kagan Paul, 1982, 302-27.

Thompson, Michael, and Aaron Wildavsky. "A Cultural Theory of Information Bias in Organizations." *Journal of Management Studies* 23, 3, (1986): 273-86.

———, and Aaron Wildavsky. "A Poverty of Distinction, From Economic Homogeneity to Cultural Heterogeneity in the Classification of Poor People." *Policy Sciences* 19, (1986): 163-199.

Thompson, Michael, Richard Ellis, and Aaron Wildavsky. *Cultural Theory*. Boulder, Colorado: Westview Press, 1990.

Tienda, Marta, and Haya Stier. "Joblessness and Shiftlessness: Labor Force Activity in Chicago's Inner City." In Christopher Jencks, and Paul E. Peterson (eds.), *The Urban Underclass*. Washington D.C.: The Brookings Institute, 1991, 135-154.

Tiffany, Donald W., James R. Cowan, and Phyllis M. Tiffany. *The Unemployed: A Socio-psychological Portrait*. Englewood Cliffs, N.J., 1970.

Timmer, Jaap, *Between Employment and Unemployment. Flexible Jobs as a Possible Strategy to Deal with Unemployment*, Paper prepared for the Conference on Poverty, Immigration and Urban Marginality in Advanced Societies, Paris, May 10-11, 1991.

U.S. Department of Commerce. *Statistical Abstract of the United States 1992: The National Data Book*. Washington D.C.: U.S. Government Printing Office, 1992.

Valentine, Charles A. *Culture and Poverty: Critique and Counter Proposals*. Chicago: University of Chicago Press, 1968.

Van Imhoff, Evert. "Alleenstaanden: Een demografische analyse" (Being Single: A Demographical Analysis). *Gezin* Jrg. 3, No. 1 (1991): 4-14.

Van der Meer, Jan. *Wat beweegt de stad? Studie naar de stedelijke dynamiek in de Rotterdamse agglomeratie* (What Moves the City? Investigations into the Urban Dynamics in the Rotterdam Metropolitan Region). Rotterdam: Dissertation, 1989.

Van der Veen, Romke J. *De sociale grenzen van beleid: Een onderzoek naar de uitvoering en effecten van het stelsel van sociale zekerheid* (The Social Limits to Policy: A Study of the Implementation and the Effects of the System of Social Security). Leiden/Antwerpen: Stenfert Kroese Uitgevers, 1990.

Van Doorn, J. A. A. "De verzorgingsmaatschappij in de praktijk" (Welfare State in Practice). In J. A. A. van Doorn, and C. J. M. Schuyt, *De stagnerende verzorgingsstaat*. Meppel: Boom, 1978, 17-47.

Van Hulst, Aad M. *Eindevaluatie Project Schuldsanering* (Evaluation of the Debt Help Project). Rotterdam: GSD (Gemeentelijke Sociale Dienst, Municipal Welfare Department), 1987.

Van Ours, Jan C., and J. S. Hagens. *Vacatures in beweging: Een verkennende analyse van de doorstroming in het vacaturebestand* (Vacancies on the Move: An Exploring Analysis of the Flow in Vacancies). Den Haag: Organisatie voor Strategisch Arbeidsmarktonderzoek, 1987.

Van Rhijn, Arie Adriaan (collected by). *Nieuw Nederland: Bijdragen van buiten bezet gebied in verband met den wederopbouw van ons land* (The New Netherlands: Contributions from Outside Occupied Territory Concerning the Reconstruction of Our Country), 1945.

——. *De na-oorlogse sociale politiek* (Post-War Social Politics). Amsterdam: Partij van den Arbeid, 1947.

Van Stolk, Bram, and Cas Wouters. *Vrouwen in tweestrijd: tussen thuis en tehuis: relatieproblemen in de verzorgingsstaat, opgetekend in een crisiscentrum* (Women in Two Minds: Between Home and Shelter: Relational Problems in the Welfare State, Recorded in a Crisis Center). Deventer: Van Loghum Slaterus, 1983.

Van Waarden, Frans. "The Historical Institutionalization of Typical National Patterns in Policy Networks Between State and Industry: A Comparison of the USA and the Netherlands." *European Journal of Political Research* 21 (1992): 131-162.

Van Zanden, Jan L. "De mythe van de achterlijkheid van de Nederlandse economie in de negentiende eeuw" (The Myth of Backwardness of the Dutch Economy in the 19th Century). *Spiegel Historiael* 24 (1989): 163-167.

———, and Richard T. Griffiths. *Economische geschiedenis van Nederland in de 20ste eeuw* (Economic History of the Netherlands in the 20th Century). Utrecht: Het Spectrum, 1989.

Vogel, David. *National Styles of Regulation. Environmental Policy in Great Britain and the United States*. Ithaca/London: Cornell U.P., 1986.

Wacquant, Loïc J. D. "The Ghetto, the State, and the New Capitalist Economy." *Dissent* (Fall 1989): 508-520.

———. "The Comparative Social Structure and Experience of Urban Exclusion: Race, Class, and Space in Chicago and Paris." In R. Lawson, C. McFate, and W. J. Wilson (eds.), *Urban Marginality and Social Policy in America and Western Europe*. Newbury Park: Sage Publications, 1992a.

———. "'The Zone': Le métier de *hustler* dans le ghetto noir américain." *Actes de la recherche en sciences sociales*, 92 (juin 1992b).

———. "Redrawing the Urban Color Line: The State of the Ghetto in the 1980's." In Craig Calhoen, and George Ritzer (eds.), *Social Problems*. New York: McGraw-Hill, 1992c.

Wacquant, Loïc J. D., and Wiliams Julius Wilson. "The Cost of Racial and Class Exclusion in the Inner City." In William Julius Wilson (ed.), *The Ghetto Underclass: Social Science Perspectives*. Vol. 501 of *Annals of the American Academy of Political and Social Sciences*, January 1989: 8-25.

Waldinger, Roger, Howard Aldrich, Robin Ward, and Associates. *Ethnic Entrepeneurs, Immigrant Business in Industrial Societies*. Newbury Park: Sage Publications (Sage Series on Race and Ethnic Relations), 1990.

Wassenberg, Arthur. "Neo-Corporatism and the Quest for Control: The Cuckoo Game." In Gerhard Lehmbruch, and Philippe Schmitter (eds.), *Patterns of Corporatist Policy-Making*. London and Beverly Hills: Sage, 1982.

Weir, Margaret, Ann Shola Orloff, and Theda Skocpol, (eds.). *The Politics of Social Policy in the United States*. Princeton: Princeton UP, 1988.

Wieringa, W. J. *Ten dienste van bedrijf en gemeenschap. Vijftig jaar boekdrukkers-organisatie* (To the Service of Company and Community. Fifty Years Organization of Bookprinters). Amsterdam: Federatie der Werkgeversorganisatiën in het boekdrukkersbedrijf, 1959.

Wildavsky, Aaron. "The Three Cultures: Explaining Anomalies in the American Welfare State." *The Public Interest* No. 69 (Fall 1982): 45-58.

———. *The Nursing Father: Moses as a Political Leader*. Tuscaloosa, University of Alabama Press, 1984.

———. "Choosing Preferences by Constructing Institutions: A Cultural Theory of Preference Formation." *American Political Science Review* Vol. 81, No. 1 (March 1987): 4-21.

Wilensky, Harold L. *The Welfare State and Equality: Structural and Ideological Roots of Public Expenditures*. Berkeley: U of C Press, 1975.

Williams, Terry M., and William Kornblum. *Growing Up Poor*. Lexington, Massachusetts: Lexington Books, 1985.

Willis, Paul E. *Learning to Labour*, Aldershot, 1977.

———. "Unemployment: The Final Inequality." *British Journal of Education* Vol. 7, No. 2 (1986): 155-170.

Wilson, William Julius. *The Truly Disadvantaged: The Inner City, the Underclass, and Public Policy.* Chicago: The University of Chicago Press 1987.

——— (ed.). *The Ghetto Underclass: Social Science Perspectives.* Vol. 501 of *Annals of The American Academy of Political and Social Science,* January 1989.

———. "Studying Inner-City Social Dislocations: The Challenge of Public Agenda Research." *American Sociological Review* Vol. 56 (February 1991a): 1-14.

———. "Public Policy Research and The Truly Disadvantaged." In Christopher Jencks, and Paul E. Peterson (eds.), *The Urban Underclass.* Washington D.C.: The Brookings Institute, 1991b, 460-481.

Wong, Roy A., Hein P. A. Kroft, and Theo J. Veerman. *Toeleiding naar de arbeidsmarkt. Een studie naar participatie en rendement van voorzieningen voor werkloze jongeren* (Guiding Unemployed Youth to the Labor Market: A Study of Participation and Efficiency of Regulations for Unemployed Youth). Leiden: A&W, 1988.

WRR (Netherlands Scientific Counsel for Government Policy). *Activerend Arbeidsmarktbeleid* (An Active Labour Market Policy). The Hague: WRR, 1987.

———. *Allochtonenbeleid* (Immigrant Policy). The Hague: WRR, 1989.

———. *Een werkend perspectief: Arbeidsparticipatie in de jaren '90* (Work in Perspective: Labour Participation in the Netherlands). The Hague: SDU, 1990.

ABOUT THE BOOK AND THE AUTHORS

The "cultures" of unemployed people in the United States and abroad are complex, varied and offer explanatory power when analyzed, as they are here, in a systematic way. The authors use case studies and survey data to devise a framework for a better understanding of the effects of welfare state policy on the chronically unemployed. They analyze the personal and political worlds behind the social mechanisms behind the welfare state. Comparing the results of this study with important ethnographic studies conducted in the United States provides unique insight into the differences and similarities between the American welfare state and the Netherlands, a highly developed European welfare state. The foreword by U.S. scholar William Julius Wilson emphasizes the universality of the method and findings presented here.

Godfried Engbersen is associate professor at the Department of General Social Sciences at the University of Utrecht, the Netherlands. Engbersen has published in the fields of the welfare state and social problems, journalism, legal aid and the unintended consequences of social policy. He has published several books, for example *Moderne Armoede* (Modern Poverty, with Romke J. van der Veen, 1987) and *Publieke Bijstandsgeheimen* (Public Welfare Secrets 1990).

Kees Schuyt is full professor in sociology at the University of Amsterdam. He has published in the following fields, Civil disobedience: *Recht, orde en burgerlijke ongehoorzaamheid* (Law, Order and Civil Disobedience 1972). Law, social justice and social policy: "The Rise of Lawyers in the Dutch Welfare State." In R. L. Abel and P. S. C. Lewis (eds.). *Lawyers in Society*. University of California Press, Berkeley/Los Angeles 1988; *Law as Communication* (1988); *De weg naar het recht* (The Road to Justice 1976); *Tussen macht en moraal* (Between Power and Morality 1983); *De verdeelde samenleving* (The Divided Society 1990); *Op zoek naar het hart van de verzorgingsstaat* (In Search of the Hart of the Welfare State 1991). Philosophy of science: *Filosofie der sociale wetenschappen* (Philosophy of the Social Sciences 1987). He was a member of the Netherlands Scientific Council for Government Policy (WRR) from 1983 to 1988.

Jaap Timmer is a researcher at the Hugo Sinzheimer Institute (Center for Socio-Legal Studies of Labor and Social Security) of the University of Amsterdam and co-author of *Een tijd zonder werk*. He is writing a dissertation titled *Arbeids-onzekerheid in twee gedaanten* (Two Faces of Labor Insecurity), about coping with the social and financial insecurity generated by situations of unemployment and working in flexible labor contracts (precarious jobs). Timmer is co-editor of a report on vulnerable categories in the Dutch welfare state. His current research focus is on the responsiveness of government agencies to the work of the Dutch National ombudsman.

Frans van Waarden is senior researcher at the Department of Political Science and Public Administration of the University of Konstanz, Germany. He has published in the fields of sociology of work and organization, labor relations, corporatism, business interest associations and public administration. Van Waarden's books, include *Fabriekslevens* (Factory Lives 1987), *Het geheim van Twente; Fabrikantenverenigingen in de oudste grootindustrie van Nederland* (The Secret of Twente; Business Associations in the Textile Industry 1987) and *Organisatiemacht van belangenverenigingen* (Organizational Power of Interest Associations 1989). With Wyn Grant and Jan Nekkers he edited *Organizing Business for War*. His current research focus is on the comparative study of the legal and political institutional bases of policy styles and policy networks of the public administration.